THE LITERATURE OF FIDELITY

THE
LITERATURE OF
FIDELITY

by

MICHAEL BLACK

BARNES & NOBLE
BOOKS
10 East 53d St., New York 10022
(a division of Harper & Row Publishers, Inc.)

Published in the U.S.A. 1975 by
HARPER & ROW PUBLISHERS, INC.
BARNES & NOBLE IMPORT DIVISION

ISBN 0-06-490440-7

Printed in Great Britain

To the memory of my parents;
to my wife and children

Contents

Preface and Acknowledgements

The nucleus of this book is four talks which I gave on BBC Radio 3 in 1971 and 1972. I took Phèdre, Emma Bovary, Anna Karenina and Connie Chatterley as four heroines who could be used, somewhat schematically, as the main pillars of an argument about the treatment of fidelity in literature; 1971 was the year of divorce law reform in England, and I wanted to make some points about moral progress. I am grateful to my producer Adrian Johnson, and the admirable technicians of the BBC for making the recording of the talks a pleasant experience.

A rewritten version of the talks appeared in *The Human World*. I am grateful to the editor, Ian Robinson, for his interest. Discussions with him have modified my views, and I gladly acknowledge that influence.

Anne McDermid of David Higham Associates heard the broadcasts and suggested they might be turned into a book – encouragement without which I might not have gone further.

This is not an academic book, so footnotes would be inappropriate. I cannot therefore acknowledge in each place the debts I owe to previous writers on the works I consider. I have listed some at the end. I must here single out one debt: to the criticism of F. R. Leavis and his wife Q. D. Leavis – that most productive and influential intellectual partnership. Anybody who writes about the books they have written about does well to start from their work, and may not get beyond it.

Cambridge, 1973   M.B.

9

And we are put on earth a little space
That we may learn to bear the beams of love
BLAKE

One should never put oneself by choice in a situation where morality and feeling are in conflict; for the spontaneous is so beautiful that it is appalling to be condemned to be for ever dominating one's own actions, and to live with oneself as one's own victim . . .

For the rest, perhaps no one has written on this subject with perfect truth; for everyone wishes to emerge with credit for his own feelings or those he inspires. So women seek to see themselves as in a novel, and men as in a history; but the human heart has never truly been penetrated in its deepest relationships. One day perhaps someone will tell it truthfully as he felt it, and all he felt; and we shall be astonished to learn that most maxims of conduct and most generalized observations are false; and that there is an unrecognized soul at the heart of the story.

MADAME DE STAEL

'On the romantic sensibility in the movements of the heart' (from De l'Allemagne)

I

Introduction

The studies in this book are, with one exception, arranged in chronological order. Each of the books or plays is concerned with love, marriage, fidelity or infidelity: and more especially with the feelings involved. I try to make the discussion an evolving one; and as we come towards the present day there are ways in which it would be possible to take the whole story as 'progress'. That is to say, the survey moves from certainties of a rigid kind, which can be cruel in their application to particular cases, towards what we think of as our tolerance—or our uncertainty. We now have liberal divorce laws; we are not so quick to condemn behaviour; we have contraceptive methods so safe that some actions no longer have their earlier consequences, so that people are now 'free' in a way they used not to be.

But we only need to think a moment to realize that laws and the daily administration of small quantities of chemicals cannot legislate for or medicate away our most intimate feelings; or that the people who now avoid marriage or hate the family because they are 'outmoded social institutions', who enter trial marriages or just live together, don't find that unhappiness is reserved for certificate-holders. The possibility of unhappiness springs from within. The most important relationships carry a possibility of pain in direct ratio to their importance, and always will. It is a consequence of being generically human, or individually a self. The thread which I follow through this book is the sense great writers have had of what it is to be a self among selves, and in direct relationships with one other self, the person one loves.

The word 'self' is used in various senses in ordinary speech, most of them related to the one I follow. This book is an extended definition, or rather a way of pursuing the manifestations of self-hood which make up so much of life. One importance of literature is that it shows so much about what it is to be human, especially in these dangerous respects: how it offers practical definitions of a depth beyond summary verbal conceptualizations. I will however risk a few words here as introduction.

'Self' can just mean 'the individual personality, continuing through a life', my self as distinct from your self in a world of unique individuals. That is only a beginning of the meanings. I am looking for something deeper, which is pointed to in some of the common phrases people use. If someone says of a certain situation 'I am not sure that I could answer for myself', we know we are in an area of danger. It could be a cry for help, suggesting 'I fear the forces within me that I cannot control'. It might be a threat, meaning 'Be what I want you to be, especially in relation to me, or I will make you suffer'. If someone says 'I feel that I owe it to myself', he may be saying 'I am not going to spare other people the consequences if my demands on life are unfulfilled'. In the first utterance we hear self-mistrust, or fear; in the second place self-love: the self-approval manifest in it may come out as anger if it feels threatened. But so it may in the first; the difference between the two messages is that in the second the speaker is putting himself behind his anger, being ready to approve it in advance. In the first case the speaker may actually be frightened of his anger, or is pretending to be frightened of it so that he can let himself go and afterwards say that he wasn't to blame; he did warn you.

Already we have slipped into the kind of complication I have in mind; where other uses of the word (he's very self-conscious; she's very self-centred; he's not very self-aware; I can't bear that self-importance; he's drunk with self-love) show that we are familiar at an everyday level with a world in which every person is a self in delicate relationships – and often out of balance – with other selves. Some of the books I discuss are by masters of the art of analysis, which is at heart self-knowledge – writers who see deeply into what it is to be a self – and I shall do well to say little more at this stage and at this very simple level, but to follow them to the deeper level. I will only add one thing here, but it is worth putting as simply. The self is both the unique nature of every individual and the thing which he or she holds in common with every other. The great writers who follow the lives of their characters to moments of crisis seem to show extreme cases: explosions or collapses of personality in which the single separate person defines the absoluteness of his individuality. This is the expression of unique qualities, the result of a unique process of growth in that individual. It is also an expression of universal selfhood. To say that we are all of the same nature is not the same as saying that we are all alike. I think the writers I talk about range themselves into those who believe in a common human nature, and those who may divide humanity into classes. Important moral consequences may follow from this tendency.

I am writing for ordinary readers; teachers and students of literature at schools and universities are 'ordinary' in their most serious reading. That is, they go to great literature in the expectation that it will do something for them other than get them a paper qualification. It will provide insight, for instance – even give access to wisdom. I don't mean that we go to the great novels and plays for a direct solution of our particular problems, or a handy set of moral maxims; I do mean that our understanding of life is deepened. If it were not so, there would be no reason to bother with literature at all, or to think one book more important than another. Since I am writing in the hope that such general readers can be reached, I have tried to be clear, and run the risk of being over-simple. I have not hesitated to say 'what happens' for readers less familiar with the plot. I hope those more familiar with the books will be patient with this exposition. It seems to me in any case that the terms in which a plot is recounted necessarily express one's own understanding of the book, and it is at this level that one starts to be right or wrong about what is going on.

2

Othello: a study of the self·I

Othello is the starting-point of this study for a number of reasons.
It comes first in time; but, more important, by exposing the naked
basic self, it provides definitions, and marks an extreme position.
The social surface of life is a crust over individual personal depths:
in certain conditions there is an eruption, an earthquake. The self
we are used to seeing splits, and there comes into view from the
depths of personality a strange and frightening element. To con-
tinue my geological figure, it bursts out as molten and damaging.
That flaring up of fire and movement throws up what is in fact very
old, very simple in its structure, unyielding and featureless. In
personal terms, we should say it was anonymous. My first chapters,
on *Othello* and *Phèdre*, are classic studies of that kind of explosion
of the self in anguished involvement with others. They help to
define both the self itself and also what we mean by 'classical'.

The discussion must start at the very moment when we decide
what *Othello* is conveying, what we make of it. There are strongly
divided views. Othello is a man – I was going to say a 'mature' man,
but that begs an essential question about what maturity is – a man
of middle age married to the much younger Desdemona. She loves
him for his masculine strength, his bravery, the sense that he has
passed through many dangers, dominated them by his courage and
resourcefulness, been tempered by them, perhaps. His being black,
being older, being a soldier, makes him strange to her in an
exciting way, but she reaches across that to something she senses
or hopes for in him: masculine courage and self-command born of
long service, knowledge of danger, strange circumstances. She finds
this turns into love for him. We may say that is the romanticism of
an intensely-feeling girl; but it is one ground of love, if what she
sees in him is really there. And why should not he respond to her
intensity, be touched by it, respond to her equal distance from his

nature: her power of feeling, and–more dangerous–her youth?
They marry, across that barrier of difference; but everyone marries
across a barrier of difference.

It happens that Othello has among his officers Iago, a man with
a disease of the personality. It is Iago's compulsion to damage
Othello as much as he can; he does so by striking at the marriage.
By a set of inspired improvizations he persuades Othello that the
innocent Desdemona is pursuing an adultery with the innocent
Cassio, another officer, who has the command Iago thinks his by
right. Othello's capacity to be jealous and suspicious turns out to
be immense and almost immediate; he kills Desdemona before he
has time to recover any kind of poise. He then has an inkling of
what he has done, and the agony of either living with or permanently
resisting that self-knowledge is more than he can face; he stabs
himself.

The question for us is, how do we react to that situation; and
how do we judge Othello himself? The division of opinion is
between those who see him as an innocent, devilishly misled by
the superhuman ingenuity of Iago, and those who say that Iago had
only to touch certain springs in Othello, that Iago's hideous instinct
led him immediately to put his fingers on the right psychic
mechanism, that he was able to do so because that instinct sprang
from his being in some ways basically *like* Othello. What then
sprang out from within Othello–the blind force of his deepest
nature–is the self in its naked destructive aspect: a murderous
power.

The first view–the noble uncomplicated soldier out of his depth
and diabolically manipulated–might be a metaphysical allegory of
the soul in the world, tempted by an external devil in the form of
Iago, and falling. It is a simple scheme, dramatically, psycho-
logically, and for that matter theologically: but it allows you to
keep a soft spot for Othello, and for that reason it is advocated by
very distinguished critics. I think they are wrong; that is not what
Shakespeare meant. I also think that people argue that way from
innocence. They can't otherwise understand Othello, so they see
him as tempted by this superhuman power, and feel his fall is not
his fault. Nobody says anything as crude, but there may also be an
impulse to concede that if Othello's jealousy had been justified, if
Desdemona really had deceived him, then it would have been
quite all right to murder her ('Look at all those people in Sicily,

B

even today'). Clichés about the *crime passionnel* cover the extenuation of murder. The academic critic can further distance the whole thing by talking about the sixteenth-century code of honour, especially in Mediterranean societies, or Othello's blackness, which made him insecure. In both cases you refuse to become involved, to make a judgement.

Not understanding Othello is a testimonial to moral qualities. I remember arguing for the dark view of Othello with that great scholar and charming man John Dover Wilson, who couldn't understand this 'modern' trend, which he knew of in the criticism of T. S. Eliot and F. R. Leavis. I could make no impression on him, and reflected afterwards that he was protected by essential innocence. To understand something, you have to find some echo of it, however distant, in yourself, and some critics find no relationship with Othello, and therefore exonerate him from responsibility for what an ordinary court of law would think a pretty humdrum crime. These critics therefore fall into sentimentality of a kind which short-circuits Shakespeare's intention, and makes for a thoroughly undramatic play. To realize Shakespeare's intention, you have to understand, that is concede your relationship with, Othello–and, if I am right, Iago, who has been found even more puzzling than Othello. Shakespeare is not merely saying 'if you have a tendency to be unreasonably jealous, learn from this example'. He is saying 'Recognize in Othello, in Iago, much more fundamental truths about being human which you had not grasped before. Admit a relationship with these two men, a kinship you will not easily concede'. If you can't admit it, you may be a candid person in the old sense of the word, as Dover Wilson transparently was. People may love you for it, but there will be a great deal you don't understand, including some of Shakespeare's plays. Alternatively, you may be an Othello or an Iago, since it's in the nature of the case that *they too* don't understand what drives them. You may find your place in the pattern by being murdered, like Desdemona, by what you don't understand; or you may be the murderer, if you can neither understand nor, therefore, restrain yourself. Somewhere you have a place in the drama, if only as uncomprehending bystander.

Strangely enough, the modern critics whom Dover Wilson didn't agree with, Eliot and Leavis, feel the same distance from Othello. If you think he is no more than a self-deceiving violent

man who saw nothing truly, least of all himself, it is natural, as
Eliot did, to dismiss him for what he called 'Bovarysme'. The
word links with a later chapter in this book, on Emma Bovary
herself. It was a shrewd perception of Eliot's to link the two, but
there are essential differences. Leavis, arguing, like Eliot, against
the tendency to see simple nobility in Othello, pointed out that the
play was a play of 'character': that is to say, that to understand
Othello's character is to understand the fatality of what happens
to him, his own powerlessness to do anything about it, the sense in
which he is not responsible, and therefore not tragic. But Shakespeare is implying that Othello's character is generically human,
that we fall into a self-deceiving trap of a related kind if we just
say 'well, thank God *I'm* not like that'. To identify part of ourselves
with Othello after an initial shrinking away, a horrified dissociation,
is to understand the play. In a fundamental, bedrock way Othello
and Iago are universal types. At the end of the play Iago's wife
Emilia, a blunt but limited person, 'puts Othello right' about
Desdemona, bursting out at him:

<blockquote>
O gull! O dolt!
As ignorant as dirt!
</blockquote>

It eases the heart to hear that said. And at that moment Othello,
under arrest, stripped of rank, is terribly diminished: a butt, a
target for hindsight wisdom and a false sense of superiority. To
allow our whole response to him to be summed up by Emilia is
part of the trap. With the whole play now behind us, if we have
entered into Othello's mind during it, we must, even if we claim
greater self-knowledge, know which part of our soul is related to
his.

Iago spends the whole play manipulating other people, so that it
might seem he is a free spirit of an experimental turn of mind, just
seeing what happens if you set people in a certain situation and
watch them respond. But he is *not* free; he is driven by an inner
compulsion–a mechanism which derives from a fear that he is
lacking in worth, and that because of this he does not have the love
or regard of others. In that state there are various compensatory
devices. One is to deny that *other* people have worth or deserve
regard: this might come out as malignant envy. In a more complicated person it might also come out as Iago's mixture of

cynicism and experimentalism. You deny that what you lack has worth anyway; you claim that your cynicism is a form of honesty that other people can't manage; you claim that the things they attach weight to are all deceptions and self-deceptions. In particular, love would be 'merely a lust of the blood and a permission of the will'—for one thing that is certain is that you aren't loved, and can't be. A sharp-eyed person of that kind—like Iago—would be quick to spot other people's personal failings, for they would be food to his cynicism. They would justify him, for he could present himself as more honest: the difference between him and other people is not that he knows he is vile, for he can't afford to face that: but he presents himself as brutally honest. He would not therefore *expect* to be loved; therefore he does not put himself at risk by investing trust or emotion in other people. Nor will they do so for him: so he embraces his poverty as a vocation. Those who love are fools; he can prove this; and his experimentalism is designed to shore up his inner abyss. But the fact is that, unknown to him, all this talk and manipulation is a *need* to him, it is as much an anxious rationalizing self-justification as any other. There are moments when he admits something like it; he admits for instance that Desdemona is good; and rather desperately he says at one moment that he loves her, for he feels obscurely both of her and of Cassio that they have 'a daily beauty' in their life that makes him ugly. That is something he cannot face squarely all the time, because to measure the distance between them and him would bring out the ultimate despair he is always fending off by rationalizing cynicism and compulsive manipulation of others. So he must damage them, even to destruction, and especially by breaking down their attachments.

You can call all this a form of jealousy. It is a condition of the lonely self feeling it *is* lonely, and reacting in desperation because it will not face that condition. The world, or other particular persons, have to be proved in the wrong, or punished. If their existence proves you wrong, they must be eliminated.

Iago's condition is identifiable and understandable. You can call it psychopathic, if you want to put a label on it (only the simplest kinds of psychopath do their own killing). You can relate it to other profound dramatic characterizations of similar conditions: Molière's Dom Juan, or Chekhov's Solyony in *Three Sisters*. The dramatic insight seems to me superior to the psychological, because you have both a clearer sense of individuality (Iago, Dom Juan and Solyony are distinct imaginations, and to enter into the people is to get behind the label) and a clearer sense of what is commonly human in their condition. *We* are not psychopaths, are we? and so we refuse to recognize the kinship.

The language Iago and Othello share gives them their peculiar kinship underneath their personal identity. It sounds in the characteristic poetry of the play, which is invariably a clue to profound meanings. There are passages which strike us as 'poetic', or 'rich' or 'deep' in a way which is not easy to account for. But allowed to sink into our consciousness, they guide our attitudes, and they can be analysed into a network of criss-crossing and merging themes.

For instance, very early in the play Othello turns to Iago and makes an odd confession:

> For know, Iago,
> But that I love the gentle Desdemona,
> I would not my unhouséd free condition
> Put into circumscription and confine
> *For the sea's worth.*

It sounds like the bachelor's hesitant farewell to his freedom (itself an insecurity, a doubt). But the phrase 'the sea's worth' gives it strangeness and richness. What the play enforces is that Desdemona *is* the 'sea's worth': as precious a thing, with her love for him, as Othello is ever to find. He doesn't know, though he has just married her, that she is worth that to him, for all his claim to love her, and his sense that she is 'gentle': so his love is a feeling, perhaps, which isn't related to any very secure sense of what she is, and ought to be to him.

Shortly after, her old father Brabantio, resigning her against his will to Othello, carries on the theme:

> Come hither, Moor:
> I here do give thee that with all my heart,
> Which, but thou hast already, with all my heart
> I would keep from thee.

This is a grudging abandonment of something precious, and

hoarded. The thought of giving, or losing, or keeping from others, leads naturally to his words to Desdemona:

> For your sake, *jewel*,
> I am glad at soul I have no other child;
> For thy escape would teach me tyranny.

The jewel and the sea recur when Desdemona lands at Cyprus and the courtly Cassio with a flourish cries

> O behold!
> The riches of the ship is come on shore!

This follows closely another of the highly charged passages of verse, again spoken by Cassio:

> Tempests themselves, high seas, and howling winds,
> The guttered rocks, and congregated sands,
> Traitors ensteeped to clog the guiltless keel,
> As having sense of beauty, do omit
> Their mortal natures, letting go safely by
> The divine Desdemona.

'Guttered' and 'congregated' strike a deep note: the first word carries the physical sense of rocks as corrugated surfaces down which water runs foaming back to the sea: but 'gutter' is a word associated with drains and poverty; linked to 'congregated', which conveys in its very pronunciation how wet sand sticks together like a barrier, it suggests a conspiracy of starving beggars and thieves. The 'jewel' is a precious cargo in a dangerous element, beset by lurking envious men. It's an ominous note: there are starving thieves in Cyprus, and they are Iago and Othello.

We hear these themes again with orchestral force in Act 3, scene 3, an immense scene, almost a play in itself. At this midpoint of the play Iago formally practices his witchcraft on Othello, releasing in him the chaotic force of his insecurity. It is an inspired improvization in which Iago produces at every turn the right impulsion to Othello's jealousy. At the end of it, Othello goes down on his knees and consecrates himself to revenge. Iago kneels as well, and swears himself to Othello's service. This parody of self-dedication—almost a marriage—has its own reality: Othello grants

Iago the post he has long sought, the post Cassio has lost through
Iago's manipulation, saying

> Now art thou my lieutenant.

Iago replies with silky calm

> I am your own for ever.

It is his highest point; but the truth is that at this moment they
have reversed roles: Othello is *his* lieutenant, and in a real sense
his, Iago's, own for ever: for Othello has embraced the true self
Iago has liberated in him: it means Desdemona's death as well as
his own; and the league he and Iago have entered into is diabolical.

Othello's aptness and Iago's skilful conducting are heard in the
concertante passages of the scene: the way in which they take
themes from each other and develop them. The pattern of the
scene, repeated over and over, is that Iago drops a hint, refuses
ostentatiously to be drawn further, and counts on Othello's insecurity to take the hint up and be dismayed by it, to enlarge on it
obsessively and give an opening for another hint. Iago enjoys being
able to protest his own scrupulousness—for instance when pressed
to 'give thy worst of thoughts the worst of words'. He couldn't do
that, he says, adding with his habitual reasonableness—who could?

> Utter my thoughts! Why, say they are vile and false—
> As where's that palace whereinto foul things
> Sometimes intrude not?

The foul things in the palace: it is another theme. It becomes
meshed with the others as Iago strikes home. Beating round the
bush, he says

> Good name in man and woman, dear my lord,

(and it sounds as if he is approaching a sexual scandal)

> Is the immediate jewel of their souls:
> Who steals my purse steals trash . . .
> But he that filches from me my good name
> Robs me of that which not enriches him
> But makes me poor indeed.

Here we have the jewel, the thieves, the distinction between true
wealth and false wealth—and real poverty.

A few lines later Iago makes his darkest utterance, and the word 'poor' sounds like an ostinato:

> Poor and content is rich, and rich enough,
> But riches fineless is as poor as winter
> To him that ever fears he shall be poor.
> Good heavens the souls of all my tribe defend
> From jealousy!

At the surface level Iago is saying 'embrace the knowledge that you are not loved, that Desdemona is false. Knowing that, you will be poor like me; that is, you will have nothing to lose, you will be at rock bottom, but secure; and you won't have to worry any more like those who *do* have something to lose'. Iago's need, his compulsion, is to bring down Othello to that level. Without emotional wealth, unloved, Iago *needs* to have people there with him, because to be the only person like him must mean he is not *worth* loving (which is the truth he cannot face). Othello does in a sense join him, to Iago's unholy joy, and he can simultaneously welcome Othello to his 'tribe' and scorn him for being led by the nose by him, Iago.

At one of the recurrent crises of the scene, where Othello drops into an abyss of mad jealousy, we hear the development of the 'foul things in the palace' theme. Othello will not embrace Iago's cynicism about his state; this is the difference between them; it is an agony he cannot argue away. He bursts out

> I had rather be a toad
> And live upon the vapour of a dungeon
> Than keep a corner in the thing I love
> For others' uses.

There is searing knowledge to be gained from Othello: more than he is conscious of himself. The 'foul thing' has here become the toad; its presence turns the former palace into a dungeon. What people have to do in the corners of dungeons produces the vapours the toad is living on. The corner for other's uses is therefore a privy, but what Othello points to but cannot name is that the 'thing' he loves is Desdemona, so that the image shifts, and *she* is the toad. What his mind is censoring into this strange form is the thought that 'their' making love to her is a fouling of her and him. The thought is too hideous to be made more explicit. But already

he has gone beyond Iago's tempting; he is thinking of her as a
common whore: the 'others' are plural.

Later he agonizes over the thought, which is both strange and
horrible, and somehow thrilling:

> What sense had I of her stolen hours of lust?
> I saw't not, thought it not, it harmed not me:
> I slept the next night well, fed well, was merry;
> I found not Cassio's kisses on her lips.
> He that is robbed, not wanting what is stolen,
> Let him not know't, and he's not robbed at all.

Here the jewel-riches theme is given a natural development: what
does it mean to 'possess' someone, or to be possessive; to think of
them as your 'own'? What does it do to you to 'know'? He takes an
extraordinary leap: if she can't be mine, she might as well be
everybody's:

> I had been happy if the general camp,
> Pioneers and all, had tasted her sweet body,
> So I had nothing known.

This is pure Othello: Iago had suggested merely that she might be
unfaithful with Cassio. Here Othello has turned his own 'not
knowing' into the grossest possibility: what's more he is saying he
would have been 'happy' if he had not 'known'. But the saying *is* a
knowing, and the word 'sweet' suggests that he is savouring the
knowledge: that he is gratified by the thought, partly in revenge.
He is imagining the possibility, and thrilled by it in ways he could
not possibly admit. It's punishment to her in imagination, and so
enjoyable; and punishment to himself. And enjoyable?

It is a kind of admission of that thought that he then veers into:

> O now for ever
> Farewell the tranquil mind! farewell content!

and then the strangely childish renunciation of his military pride
and office. If the general camp *has* tasted her sweet body, then they
are all laughing at him and he cannot command them, cannot even
face them:

> Farewell the pluméd troops and the big wars!

He calls to mind all the things to which he really thrilled; all the things that gave him his social identity, his status, his pride. For a minute he thrills to them all again, and then he shuts them away in imagination for ever, like an angry child kicking over his favourite toys because he is upset:

> Farewell! Othello's occupation's gone.

The exchange takes its further turn down the spiral. Iago with his deathly instinct picks up the thrill implicit in the thought of the general camp enjoying the sweet body, and the ambiguity in Othello's repeated 'give me the ocular proof'; 'make me to see't', 'would I were satisfied'. With calm relish he puts his question:

> I see, sir, you are eaten up with passion:
> I do repent me that I put it to you.
> You would be satisfied?

Othello, bull-like, replies

> Would? nay, and will.

Iago continues to be interested and reasonable, as if pursuing a novel thought in a purely speculative way:

> And may. But how? How satisfied, my lord?

He slips his trap:

> Would you, the supervisor, grossly gape on—
> Behold her tupped?

The hideous monosyllable links back with the very first scene of the play, where Iago made innocent farmyard matings the vehicle of coarse and voyeurist references to Othello and Desdemona ('Even now, even very now, an old black ram/Is tupping your white ewe', and 'You'll have your daughter covered with a Barbary horse'; and 'the beast with two backs'). Iago has found a responsive audience this time: the old black ram himself. Othello, touched on that nerve, cries out

> Death and damnation! O!

Iago knowing exactly what he is doing, keeps his probe on the nerve. He goes on in his bland way:

> It were a tedious difficulty, I think
> To bring them to that prospect: . . .

(of course, we know they're doing it, but it's unreasonable to
expect to catch them at it, to be there, watching)

> . . . Damn them then
> If ever mortal eyes do see them bolster
> More than their own! . . .

A brothel-performance is hardly to be expected, but the idea is
excitingly entertained, even while it is damned. He goes on with
his joyous speculation:

> . . . What then? how then?
> What shall I say? Where's satisfaction?
> It is impossible you should see this
> Were they as prime as goats, as hot as monkeys,
> As salt as wolves in pride, and fools as gross
> As ignorance made drunk . . .

This is soiling. Othello is made to go on seeing it, and seeing it
overlaid with these animal comparisons which degrade Desdemona
and mock him. He makes no protest. It is of course important to
dehumanize Desdemona, so that her murder seems like pest-
control.

Iago concludes:

> . . . But yet, I say,
> If imputation and strong circumstance
> Which lead directly to the door of truth
> Will give you satisfaction, you might have't.

All I can give you is reasonable circumstantial evidence: don't
expect to *see*. But saying that, Iago pursues Othello's complex of
horrified reactions in the phrase 'to the door of truth'. At that door
one looks through the keyhole, to see the bestial act: and there is
'satisfaction', linked ambiguously with 'knowing'.

Goaded on like this, Othello finally says 'Now do I see 'tis true'.
He sees nothing, of course; it has all been the merest and basest
insinuation of a kind that a man secure in his own self-regard and
his assurance of being loved would never stoop to consider. But
something is liberated in Othello, and its expression is inevitably a
sea-image:

> Never Iago, like to the Pontic sea,
> Whose icy currents and compulsive course
> Ne'er feels retiring ebb, but keeps due on
> To the Propontic and the Hellespont; . . .

He contemplates the coldness and violence, the inevitability of the tide churning through the narrows, he feels swept on by its blind purposefulness; he becomes that impersonal racing force. For the whirl of his own chaotic feelings is given a tide, a channel and a speed by his jealousy; his liberated self organizes itself into that movement, which gives him back a meaning and a dignity. He is identifying himself with his madness, and congratulating himself on it.

> ... Even so my bloody thoughts, with violent pace
> Shall ne'er look back, ne'er ebb to humble love
> Till that a capable and wide revenge
> Swallow them up.

The tide has turned to blood, 'their' blood, which also flows only one way when shed–it too has no ebb. At the thought he feels a release; he is out in the open sea, 'capable and wide', and with yet another kind of satisfaction he sees the bodies turn under the surface and sink. He's there; and in this joy, this satisfaction, he goes down on his knees with Iago and consecrates his new self to that consummation. It is a moment of breath-taking theatricality, and immense human depth.

When Othello meets Desdemona face to face and alone, in the next act, his state is such that he cannot communicate with her, only pour out what is in him. It comes out as a tangled mass of themes we are now familiar with. His grief, his rage, his fundamental confusion produce a choked torrent. He starts

> Had it pleased heaven
> To try me with affliction; had they rained
> All kind of sores and shames on my bare head, ...

He sees himself as Job, tormented by God for inscrutable reasons, plagued with 'sore boils'. But the Biblical sores turn into a different kind, and the word 'rained' becomes active. But he is not out on a moor like Lear, he is back in that dungeon; the rain is sewage again, and he is chained upright in its rising tide, so he goes on

> ... Steeped me in poverty to the very lips ...

(Iago's 'poverty' has become a threat to his life: he dare hardly move his lips or it will come pouring in)

> . . . Given to captivity me and my utmost hopes,
> I should have found in some place in my soul
> A drop of patience . . .

The 'some place in my soul' links back to 'the corner in the thing
I love', the notion either of hugging something all to oneself, or
more desperately trying to keep a small piece of it for oneself. That
general idea, and the drop of 'patience', which is a pure element,
generates the later lines:

> But there where I have garnered up my heart,
> Where either I must live or bear no life,
> The fountain from the which my current runs,
> Or else dries up–to be discarded thence! . . .

One's heart, for a moment, goes right out to him. There's a
possessive element in it, and also a dependent element, but this is
an anguished truth about his *need* for her, for what she means to
him, what he cannot live without, and the life-supplying current of
his feeling is direct, and for a minute clear. This is his love,
imperfect perhaps, and potentially destructive, but love. As for
need: do you recognize that as a claim, or resist it as a demand? In
his case it is compulsive, and twists easily into a horror, so that he
runs on:

> Or keep it as a cistern for foul toads
> To knot and gender in!

It's her he means again; she and the 'others', knotting and
gendering. So his fountains meant for pure water become sewers,
his garner meant for harvested corn becomes a dungeon; his
'current' is forced to become the 'icy compulsive course', the
murderous tide that kills her.

At the very end of the play, with Desdemona dead, his equals
stand there horrified, unable to comprehend him. The coarse
Emilia shouts the truth in his face. He puts his dignity back on as
best he can, his self-command, and attempts a last performance in
his old social self:

> Soft you; a word or two before you go.

That's the note we recognize in the first two acts–calm command:

> I have done the state some service, and they know't.
> No more of that. I pray you in your letters,
> When you shall these unlucky deeds relate,

('unlucky' begs enormous questions)

> Speak of me as I am; . . .

(that begs another. 'He's that he is', Iago had said of him, from a deep knowledge)

> . . . Nothing extenuate,
> Nor set down aught in malice. Then must you speak

(he goes on, wanting to write their account for them)

> Of one that loved not wisely but too well;

(an utter falsehood, unless you think of love as a disease)

> Of one not easily jealous . . .

(false again)

> . . . but, being wrought,
> Perplexed in the extreme;

(and that is nearer the truth; but he comes right up to it in the last transformation of the jewel image:)

> of one whose hand,
> Like the base Indian, threw a pearl away
> Richer than all his tribe. . . .

That is a recognition of his act, his guilt, the value of Desdemona, the 'sea's worth'. The tribe is the one Iago knew he belonged to (p. 24). In that knowledge, Othello kills himself; the last act of the self being a self-punishment which follows or inhibits self-recognition, avoids the need to build another self, or recognizes the impossibility. It's inevitable that the last words of the play are directed to Iago, and bring the play's harmony to a dark unresolved clash:

> O Spartan dog,
> More fell than anguish, hunger or the sea . . .

'Spartan' conveys the willed and brutal poverty Iago preaches; the Spartans were human, but a dog is not: this kind of dog attacks people for food. As for 'anguish, hunger and the sea', they are totally impersonal enemies of the personal and the human. The mystery conveyed by Iago and Othello is that individual people have this elemental force in them, embody it. It is their self.

3

Othello: a study of the self · II

Othello is a strange play in that only two centres of consciousness—
Othello's and Iago's—are explored in depth; and we want to feel
closely related to neither of them. Our impulse is to keep a
distance from Othello's agonized obsession, to feel that Iago is an
inhuman mystery. It is a play of supreme dramatic skill, with a
good deal of activity and a painfully mounting tension: we could
take it as a kind of thriller, and leave the theatre feeling uninvolved,
as we do after other thrillers—except that our sense of justice is
outraged, and so we go over it in our minds, to find the deeper
meaning. If we don't accept the defence of 'one who loved not
wisely but too well', it is because a self-defensive instinct on our
own part asks 'but what kind of love is that, if it leads to the murder
on unjustified suspicion of an innocent by the person to whom she
ought to have been most precious?'

There's a question begged, of course. Supposing that there had
been grounds for jealousy, that she *had* been deceiving him, what
then would have been Othello's appropriate response? We may not
have clearcut answers of our own, but there are more or less agreed
or conventional or convinced social judgements about the act,
adultery is the technical term, and it is common observation that
deceived husbands or wives are deeply grieved, or angry, or
jealous. What do we think of that—being jealous? Is it just natural,
or a defect of the personality?

But Shakespeare has deliberately taken the case of unfounded
jealousy bordering on madness and leading to violence, and I can
only think he did so because the case poses in an extreme form
something about human relationships that he wanted to identify
and analyse. It is a lesson about the self, and its dangerousness,
especially in people who are instinctive, unself-conscious, unself-
critical: who cannot control themselves.

Each of us thinks that his self is unique and differentiating, what

31

makes me me, and yet the uses of the word and our knowledge of the world tell us that selfhood is what links us all at the lowest level of our common humanity. For that reason I use the traditional word, and don't resort to technical psychological terms. What 'self' reminds us of is that we are all one self each, and that it may be a misleading dodge to call the common element the 'id'–or some other word–and the personal element the ego, and the censoring self-controlling element the superego. For one thing it is morally equivocal; if you do something uncontrolled you can, after the event, excuse yourself on the ground that that was the universal anonymous bursting out, and you're very sorry but it is now back in the kennel, and the real you is in command again. But observers are under no illusion: they watch the outburst, and from their knowledge they say that that is X 'showing himself in his true colours'. If they know you very well and are inclined to excuse you, they may say 'Ah, that's old X, all right'. They don't say it was 'it'; they say it was you. And who, controlling himself, ever doubted that it was himself he was controlling? Yet it is a question.

The paradox is that this deepest and most personal level is universal and perhaps therefore anonymous. It takes a poetic dramatist, a Shakespeare, to show that an Othello is peculiarly himself, that he has a strange fellow-feeling with an Iago, shown by their capacity to speak in related but unique poetic styles, and that he is human and therefore a brother. That is the deep meaning, I think, of Othello's being black: not that anything is implied about being a Negro, but that his blackness singles Othello out as the focus of interest in this dramatic world; that also his blackness, being something he can do nothing about, being his condition, makes us ask the deep moral question whether he could do as little about his character, which is revealed as it is; and that beneath the black skin, beneath his separate identity, beneath that explosive character, he is related to us all. His poetry, as critics point out, is recognizably his 'style'; but we understand it. If you say simply, he is like that: being what he is, he did what he was bound to do, you make character a fatality, a blind fate. But the law knows no such plea; you cannot murder a wife and plead that your temperament drove you to it; it might be a statement of the case, but the law necessarily assumes that adults are morally responsible. For the same reason you cannot plead the diabolical temptation of a psychopath whom you listened to, for that is to cast your responsibility aside in another way. Iagos are only listened to to that effect by Othellos. *Othello* the play remains a tragedy, I have suggested, if we don't dismiss Othello as a freakish case or turn aside from him, indifferent, as we might from a newspaper account of the same crime. If we enter into him as he turns his horrifying feelings into words, we learn what it is to be him; equally we learn what it is to be Iago. It is an essential part of the situation that they don't have self-knowledge or enough control to see what they are and what they are doing until it is too late—if they ever fully admit it. If we say that 'tragedy' is a word that must be reserved for the character who knows what he is doing; who is in a sense—almost a religious sense—converted to the necessity of death since he also knows that the force he brings down upon him in punishment is as necessary as the force he embodies—then Othello is not tragic in that sense. But it is too narrow a definition: the world contains more Othellos than tragic heroes of the other sort, and most of us are more closely related to Othello.

But it could be put this way: life does seem at times a device for making people pay bitterly for being what they are; and most people, looking back on their experience, say 'If I had known then what I know now . . .'. If knowledge comes too late, it is because the self wards knowledge off at the time. It won't have it, because it is self-defensive, and self-knowledge is its greatest threat (and it is nearly always self-knowledge that we lacked). In that sense therefore, Othello, who has a glimpse of what he has done, too late to be anything but annihilated by that knowledge, represents a daily kind of tragedy.

To generalize, for a moment: the basic self, uncomplicated by self-awareness, is inevitably insecure, either dominant or dependent. That implies relationship, which is necessary because of the fear of solitude: the need either to own or to belong. Dependence produces the need to cling, dominance the need to hold down the other. Hence two kinds of possessiveness, lest the other person should be lost. For an insecure self, that is always a threat; hence fear of the end of the relationship, hence an anticipatory readiness to punish. There follows self-justification in that stance, therefore a readiness to release a justifying anger and hatred, from which the punishment may flow.

Associated with all this is a fear of giving, though it is a trite

c

piece of folk wisdom that loving is giving (not less true for being trite). Miserliness and poverty of feeling for the other person (directly incorporated in the shared imagery of Iago and Othello) leads to a hoarding of feeling which is 'garnered up' as Othello put it, referred inwards to the self, ready to become intense self-pity and self-dramatization. There is a related instinct to take selfishly in the sexual relationship, to be always ravishing the other; but this can be inverted into the other kind of inability to give, frigidity. It is allied to the inability to give other things in the relationship: especially respect and tolerance for a mature person, delight in the spontaneity of a young person; the inability to give the other person their freedom; the inability to forgive. Knowing is substituted for giving–or rather one kind, a false one, of 'knowing'. It's striking how often Iago and Othello touch on knowing: Iago insisting slyly that it's best to know the worst, so that you can't be damaged further; Othello wanting to 'know' but unable to bear the knowledge, and finally losing all touch with reality, and all sight of Desdemona's identity and worth. But if you are really to own, to control, you must want to know what the other person is, but want at the same time to find them what you need them to be; and above all they must be finished creatures, not growing or changing and so constantly escaping knowledge and control. That is an anguished preoccupation: knowing but fearing knowledge. At the least you must always know what the other is doing–be watchful, suspicious–so that you know whether the other is abusing the 'trust' you don't give them; whether they are growing out of the dominance. If anything happens to them, you must know of it, pick it over, and incorporate it into your knowledge of them, including your sexual knowledge. This gives a peculiar thrill of vicarious living, of voyeurism. I use the word deliberately: we have seen it in Othello's case. It is important that Othello is not dismissed as merely perverse. That thrill of knowing is at the heart of sadism as well, and Iago's 'what if I were to do this; what would he do; and how would I feel, doing it and watching it?' is the sadistic form of 'knowing'.

'Knowing' is finally a way of not knowing–that is to say, of not admitting that the other person escapes one's knowledge, is beyond it, is other, finally a mystery, fundamentally separate. 'Knowing' draws the blind on that perception; it cannot accept, still less rejoice in that uniqueness, because it is a threat to one's need to be

supported by the solidarity of other people like oneself (Iago's case)
or to have one other person in one's possession (Othello's case).
Hence the inability to relax demands on the other, to let them go
if they must, to trust that they might not *want* that freedom. That
would be a selfless love, or as near selfless as one gets; and from
outside it might look like indifference. Hence the paradox in the
prayer book: whose service is perfect freedom.

I set all that down analytically and baldly, as familiar experience,
everyday knowledge. It helps to throw into relief Shakespeare's
unique power to embody generalized perceptions into intensely
imagined dramatic situations, where the characters have the individual life and depth given them by their own language. In
Othello the figures of speech have a corrosive force we can hardly
bear to feel. The jealousy is forced on us as a physical thing,
repulsive in a way, but also splendid in its truth, its own depth,
richness and coherence. Our horrified thrill when we get the
meaning is no distant relation of Othello's.

There is a last thing we are forced to contemplate. The end of
this knowing and owning is violence, murder. And that violence is
related to the predatory kind of sexuality. Shakespeare shows us
that too. What Othello finally inflicts on Desdemona is an ultimate
sexual act. He knows before he kills her how he desires her. 'I'll
not expostulate with her', he says, 'lest her body and beauty
unprovide my mind again.' Meaning to murder her, he might
merely force her: the acts are related. At the last, all the play's
images of scent, sweet or disgusting, converge in an implicit sexual
fantasy, as he kisses her before smothering her:

> When I have plucked the rose
> I cannot give it vital growth again;
> It needs must wither. I'll smell it on the tree.
> O balmy breath, that dost almost persuade
> Justice to break her sword! One more, one more.
> Be thus when thou art dead, and I will kill thee
> And love thee after.

Most readers or spectators hear the anguish, which is there; and
they feel the love—of a kind. They think it touching, and in a
complicated way it is. But it is also a fantasy of necrophily, to add
to the other 'perverse' elements in his feeling. To kill someone is
to have the ultimate knowledge (in the sexual sense of the word,

too); to exert the final control, to arrest all change, to deprive all rivals, in a supreme act of will. It cancels out all acts by the other person, so that the self finally and supremely imposes itself. In peace, it can enjoy the other person; only she happens to be a corpse.

Other writers knew the same thing; Lawrence, for instance:

> The moment [Gerald] saw Gudrun, something jolted in his soul. She was looking rather lofty and superb, smiling slowly and graciously to the Germans. A sudden desire leapt in his heart to kill her. He thought, what a perfect voluptuous fulfilment it would be to kill her. His mind was absent all the evening, estranged by the snow and his passion. But he kept the idea constant within him, what a perfect voluptuous consummation it would be to strangle her, to strangle every spark of life out of her, till she lay completely inert, soft, relaxed for ever, a soft heap lying dead between his hands, utterly dead. Then he would have had her finally and for ever, there would be such a perfect voluptuous finality.
>
> (*Women in Love*, xxx)

Baudelaire knew it too. He once planned a play about a drunkard, estranged from his wife, jealous of her, and envious of her capacity to live more successfully. He plots her death, succeeds, and has an access of longing for her afterwards, wanting to violate the corpse. Baudelaire explained the plot to friends; the mistress of one of them, a conventionally-minded person, was very shocked. 'Ah Madame', Baudelaire said smoothly, 'we should all feel like that in those circumstances. Anyone who didn't would be very odd.'

If we seem a long way from 'normality', we are not. I am suggesting that Othello and Lawrence's Gerald Crich are representative human beings who in a sense explore on our behalf the further reaches of possessive love, which is a general enough thing, even if it leads to frustration and unhappiness more often than murder. We ought also to remember that it affects parent-child relationships as often as man-woman relationships. Who has not seen parents dominating or dependent on children: living their lives for them, using them to supply something otherwise lacking in their own lives, unwilling to lose them, jealous of their attachments, or jealous simply of their talents and their youth? Since I am in this part of the book setting up criteria, key experiences which set the limits of the whole enquiry, I set down two supreme things, which both come from parent-child relationships. The first comes from the Bible:

And he said, A certain man had two sons:

And the younger of them said to his father, Father, give me the portion of goods that falleth to me. And he divided unto them his living.

And not many days after the younger son gathered all together, and took his journey into a far country, and there wasted his substance with riotous living.

And when he had spent all, there arose a mighty famine in that land; and he began to be in want.

And he went and joined himself to a citizen of that country; and he sent him into his fields to feed swine.

And he would fain have filled his belly with the husks that the swine did eat: and no man gave unto him.

And when he came to himself, he said, How many hired servants of my father's have bread enough and to spare, and I perish with hunger!

I will arise and go to my father, and will say unto him, Father, I have sinned against heaven, and before thee,

And am no more worthy to be called thy son: make me as one of thy hired servants.

And he arose, and came to his father. But when he was yet a great way off, his father saw him, and had compassion, and ran, and fell on his neck, and kissed him.

And the son said unto him, Father, I have sinned against heaven, and in thy sight, and am no more worthy to be called thy son.

But the father said to his servants, Bring forth the best robe, and put it on him; and put a ring on his hand, and shoes on his feet:

And bring hither the fatted calf, and kill it; and let us eat, and be merry:

For this my son was dead, and is alive again; he was lost, and is found. And they began to be merry.

Now his elder son was in the field: and as he came and drew nigh to the house, he heard musick and dancing.

And he called one of the servants, and asked what these things meant.

And he said unto him, Thy brother is come; and thy father hath killed the fatted calf, because he hath received him safe and sound.

And he was angry, and would not go in: therefore came his father out, and intreated him.

And he answering said to his father, Lo, these many years do I serve thee, neither transgressed I at any time thy commandment: and yet thou never gavest me a kid, that I might make merry with my friends:

But as soon as this thy son was come, which hath devoured thy living with harlots, thou hast killed for him the fatted calf.

And he said unto him, Son, thou art ever with me, and all that I have is thine.

It was meet that we should make merry, and be glad: for this thy brother was dead, and is alive again; and was lost, and is found.

The religious truth is founded on human truth. The son's behaviour is at first self-seeking; he makes demands; he wants his 'fulfilment'. The father gives him what he wants. Unsatisfied, the son returns; will he have lost his father's love? Notice that the father sees him 'when he was yet a great way off'; not pursuing, he had been hoping; he was watching. The son makes his abasement, but it is neither self-excusing nor self-punishing: merely just. The father does not then 'feel that he owes it to himself' to sermonize, to insist on being one-up; he does the equally pure thing. Nor does he use the word 'forgive'. The other son, very humanly, feels slighted, and that is the operation of the self. Beautifully, the father puts him right.

These are gestures and words for the reaching out between selves, the ability to meet, to relax demands, to give. The father in the story is God, and the story gives a meaning to the statement that God is love; but human fathers can manage that, though it may have to win its way through failings of a terrible kind. I am thinking of the scene in *Lear*, which is perhaps Shakespeare's parable about prodigal fathers. Things happen in the play as fearful as Desdemona's death; Lear's experiences spring directly from the first scene, in which Cordelia, a complicated self, will not meet the demands of Lear her father, another complicated self.

Lear half flings off, is half cast out; he spends most of the play at
the mercy of his self, pitying himself, threatening punishment,
blind to his failings, almost out of human reach. Cordelia having
learnt self-knowledge, rescues him for a moment, waking him out
of sleep and madness:

> *Cordelia.* How does my royal lord? How fares your Majesty?
> *Lear.* You do me wrong to take me out o'th'grave:
>   Thou art a soul in bliss; but I am bound
>   Upon a wheel of fire, that mine own tears
>   Do scald like molten lead.
> *Cordelia.*   Sir, do you know me?
> *Lear.* You are a spirit, I know; when did you die?
> *Cordelia.* Still, still, far wide!
> *Doctor.* He's scarce awake; let him alone awhile.
> *Lear.* Where have I been? Where am I?
>   Fair daylight?
>   I am mightily abused; I should e'en die with pity
>   To see another thus. I know not what to say.
>   I will not swear these are my hands: let's see;
>   I feel this pin prick. Would I were assured
>   Of my condition!
> *Cordelia.*   [*Kneels*] O, look upon me, sir,
>   And hold your hand in benediction o'er me;
>   No, sir, you must not kneel.
> *Lear.*   Pray do not mock me;
>   I am a very foolish fond old man,
>   Fourscore and upward, not an hour more nor less;
>   And, to deal plainly,
>   I fear I am not in my perfect mind.
>   Methinks I should know you, and know this man,
>   Yet I am doubtful: for I am mainly ignorant
>   What place this is; and all the skill I have
>   Remembers not these garments, nor I know not
>   Where I did lodge last night. Do not laugh at me,
>   For (as I am a man) I think this lady
>   To be my child Cordelia.
> *Cordelia.*   And so I am: I am!
> *Lear.* Be your tears wet? Yes, faith: I pray weep not.
>   If you have poison for me, I will drink it:

> I know you do not love me, for your sisters
> Have (as I do remember) done me wrong;
> You have some cause; they have not.
> *Cordelia.*   No cause, no cause.

The last example comes from adult sexual love. Tolstoy's Prince
Andrew in *War and Peace* lies mortally wounded after Borodino.
Natasha, who had injured him by her unfaithfulness, approaches
him in his delirium.

> 'It is my shirt, no doubt, that has been left on the table. But
> then how is it that everything is swelling and spreading and
> spinning round me? Why that monotonous voice singing in
> time?' said the hapless sufferer in aggravated anguish–and on a
> sudden his thoughts and ideas were clearer and stronger than ever.
> 'Yes–Love! Not selfish love, but love such as I then knew it for
> the first time in my life, when dying I saw my enemy by my side,
> and could love even him! It is the very essence of the soul which
> does not cling to only one object of its affection–and that is what
> I now feel. Love of one's neighbour, of one's enemy, of each and
> all, is the love of God in all His manifestations! To love those near
> and dear to us is human love; but to love one's enemy is almost
> divine. That was the reason of my gladness when I found that I
> loved that man. Where is he? Is he still living? Human love may
> turn to hatred, but divine love is perennial. How many people I
> have hated in the course of my life! And did I not hate most of all
> her whom I had loved most of all? . . .'
> The image of Natasha rose before him, not in the fascination of
> her external charms alone; he saw into her soul, he understood
> her anguish, her shame and repentance; and he reproached
> himself for his own cruelty in having thrown her off.
> 'If only I might see her,' thought he. 'If only I could look into
> her eyes once more and tell her . . . Oh! that fly!' And fancy again
> bore him away into the world of hallucination mingling with
> reality, in which he saw, as through a mist, the structure built up
> from his face, the candle burning in a red halo, and the sphinx
> watching near the door.
> Presently he heard a slight noise, a breath of cooler air fanned
> his face, and another white figure, a second sphinx, appeared in
> the doorway. Its face was pale, and its eyes shone like the eyes of
> Natasha.

'Oh! how weary I am of this delirium!' thought Prince Andrew, trying to shake off this vision.

But the vision did not vanish–it came nearer–it seemed to be real. Prince Andrew made a great effort to return to the realm of pure thought, but his delusions were too strong for him. The murmuring voice still hummed on; something weighed on his chest–and that strange figure was still gazing at him. Collecting all his strength to recover his wits he moved–there was a ringing in his ears, he saw no more, and lost consciousness. When he came to himself Natasha–Natasha in the flesh–she whom he most longed to love with that pure, divine passion that had just been revealed to him, was there, on her knees, by his side. He recognized her so completely, that he felt no surprise, only a sense of ineffable gladness. Natasha was too terrified to dare to move; she tried to smother her sobs and her pale face quivered.

Prince Andrew gave a deep sigh of relief, smiled, and put out his hand.

'You?' he said. 'What happiness!'

Natasha eagerly went closer, took his hand very gently and touched it with her lips.

'Forgive me,' she murmured, looking up. 'Forgive me.'

'I love you,' he said.

'Forgive me.'

'What have I to forgive?'

'Forgive me for what I did,' said Natasha, in a low voice, and with a painful effort.

'I love you better than I did before,' replied Prince Andrew.

These are things we can set beside *Othello*: equal human capacities. The self is a shell; it cuts people off from others; it is resistant to the needs and natures of others. Insidiously, it protects that isolation; it will not be open and it will not grow or change. Nonetheless people can get through to each other, either by grace of personality or by an effort of will. The spontaneous gesture might seem to us more pure, more valuable; but people who know what they ought to do and make themselves do it have their own kind of heroism. A parent, especially perhaps a mother, can identify a need in the child and spontaneously give the child its satisfaction. That is an instinct or a gift of nature; we recognize good kinds of spontaneity and treasure them. But in other relationships the self operates to block that feeling; spontaneity then becomes anger or spite or vengefulness. The consciousness that can identify bad urges, repress them, and either let the good urges through or act as if it had the good urges is not spontaneous, may seem too willed; but it is doing a recognizably right thing. It is the good kind of puritanism.

Either way, 'getting through' or reaching across becomes deeply important, and the gestures in which it is embodied–the father running to the prodigal, Lear and Cordelia kneeling to each other– express profound meanings. This is love in its positive form; images for the capacity come from parental or sexual love. People can break the shell, or drop the defences, and meet in their naked-ness, and bodily union in its mutuality is the allegory and the accompaniment of a good love–just as predatory sexuality is the allegory and accompaniment of the other kind. Alternatively people can manage these momentary gestures or even live long lives of outgoing or supportive affection, as children, or parents, or friends. It is then, paradoxically, that the self is fulfilled, for it discovers that its happiness lies outside itself: in the world, or in another person. It is no accident that my three examples have to do with the restoration of what had been lost by the self's impulse to refer its satisfaction inward, to be demanding; and that the person who finds it again now knows its worth and its separateness from his self and its demands. Othello, on the other hand, threw his pearl away, not knowing it was richer than all his tribe.

4

Phèdre and knowledge of the self · I

One reason why *Othello* stands at the beginning of this enquiry is that he represents total unself-consciousness. The absence of self-knowledge means the absence of self-criticism and therefore of self-control. This liberates a dreadful spontaneity: the self is free to make its demands unchecked, and to inflict its punishments when the demands are not met. In Othello's case we are shown the self feeding on lies, self-deceptions and shadows, resistant to reality. When it is suggested or discovered that the world and other people are not as the self would imagine them, it kills and then turns on itself and destroys itself. The only alternative is to construct another self; that is to say, to grow. One basic truth about the self, and not only in neurosis, is that it feeds itself on its own projections and protects itself against the reality that would convict it of being wrong and might therefore annihilate it. Growth breaks down that self-protectiveness, and is resisted for that reason.

We all see this every day, usually in mild forms. We also see it in ourselves. Self-consciousness introduces a new element: the possibility of some self-knowledge. I say 'some' self-knowledge because of the limitation that all self-aware people face: they know that they cannot see themselves as other people see them, because they know that self-interest, self-love, make sure that they don't; and this consciousness leads to a large part of adult mental life. If we weren't a self we should be a machine or a chaos; but to be merely a self is to avoid one chaos by imposing our pattern on the entire universe, and that is another kind of chaos. Because we are selves we can never know the truth about ourselves, even though we may know ourselves from the inside better than anyone knows us from outside. Yet we must try to manage some balance between an outside knowledge–which might be hostile, and annihilating–and our inside knowledge which can fatally mislead us.

The search for that knowledge, that balance, is the leading

43

principle of classical French literature. The great moralists and the great dramatists are united in this. Seventeenth-century France provides the unequalled example of the literature of a conscious society formulating and exploring that society's group ideals. That *is*, really, what we mean by a classical literature: not principally that it aims at perfecting conventional forms in a conventional language, but that it does so because these are group achievements, and much more because they express the highest reaches of the group consciousness. Classical France was concerned with this basic interaction between the self, naturally inclined to egoism, and the society which must correct that egoism or be damaged by it. The possibility of diminishing blind conflict is offered by self-knowledge. The group invites the self to recognize that it *is* a self, basically like other selves, with the same needs; that these needs, pursued at the cost of others, become anti-social; that society has no option but to correct, or if necessary to destroy the anti-social self; that if it would learn to avoid wasteful conflict, possibly destruction, the self must (so far as it can) know, watch, and control itself. Art is a means to that end, especially the art of the introspective moralist and the dramatist. The one is gifted with self-knowledge above the ordinary. He is able to record his inner goings on, and to say like Montaigne to the reader, 'Observe both how I am peculiarly me, a person of great complexity, and also in many ways representative of all humanity. Telling you about myself, I tell you something about yourself. I find myself, and you find me, intrinsically interesting, and I am not despicable, though I have my merely human impulses, like you. I can manage this balance between self-esteem and disinterestedness'. The drama, more importantly, is able to take that body of self-knowledge, and project it into the active clash of imagined personalities, saying 'observe this, and agree that it is true of life as you know it. People conflict in these ways, and at the heart of the conflict is mistaken self-love, a distorted personal view of the world'. This can be said in two voices. The voice of the comic dramatist essentially takes the side of society; offers the conflict as something where our social wisdom alienates us from the mistaken person and makes him seem laughable. The tragic dramatist manages a more difficult balance: he enters into the self of the sacrificial hero who is to suffer to demonstrate the inevitability of the things he rebels against. The dramatist sees through that hero's eyes, and shows the personal inevitability of his opposition to what defeats him. Our response is complex: we acquiesce in his defeat or death, but we also identify ourselves with him. A barrier is broken down. We are made more aware of our common humanity; we feel that the hero has taken upon him some of our burden; that in some way he has been killed for our better health. This is not an easy matter of ridding society of an irritant; much more a matter of contemplating what is both personal and shared, and how that personal element is the material of society, and in its extreme forms either a heroic achievement or a danger.

In any society which identifies the concept 'passionate love' (not all do, or have done), love is likely to be one staple concern of the drama. At any rate a society of self-conscious people will recognize that among the most crucial relationships for the self are its relationships with the one other self to which it looks for self-validation. We use the people we love partly as mirrors, partly as windows, looking for our reflection in them, looking for their valuation of us, and through them the world's valuation of us. If they are doing the same with us, a set of relationships is set up in which people are either confirmed, corrected, or devastated in their capacity to esteem themselves. The relationship will express their own natures, whether they know it or not.

One distinguishing feature of drama brings home that phrase about 'expressing their nature'. There is no narrator, as there is in a novel, to say 'as he said that, he was thinking . . .', or 'he remembered at that point . . .; he felt he couldn't say what he had meant to say, and so said . . .', or 'he was exasperated by this familiar trick of her nature, and so he spoke more harshly than he meant'. If he is dealing with a simple, rather crude reaction–or himself being crude–the novelist can offer explanations like 'he enjoyed saying this because he knew it hurt'. In a more complex situation he may point to subtler things, such as 'he had tried to avoid saying this, because it would be painful to both of them. But now that it was said, he felt relieved'. In either case he sees that we get the point by stepping in and making it explicit.

These things relate to the interior workings of the self, which come out, whether we know it or not, in everything we say or do. According to our awareness or self-awareness, we watch this happening in everyday exchanges; we infer the reasons, for we have no novelist to draw them to our attention. The mature drama is an art based on such inferences; a very large part of our understanding has to come from our saying to ourselves 'Why does he put it like that? What is his motivation?' and 'Why, when he has just said that, does she say this?' People do it all the time in daily life, and there are times of great weight when they watch the face and eyes of the person they are talking to because it is desperately important to know why they are putting it like that–what is their deeper meaning, and what does this mean for the relationship. At crises people hardly know what to say because their words carry so much weight, and they are torn between deep urges from the self (including panic, rage and pain), their verbal incapacity, and their sense of what the occasion is doing for their lives. At that sort of moment two people listen to each other's words with dread, half unable to hear what is said, half reading into it fearful meanings born of their own insecurities.

All this is the basic material of Racine's drama; one reason why he is virtually untranslatable. But even in translation we can feel ourselves into his situations, and get a sense of the anguish with which his characters approach each other. 'What fearful thing am I about to learn; what hideous indiscretion am I likely to commit? Can I either bear or conceal the truth? I doubt if I can answer for myself.' That panic and despair underlies almost every exchange. There are no neutral situations: every character either has power over another or fears him; has something to conceal which it would also terribly relieve him to reveal–typically a declaration of a ravening and abject kind of love, for someone who may despise it or be repelled by it, or be insultingly indifferent to it.

All this we, the spectators, have to infer. All we have to go on is what the people say and do, and our capacity to interpret it, to infer the reason for it. All Racine has to do this with is his language, his poetry, to which our ears are not accustomed. We hear the formality of it, both in the verse-form and in the ceremonial forms of address. It takes a keen ear to catch what is writhing underneath; all the more so in that the images don't have Shakespeare's richness and relief. Iago's and Othello's strange images of 'poverty' are resonant; one doesn't instantly understand, but can't ignore them; they have to be entered into and interpreted or part of the play goes dead. Racine's images often look like clichés; you think you do understand them, and that they function at a very low level of power, and so you may pass over them as negligible. But they carry great moral weight.

To take a tiny example: Phèdre's lady in waiting and former nurse Oenone at one moment says to her: '*Et quel affreux dessein avez-vous enfanté?*' –literally, 'what hideous plan have you brought to birth?' The combination of the word *affreux* and the near cliché *enfanté* leads to the notion of the monstrous birth, and the unimportant phrase connects with a whole network of images which holds the play together. At some moment, every character is seen by some other character as a monster. It's a familiar piece of abuse, in English too. What gives the word weight is the power of the whole play, turning the cliché into specific meaning; also the mythical framework behind the play; and the appalling bursting-in of a real and hideous monster at the end of the play. It has been summoned by Thésée, Phèdre's husband; it slays his son Hippolyte. Thésée has cursed Hippolyte because Phèdre has let him be falsely accused of the attempted rape of her, his stepmother. It is she who loves him, desperately and, since he is her stepson, sinfully. In the course of the play she has declared her love for him; he has responded with repulsion; her rejection, her shame, her wounded pride, make her accuse him before he can accuse her. Thésée, a man notorious for his own infidelities, is quick to be jealous; he has a deep motive for wanting to judge his son as sexually rapacious as himself; he had felt criticized by Hippolyte's ostentatious virginity; he had long before been granted a wish by Neptune, and he now uses that gift to curse his son and call down his death. The monster appears as the answer to that prayer; and it hideously carries out his wish. It does more; it symbolizes something in all the characters; their own monstrosity.

Thésée is better known to us as Theseus, the mythical hero who rid Crete of the Minotaur. That was a half-human monster that lurked at the end of a labyrinth. Young men and girls were annually sacrificed to it: driven into the labyrinth, they were killed at the end of it. That myth gives Racine a powerful element in the imagery of the play. The monster is the self, the labyrinth is the recesses of the personality. The person you love is either your prey or your executioner: at the end of the labyrinth you will either kill or be killed.

The recurrent pattern of the play is the confrontation between two people, one loving another but not necessarily loved in return. The interview is an ordeal in which one tries to restrain himself from some dangerous confession or action. He knows, or she knows, what the danger is: there is knowledge and self-judgement involved. But the resistance is vain; something bursts out; the thing is said or done. The character concerned, horrified, falls into bitter self-judgement, or self-punishment.

There are four such occasions in the play. First, as a kind of relief and self-punishing exposure, Phèdre cannot resist telling her nurse and confidante Oenone of her love for Hippolyte: it is a fatal indiscretion, setting the whole action in motion. Then Hippolyte is amazed to find himself blurting out his love for Aricie, a young woman, half-ward, half-prisoner of Thésée, a member of a family who are dynastic enemies. We see the pattern supremely in the climactic scene when Phèdre slips into confessing her love to Hippolyte himself. Finally Thésée, looking for an adequate response to the charge of attempted rape, bursts out into the curse that causes his son's death. All try to hold back; none is able; the monster in them breaks out, and leaves them amazed. They had not known what they were capable of. If one asks oneself what kind of man uses a gift from the gods to curse his son, the answer is, the same kind as all the people in the play.

It is the third occasion which most completely demonstrates Racine's skill—which is another way of saying it shows his insight into the way people's minds work, the way in particular in which their selves sway their words, their reactions to the words of others, and finally their actions.

Phèdre enters; and the mere sight of Hippolyte acts on her like a physical thing:

> He is here. My blood retreats toward my heart
> I see him, and forget what I should speak.

Recovering her poise somewhat, she addresses Hippolyte formally. He is leaving; she is both paying him a courtly farewell, and commending to his care her children by Thésée (it is thought that Thésée is dead; that Hippolyte is about to become his successor. The fate of her children under the new reign is a legitimate concern). Urging Hippolyte to look kindly on her son, Phèdre suggests that the child will soon be completely orphaned, which is her way of hinting that her passion will drive her to suicide: it is the only way of stilling it. This is the first of several hints that Hippolyte simply doesn't respond to: he is not privy to Phèdre's inmost thoughts; indeed he is indifferent to her; and that wounding indifference is a goad to her. She says, ending the speech about her son, that of course she is undertaking a difficult office, since Hippolyte could, perhaps might, strike back at her through the child. Once again Hippolyte fails to see the point: he's surprised she should have thought of it, and merely says he has no low vengefulness in him.

Phèdre can't leave it at that; she has to press on and say why. She has persecuted Hippolyte, she reminds him; had him exiled; even forbade people to mention his name in her presence. That might seem a very striking antagonism, she says, and yet, and she cannot but drop another hint, if he could have looked into her heart, he might understand, and perhaps forgive. Hippolyte shrugs; it was, he says, the normal action of a stepmother; some women might have behaved even worse.

That stings her, and she can't now prevent herself from saying that she was far from being merely the conventional oppressive stepmother. Bitterly, she says Heaven has deigned to except her from that general rule. It is another deep trouble that devours her. She is now very near some disastrous verge.

But Hippolyte is armoured against hints; he doesn't in fact even like her, just the reverse, so he has no sympathetic insight which might catch the meanings she is desperately signalling. Thinking that she merely feels her bereavement, he offers a conventional comfort: perhaps Thésée isn't dead after all.

Phèdre is not moved at Thésée's death; indeed if he is dead her love for Hippolyte becomes less sinful and she is mad enough to hope it might be returned. With some urgency she says no: Thésée is dead, he must be; and then, as she looks in her agony at Hippolyte, something happens to her. She had always been conscious of the resemblance between Thésée and his son; in her long struggle with her passion it had been a dreadful reminder (and there was just a hint in something she had said earlier to Oenone, that she had been aware of it in Thésée's love-making and it was a torture to her). Now that she looks at the younger man, strangely like the older man, but the one she actually loves; and thinking

D

that the older one is dead, and she is free, a substitution takes place in her mind:

> But did I say that he is dead?
> He breathes again in you; I see the king.
> See him, speak to him, thrill. . . .

Horrified, she sees what she is doing, realizes she has gone infinitely too far. Tortured, she breaks off:

> My mind is wandering,
> My lord, my madness speaks the thing it should not.

It's an appalling moment, but Hippolyte is armoured by his indifference to her, or his dislike of her, and his mere wish to get away. He isn't even really listening very hard, and he says yes, of course, I see how you must have loved him, you still think of him as there, talking to you.

Reprieved, in her infinite relief Phèdre takes the saving line with gratitude; but she is now so off her balance that she goes on pouring herself out. Oh yes, she says, I burn for him, I long for him. Her eyes still on Hippolyte, she rushes on: I don't think of him as he was at the end of his life, an adulterer, a trivial womanizer, I think of him

> faithful, fine,
> Sometimes aloof, . . .
> [like you now, that is]
> . . . and pure, gallant and gay,
> Young, stealing every heart upon his road –

She slips back into her trance as she goes on. 'Just as I see you now', she says, and noticing that he is beginning to be embarrassed, to blush, she says she remembers that Thésée too was once able to blush, when she first saw him in Crete. Hippolyte is blushing either because it is his peculiarity to think of his father's easy sexuality with repulsion, and here is his middle-aged wife going into raptures about it and he feels disgust; or he is finally seeing where that same middle-aged wife is proceeding; perhaps both. He begins to have an inkling of the situation he is in.

But she is finally lost in her dream. Thésée came to Crete to kill the Minotaur, to free the land of that monster; both of the daughters of King Minos – Ariane and Phèdre – loved him. Where

were you then, she wonders out loud, why did he come without
you? *You* could have slain the monster, for all the windings of the
labyrinth; for my sister could have done for you what she did for
Thésée, given him the thread with which he entered the labyrinth,
paying it out from the spindle she held (and that was the myth).
But no, she goes on; if it had been *you*, *I* should have had that idea.
I should have taught you the way through the labyrinth. Indeed,
I'd have gone in with you, I'd have walked before you, and
we'd either have come out together victorious, or have died
together.

The labyrinth shows itself as a profound sexual metaphor: I
would have initiated you in that mystery, Phèdre implies. We
should have loved each other mutually and successfully, or died.

Hippolyte can no longer fail to see the point. He is thunderstruck.
What are you saying, he bursts out; have you forgotten that
Thésée is your husband and my father? Phèdre is gifted with a
sudden return of self-command: and why should you think I have
forgotten? she snaps back. Do you suppose I have no regard for
my honour? (It's a bitter irony.)

Hippolyte is halted by that. Then, he thinks, he doesn't really
care; he doesn't want to pursue the matter; he just wants to get
away, out of this now hideously embarrassing interview. He offers
some sort of apology: of course I must have misunderstood, he
says; I am so embarrassed, allow me to go. That, of course–that
fundamental indifference–that he should have glimpsed the truth,
have hated it, and have just wanted to forget it and to get away–
is the final humiliation for Phèdre. He has seen her love, he can't
have mistaken it, and he has leapt back revolted like a man who has
put his hand on a slug, or on the face of a corpse in the dark. It is
that which splits her final reserves of control right open. No, she
says, you shall look, you shall face the madness of it. I love you.
She launches into an enormous and deeply touching speech, a
mixture of anger, shame and bitterness, saying how long and how
bitterly she has resisted her love for him, and how she hates herself
for it; how she exiled him to be free of the torture of his presence;
how she tried to make him hate her; how she only loved him the
more. What torture it had been to her he could have seen–had he
even cared to look at her. She had on this occasion meant only to
speak to him of her child, and had found herself able to talk only of
him. Seeing his shock and loathing, she is urged to turn it into an

instrument of self-punishment, and the solution of the whole entanglement. Rid the universe of this new monster, she says, and she tries to whip up his anger by her self-scorning. What! she says, the widow of Thésée dares to love Hippolyte; it is monstrous, and the monster must be annihilated. Frenzied, she begs for death, and in the heaving rhythms of her last ecstatic words, as she bares her breast to him, we hear with horror the sexuality in her anguish – a new kind of satisfaction is offered her; the only way in which Hippolyte would consent to pleasure her is by killing her, and she goes into throes of exquisite anticipation, her eyes shut, feeling his hand coming towards her. Robert Lowell brings this out neatly in his translation:

> look, this monster, ravenous
> for her execution, will not flinch.
> I want your sword's spasmodic final inch.

But in the French the sexuality only comes out in the gasping rhythm; it is unconscious. Lowell makes it verbal and conceptual, and inappropriately witty: but he makes the point.

At the end of the scene Phèdre is bundled off in a state of collapse. She has exposed herself totally. How could anyone have that burst out of them and ever hope to recover self-command – let alone self-approval? From that wincing ignominy she never comes back; and the sense that Hippolyte has seen that nakedness and rejected it means that she can't, at a crucial later moment, face him again. She assumes that he must be hideously laughing at her, or boasting coarsely to others of his command over her; rejected love turns automatically to its complementary opposite, punitive hate; she allows Oenone to accuse him of rape, and his death follows.

By a subtle further twist, what confirms her guilt is jealousy. Appalled at what has happened, she is about to intercede on Hippolyte's behalf with Thésée, perhaps to confess her own guilt, when Thésée mentions as something he doesn't believe – a mere dodge to divert his wrath – that Hippolyte says he loves Aricie, not her. Phèdre is as it were, pole-axed: her good intentions drop dead. She is instantly ready to believe, because now she manufactures (perverse consolation) one reason for Hippolyte's indifference to her. She drops into an abyss of jealousy, and lets Hippolyte die. She thus becomes deeply and touchingly representative of her kind of love. She is both the adulteress in intention and the offended party; she loves where she should not, but is also jealous. And indeed that kind of love and jealousy are the two aspects of possessiveness. As with Othello, the desire to have becomes the desire to own and control; thwarted, it becomes the desire to punish and finally to destroy what you can't have. She and Othello both do this. Racine, like Shakespeare, shows the suffering that goes with all this, and again shows it from within, so that, feeling for her, we are shown something potential in ourselves. There is also a generous kind of envy in Phèdre: at one moment she imagines what it might be like to be Hippolyte and Aricie, mutually loving; that is, with a love for each other which is returned and approved and therefore freely flowing outward, spontaneous, unforced, unchecked. It is only a fantasy, and reflects bitterly on her own rejected love. But it is some kind of reminder both of the joys and the risks of love: commitment to another person is commitment to the pain that person may cause you if he finds his good, but not, or no longer, in you. For her this is real pain, and pure pain, and for us a profound lesson. In Othello's case the jealousy was mere self-delusion. We are with Phèdre for a deep moment: but then, since she is a self, the distorting currents of her anger warp her insights. She wants Aricie killed too, for a horrifying moment; and then she comes to, asks herself who she is and what she is doing, judges herself, and punishes herself. She takes poison, confesses to Thésée, and dies. He feels no sympathy for her, but repulsion, and the play ends. It would be a mistake to say that she reaches a just view of herself and her crime: she is as passionate and self-driven in her suicide, as self-lacerating in her confession, as ever. She is locked within her passion, which is identified with her self; and death is not a solution; it is a violent short-circuit which ends an intolerable agony. It is not an expiation, but a vengeance taken on the self. If she speaks a kind of truth at the end, it is the truth seen through the still active workings of a corrosive passion.

5

Phèdre and knowledge of the self·II

Among the questions posed by *Phèdre* is this: the monstrous
element which breaks out of people, harming them and others–is
this the identity, or does it come from so far below the indivi-
duating principle as to be, as geologists put it, an intrusion? But
that begs the question: from where? The volcanic depth is finally
personal, unless you call that common stratum the 'collective
unconscious' or some other psychological myth.

The characters in the play find themselves, in horror, wanting to
dissociate themselves from their action, yet no more justified in
doing so than they are willing to identify themselves with what
they've done. Phèdre puts it for them when she says '*Mes fureurs
au-dehors ont osé se répandre*'–My mad passions have dared to
burst into the outside world. They are *her* passions, she knows, but
it was *they* who broke out; she looks at them now, appalled, as a
separate thing. Where does she, the essential her, stand in this? All
she knows is that she is driven and torn; is it even true that in
moments of abandon she 'lets herself go'? Isn't she, rather, carried
off by this monster within? We are back with the familiar phrase: I
am not sure that I can answer for myself.

But we have, now, other related words given to us by our more
recent culture: we ask whether we can distinguish between that
self, the ego–the *moi* as it was called in seventeenth-century
France–and something more proper to us as individual recogniz-
able persons, the identity. The self, we see, is universal, anonymous,
closed, self-protective, and in a bad sense stable. If the world is
to be a tolerable place, we *need* the identity: open, capable of
growth, the unique organism, the single blossom which grows
out from the universal stem. It could be something to be respected
rather than something to be feared and controlled; something
in yourself to which you own a duty; and you would want that
to be compatible with social duty. A good society is composed

of, or encourages, growing identities, which pursue their own development.

Racine had no such words or ideas available to him. Nor had his society, and they are not to be found in its literature. Just the opposite: the distinction between self and identity would have been resisted as an unreal and dangerous illusion powerfully illustrating the self-deception that literature concerned itself with. Since this literature shows an unrivalled insight into what happens inside people, and how that affects their social life, and since Racine in particular was well able to subvert the psychology of his own age, we need to keep him in view as a profound negative voice when we offer ourselves the comfort implied by the distinction between self and identity, or egoism and proper self-fulfilment.

Because she is self-conscious, Phèdre is not just a blind self; and we have to recognize that she is representative of ourselves in a higher way than Othello. It is a real question whether the self that bursts out of her *is* her, because it is the thing that bursts out of other characters too. Indeed it is what bursts out of Othello, universal, anonymous. But that *is* her, as much as the person of moral fineness who recognizes, deplores and finally punishes that self. She may have divided impulses, but they are present to one self-consciousness, hers; and she is one moral agent, identified with her crime as well as her conscience.

In that way *Phèdre* comes down, though equivocally, on the side of the social sanction. The only over-reaching that is admired in this society is over-reaching *by* the self *of* the self; the transcendence of the individual impulse; the reassertion in heroic form of the approved social judgement. The recurrence of that preoccupation in French classical literature leads to the obvious thought: if it was such an obsessive theme, it must have been felt to be a constant and dangerous struggle. People go on asserting things when they fear the opposite. Racine's position is equivocal in that while assenting to the ideal he demonstrated that some people–and they were the best people–couldn't rise to it; perhaps none could but emotional imbeciles; and rising to the ideal would be such a violence, the cost so great, that the ideal is substantially shaken.

In this kind of concern love is obviously a crucial experience: it is either the cement holding the building together, or the explosive which brings it down. It would be so in any scheme of social and emotional relationships, because the flow of feeling between the self and other selves is here at its most intense. The individual and the social are both focused here: the whole sense of identity (in the common sense of the word) is involved. What was it Othello said?– 'The fountain from the which my current runs,/Or else dries up– to be discarded thence!'–that deprivation is a blow at the roots. The whole sense of meaning and purpose in life is involved. In this or any other society, how are two selves to be related: what mutual obligation is involved; what demands are proper; how does the society endorse those bonds? Is a settled relationship to be taken as a contract, so that demands become rights? What if something happens to threaten that relationship? All that is familiar, like the thought that the social institution, marriage, formalizes it all, and can be simultaneously the expression of the ideal of responsible commitment, and the answer to the normal need for security and continuance; but also of the low wish to insure the self, to control others, and at the worst to be in a position to punish them. It sets a stop to one kind of growth–which is change–and so thwarts another natural need. In that respect the seventeenth-century was consistent: you grow to maturity, and before maturity you are not responsible. Once grown, the inner life is not a matter of further growth in the direction of change; it is a matter of vigilance, of struggle. In the emotional life it will be struggle against temptation, which is sin. Your obligation is not to yourself, it is to others, to the community, and to God.

It was expressed in a psychology and a philosophy. We are divided entities by nature, and conflict is therefore to be expected. We have a heart and a head, senses and reason, impulses and obligations. Above all, we have a will, and it is the function of the will to carry out the commands of the conscience. In Descartes' terms the 'senses' may be charmed and the 'heart' give way: that is love. But if the 'reason' cannot approve, the 'will' must stand firm. A justified love is not only acceptable but obligatory: if you are free, your senses charmed, your heart captivated, and your reason tells you that the other person (also free) is 'estimable' because of his moral and social qualities, then it would be a failing in you–a lack of judgement and right feeling–*not* to love. But if the very same people with the same qualities and inclinations are not free, then their love is a sin. It happens, of course; it is the stuff of life (and literature) but the only course the world can sanction is silence and renunciation. Manage that, and the world approves; fail, and the world condemns. The feeling is the same in all cases: if you are free it is a good feeling, and if you aren't it is a bad feeling. No inconsistency is felt here, because the age had a sense of tragedy. If you are overtaken by that situation and fail in it, people of the world know enough to feel for you; but they will also feel your suffering is justified.

It is a heroic ideal. Whether you think it is 'positive' or 'negative' will depend on your own orientation. Racine at any rate shows the laceration and the cost. Moreover, to those who listen for what he doesn't say explicitly, he conveys a message of despair to seventeenth-century hearts, and perhaps to ours as well: the message implicit in the monstrosity of the self.

Self-knowledge is necessarily associated with the will, which exercises itself in self-control. In this literature the conjunction was asserted with a heroic certainty which now seems suspect – partly because we have learnt reasons to distrust the will, partly because it seems too easy. Racine recalls his century to reality in this respect – but to his reality. Suppose, he implies, that the will comes out not as the impulse to self-knowledge and self-control, but as the impulse to self-assertion concealed as an impulse to self-surrender – all this being something the consciousness will not even acknowledge, which it therefore won't answer for? Isn't that what happens in *Phèdre* and don't we recognize it as more probable, at any rate more frequent – more *human?* The monstrous element in Phèdre, the *fureur* before which she is powerless; isn't *that* her will at a level so deep that she doesn't recognize it, is indeed shocked by it in her social self, and feels an impulse to dissociate herself from it, and not to acknowledge responsibility for it? And, really, though people will always be made to pay by those around them, *can* they help it? We said, in Othello's case, that his responsibility is problematical, because he had no self-consciousness; here however is Phèdre, profoundly self-conscious, and yet the self, the will, can always find a level at which it eludes self-consciousness, or dupes it, or overbears it.

The will is, typically, the assertion of the self, asserting its hold on others, and archetypally in love. The sad self-knowledge Phèdre shows is necessarily partial: indeed one thing the seventeenth-century French knew well was that the introspective self was always doomed to the extreme refinements of self-deception (all the more reason for clinging to the social judgement). To the end of the play–even in her final self-punishment–Phèdre never breaks out of her ego-bound state. That was not, for Racine, conceivable. Her self-judgement is tainted by her assenting to her condition (and vice-versa). She assents to it even when she kills herself, for she identifies herself with the guilt she punishes, thus showing that the self *is* one.

There are other respects in which Racine undermines the psychology of the time and the moral certitudes of his audience. He shows that what goes on inside people is not a mechanical interplay of polarities where the governing part, the reason–up in the head and handling the controls–switches off the inclinations of another part, the senses. Above all, the will isn't where they thought it was: or it is divided. One powerful will, the unconscious one, is set against the other, the conscious one. Yet if there is conflict, even polarity of impulses, there is no justification for seeing the self as ultimately anything but a single person, however torn. Phèdre is her self, one self; she is driven by things she does not fully know and cannot therefore control: but her single self-hood is proved when she can only thwart these things by self-destruction.

Perhaps the social code of French classicism answers well to the theoretical needs of a world which looks to prohibitions and defences against the dangerous upsurge of the uncontrollable. But that word expresses the paradox that Racine revealed; the stable door may be carefully and regularly locked; but what is the point when the horses are stolen in advance? The rules are known, and so, now, is the impossibility of subjecting the self to those rules.

One point at which one might try to subvert Racine's case is precisely his hopelessness about the self in love. He is categorical about this: it is another permeating element in the imagery of the play. Love is a disaster, a disease of the mind, a black magic; what the self is looking for in order to create most damage. If you want to do real harm to people, the best thing you can do is fall in love with them (read his plays, and see what happens). Adultery is the perfect means, since you can do other people harm as well, and with a rigid marriage-code giving no freedom for manoeuvre the damaging futility of the whole thing is built-in. Love sets the predatory ego loose on the loved one; and since in Racine's world nobody understands anybody and nobody can forgive, the love will probably not be returned, but it will be punished. It is obsessive and possessive passion entirely: a self-fuelling of the self-consuming ego, a cancer of the personality, the monstrosity of the will. The restricting poles within which it oscillates are predatoriness and its opposite, punishing hate.

There is a total lack of generosity, openness, or disinterested love—except perhaps Hippolyte's love for Aricie, which is cut off; or Oenone's faithfulness to Phèdre. Oenone is cast off for it, and cursed. We listen to Phèdre's last words to her, or Thésée's words as he turns from Phèdre's body, with a shudder. What a world! The shut in-ness of each ego, the inability of one person to reach another, the destructiveness of the attempt, that is the overwhelming impression. There is passionate attachment, but it is shown as an assault on the other person, a hunt for a wild beast, a search through a labyrinth for someone dangerous, who may have to be killed. Exchanges between characters answer to our clichés for the failures of social life. They talk to a brick wall, set traps, fence, fish, talk at cross-purposes, give a piece of their mind often enough. They never come heart to heart. There is no mutuality, no graciousness, no forgiveness.

It is the world of melancholia, of breakdown, raised to high art, and denied the comfort of religion, though furnished with some of religion's horrors. The thought leads to *King Lear*. There too we are led to the same breakdown, to madness, but through it, to the possibility of openness, forgiveness and growth. Nowhere in *Phèdre*, or in Racine as a whole, is there a counterpart to the scene quoted on p. 39, where two people, reconciled, ultimately meet each other in their love, having transcended the old defensive ego with its demands and its closed wall of self-reference. For Racine that is inconceivable. I suppose he would exclude it as a rare, a miraculous occurrence. He would say he was concerned with normal behaviour.

'Normal' begs a question, perhaps. What is normal is not as extreme as either *Phèdre* or *Lear*. But that they show extreme ends of the range suggests that one is as human as the other; they are both possibilities to be kept in mind.

In English and American literature there is not a classical moral position so crystallized, explored with comparable depth at a single period, and in the drama. What we have instead is the tradition of the novel, from Richardson to D. H. Lawrence. What the novel in English 'does', to put it crudely, is to set off against each other the Anglo-Saxon moral tradition, largely puritan, and the dynamic complex of impulses which we sum up as 'romanticism'. Over the two hundred years that separate Richardson from Lawrence we see explored in great depth first this area, then that, of moral and social life as a whole. Obviously this was not a planned process, but it would be foolish to say it was not conscious. There are also ways in which the tradition broadens out and becomes a European one, for the novelists had eager readers in other countries, including the novelists of those countries: Rousseau, Goethe and Tolstoy read Richardson, Sterne and Dickens; Henry James in his turn read Flaubert and Turgenev, as well as Hawthorne and George Eliot; Lawrence read Tolstoy. The novel becomes the main organ of western literary consciousness, taking over from the poetic drama of Shakespeare and Racine.

A historical point I can touch on only briefly here is that the classical moral position in England in the seventeenth century was also a religious one; it finds its literary expression at the popular level in *Pilgrim's Progress* and in the Bible of 1611. There was very little expression at the level of high art; Milton's, Marvell's and Herbert's poetry, principally. It was in the following century that it began to find expression in the middle-class art-form, the novel; which is not a social art in the same way as the theatre, since it does not physically assemble an audience and operate on the consciousness of the group. It appeals to the solitary silent reader: appeals to him as social being certainly, but because of the novelist's freedom to say explicitly what his characters' struggles are, appeals to him primarily as single conscience, with similar internal conflicts.

The puritan conscience is the source of the English novel. The Protestant habit of personal self-examination is a variant of the Christian notion of the soul's accountability, so English puritanism is the Protestant equivalent of the French tradition of introspection, both Catholic and humanist. In both, the old prescription 'know thyself' is put to the service of right conduct in a life which enforces difficult decisions and offers temptations. So far as sexual morality is concerned, English puritanism and French classicism share common standards. That is to say, they affirm the Christian view of marriage as a social contract made sacramental. Adultery therefore did not merely injure a partner emotionally, it was a sin and offensive to God; a crime, and offensive to the community. It could not have been the intention, but possessiveness, jealousy and punitive anger are thus endorsed by the state and the church. It ceases to be a question whether jealousy in offended spouses is 'natural' and therefore expected and therefore right. The social attitude is that your rights have been offended and you may react accordingly. If the parables teach a better course, institutional Christianity took a harsh view.

But we ought not to take easy anti-puritanical attitudes. Puritanism at its best means the sensitive conscience aware that there is a moral element in all important decisions; that life is a constant choice between courses of action; that the self will always be trying to betray one into the easy, the selfish, the flattering or the sinful course; that one must be vigilant. That is as much a ground of sensitive behaviour, aware of others' needs, as it can be a ground of pharisaism. Indeed, the pharisee is a *failed* puritan, since he has fallen to the last but one enemy, who is self-deception. For that reason, the danger of puritanism at its best is not that it produces the sanctimonious, the narrowly bigoted and the prurient reprovers of others' sins, but that it produces the morally self-crippled, the nobly inhibited, the self-reproving and the self-distrusting. Here it links hands with the secular tradition of introspection. In both cases self-examination can lead to a kind of paralysis. The ordinary introspective, aware of the impurity of motive and the pull of the ego, can fall into painful self-irony, or inhibiting self-consciousness. He may get to the point where he no longer knows what he does feel; may doubt his capacity to feel at all, and be as effectively locked within his paralysed ego as the mere active egoist in his outgoing one. The religious puritan will have an equal distrust of his motives linked with a more powerful sense of sin. His natural impulses may be labelled as carnal temptations, and he may avoid as concupiscence what the other fears may be insincere or merely impulsive. In both cases love will be an area of enormous difficulty because they will be unable to let themselves go; will feel that they mustn't, or daren't, or can't.

That brings us back to Racine. I revert to him at the end of this discussion of classicism and puritanism because he is subversive of what he seems to be upholding. Where the Christian would say either 'watch and pray' or in a moment of hopeful mysticism 'God is love', Racine replies that you may watch and pray, but the devil *will* devour you; he is inside the castle. As for love, love is hell. If God is love, his love seems painfully like human love. Where the secular introspective would say 'know yourself, and try to act well; struggle to resist your natural self', Racine would reply that the self knows how to elude that knowledge. Where inhibited puritan and humanist both feel that they mustn't let go, Racine shows that in the end we all do. The alternative is not to live; life is letting go and suffering the consequences. In a way, letting go is a relief, and the certainty that you will be punished for it heightens the ecstasy.

Turn, then, to a flat statement of the opposing ideal: to Lawrence's Rupert Birkin in *Women in Love* urging that two people in love must learn to leave the self behind 'so that that which is perfectly ourselves may take place in us'. For Racine that which is perfectly ourselves is far too dangerous to be let loose; when it bursts out it is a monster. He had also some very telling replies. Do we *know* what is perfectly ourselves? Not if we think of it as a becoming; we have no gift of prophecy at any stage, and cannot say what we are to be. And if we value spontaneity, we cannot will ourselves to be this or that. Racine would be sceptical; our self-love will naturally form or distort our ambitions for ourselves; and as for being merely spontaneous—that is to let half the world, the monsters, prey on the other half, the innocent, like Othello on Desdemona. How might our perfect selves be expressed? Perhaps in terms of natural need fulfilled. I can imagine him replying 'You are going to tell me that *your* needs are needs, and must be fulfilled; but that *my* needs are demands, which must be resisted. Who are you to say that? You speak from the centre of your self like everyone else.' It is the answer of the angry, or faithful spouse to the pleading, or unfaithful one. It can only be answered from a totally different standpoint: the one implicit in the parable, the passage from *King Lear*, the one from *War and Peace*. If A has needs, they cannot be fulfilled at B's expense, or they become demands. Will B then *give* that fulfilment; in which case B truly loves A? For a parent, it is often easy; for a spouse, often hard. But that is a sacrifice, and we may be back with puritan self-repression. The deeper question is, can both A and B meet each other on the ground of love, and find a way through?

It is not just a question of the emotional life, either, as Lawrence knew. Here is another passage from the same book. Birkin is speaking to Gerald Crich:

'I hate standards. But they're necessary for the common ruck. Anybody who is anything can just be himself and do as he likes.'

'But what do you mean by being himself?' said Gerald. 'Is that an aphorism or a cliché?'

'I mean just doing what you want to do. I think it was perfect good form in Laura to bolt from Lupton to the church door. It was almost a masterpiece in good form. It's the hardest thing in the world to act spontaneously on one's impulses – and it's the only really gentlemanly thing to do – provided you're fit to do it.'

'You don't expect me to take you seriously, do you?' asked Gerald.

'Yes, Gerald, you're one of the very few people I do expect that of.'

'Then I'm afraid I can't come up to your expectations here, at any rate. You think people should just do as they like.'

'I think they always do. But I should like them to like the purely individual thing in themselves, which makes them act in singleness. And they only like to do the collective thing.'

'And I,' said Gerald grimly, 'shouldn't like to be in a world of people who acted individually and spontaneously, as you call it. We should have everybody cutting everybody else's throat in five minutes.'

'That means *you* would like to be cutting everybody's throat,' said Birkin.

'How does that follow?' asked Gerald crossly.

'No man,' said Birkin, 'cuts another man's throat unless he wants to cut it, and unless the other man wants it cutting. This is a complete truth. It takes two people to make a murder: a murderer and a murderee. And a murderee is a man who is murderable. And a man who is murderable is a man who in a profound if hidden lust desires to be murdered.'

'Sometimes you talk pure nonsense,' said Gerald to Birkin. 'As a matter of fact none of us wants our throats cut, and most other people would like to cut it for us – some time or other – '

'It's a nasty view of things, Gerald,' said Birkin, 'and no wonder you are afraid of yourself and your own unhappiness.'

Lawrence knew that 'just doing what you want to do' might include wanting to murder someone. I have quoted the passage in which Gerald echoes Othello (p. 36). Presumably if you have those urges you are one of 'the common ruck' for whom 'standards' are 'necessary'. The implication is that a few people have grown beyond that stage, and can be perfectly themselves, acting spontaneously on their impulses. They do not want to be murderers or murderees because they do not have the deficiencies of either group: aggressiveness or passiveness. What do we think about that? At best it is an ethic for an aristocracy, the perfectly themselves. Racine was not offering an ethic for an aristocracy: indeed his aristocrats are typified by Phèdre, who is a person of quality in all senses of the old phrase. She is not immune from the urges of the 'ruck'. It is suggested that through her we see the universal: how people are and remain; and that is what we have to live with.

6

Emma Bovary and the dream of self-fulfilment

It would make a neat contrast if *Madame Bovary* could simply be presented as a romantic counterstatement to the classical position. But it is not possible. Flaubert's attitudes are as complicated as Racine's—more so, perhaps; and there is the usual difficulty that what his book does to us as we read it is more complex than what he expected it to do, and that we find ourselves discussing him as he is revealed in it as well as his heroine and her story.

Theoretically, a 'romantic revolt' would simply overturn the classical viewpoint. The intense individual feeling, the sacredness of spontaneity, the rights of the heart, the authenticity of passion, would take the place of the inhibiting conscience or desiccating self-consciousness, the social judgement. The self-distrusting introvert would feel himself flooded with the spring of passion, would find with joy that at last he knew what he felt and could go with the current; the naturally spontaneous would, as always, go with their spontaneous feelings, and those who knew them would love them for it. But the introspective tradition carries itself forward into romanticism with undiminished power for inhibition, and people remain social beings whose spontaneous actions affect other people; life is not slow to produce consequences and difficulties. So far as French literature is concerned, uninhibited romanticism is undermined in advance by the achievements of classicism— especially classicism's power to grasp and present the human intransigence which undermines classicism as well. Racine can be presented as a romantic; but really he saps both terms.

We find in the greatest works of French romanticism the same analytical gift, and the same tragic potential. At the superficial level one can say that Flaubert proved himself able—though *Madame Bovary* was prosecuted for obscenity—to deal with an everyday adultery in a way which explores it with some care. He didn't at any rate feel that this was a taboo subject. Whether he presented it 'sympathetically' is a hard question to answer. Emma Bovary finally kills herself in a horrifying way, having ruined herself and her husband, and having finally undergone a moral decline, a kind of addictive dissolution as with drink or drugs. There's no suggestion that adultery itself is endorsed–either taken lightly in the coarse sense of 'a bit on the side', or in the more serious sense of necessary self-fulfilment taken at the expense of a dissatisfying marriage. Indeed, if you ask where Flaubert did stand, there is no easy answer: he refers you blandly to his subtitle, a study of provincial life. But does Emma embody some idea of provincialism, and is she really frustrated and finally broken by it? Where does Flaubert stand in relation to *her*?

Emma Bovary is presented by Flaubert as 'romantic' in a limited and pejorative sense of the word. Though she is frustrated in her marriage, she is not a nature deep enough fully to express an ideal of self-fulfilment. That would imply a new feeling for the needs of and the possibilities open to the self, but it couldn't be expressed as a crude egoism, a demand for life satisfaction, since anyone but a crude egoist has the task–as *part* of self-fulfilment–of relating his or her needs to those of others. We are social beings: we need relationships. Values have to be grown into, and in a harmonious life the values which win a free personal adherence will chime with social ones. Merely imposed values, a rule-book, are dead, and therefore not felt as values. The 'classical moment' of the French seventeenth century saw the coincidence of the feelings of persons as individuals and persons in the group; the values were social and their need passionately felt. But when the moment passes, dead rules are imposed on living people. When that balance changes, the latent conflict between the self and the community is converted into romanticism, or romanticisms of various kinds. The moral sense moves outward from the individual feeling, not inward from the group judgement. The key virtues become spontaneity and the power of growth. But the centre of consciousness, the imagination, is also the self. The dangerousness of pure spontaneity needs no stressing: the innocence that could survive the inevitable conflicts unchanged would be a kind of imbecility; it would itself need to grow into a self-responsible strength of will.

The love relationship would be a crucial area both of that testing and that growth; and–to come to the point–the mistaken marriage, grown out of, resisted and broken if it cannot itself grow and becomes merely restrictive, would be an archetypal romantic situation. The adulterous passion, felt as liberation, awakening, spontaneous growth, authentication of the self, is the natural correlative. But the need to have an unforced but responsible relationship–to love and be loved–either in marriage or out of it, brings into play the dangerous impulses of the self about which Racine was most deeply disheartened.

And there is the question of children. In every age before our own, to be married was to embark at once on the rearing of a family. These, in the moral scheme, are unformed consciousnesses who expect to be cherished, and who are damaged by insecurity. According to the adult's sense of responsibility to them they are either a burden, a clog, or an irresistible claim.

Emma Bovary has a need; it is a question for us what the need is. She is not satisfied by the life she lives or the society she lives in, or by the regard of those who respect, love or need her. She is irritated by them because they are small; and so was Flaubert, who wrote them off as mere bourgeois. Perhaps what she needs most is to *feel*. She is like a dangerous weapon loaded with emotion and needing a target; she is almost summed up as a will to discharge that explosive power. She discharges herself not at her husband, but at two other men, her successive lovers. But that's not quite true either, for if she was truly aiming at them, she would see them; but she is almost unaware of them as people, and that is how she can fail to see that one is brutally empty, selfish, vain and predatory, and that the other is immature and weakly unresponsive to her own deep need. They fail her; in a sense they just aren't there where she needs them to be; but they are the illusory targets at which she fires herself. The people injured are herself, her husband, her child. She has an exasperated hyperconsciousness, but no real knowledge of anything, least of all herself. She is in the deepest sense irresponsible, since she proves no more responsible to herself than she does to others. She can't therefore stand as an example of dangerous self-fulfilment; she represents the romantic ideal blighted at the root, a case fundamentally less sympathetic than Phèdre's. What did Flaubert think he was doing?

For years he was thought of as the Olympian literary master, aloof, uninvolved, presenting his characters playing out their little tragedy, elaborating the beauty of his 'style' and permeating the whole with irony. It's a contemptible ideal in itself—an ideal of the 'literary', the uninvolved, the inhuman. But then it was never true, and to do him justice, Flaubert didn't claim it as true for himself. We have reacted away from that, and away from him in consequence. It is a convention now to decry Flaubert, citing Lawrence's devastating remark that 'he stood away from life as from a leprosy'. Certainly Flaubert is a prime example of what Nietzsche called 'the great nausea', but 'stood away' suggests mere withdrawal; it needs completing by other remarks of Lawrence's in the same essay, especially the symbolic force of the story *St Julien the Hospitaller*, where in the central incident St Julien kisses a leper 'and naked clasps the leprous awful body against his own'. Yes, one thinks, that's it; that is Flaubert on both life and leprosy; there we have the grief, horror and fascinated repulsion, the whole complex behind the so-called Olympian attitude: and as well as being contemptible, it was ludicrously inappropriate; how could it ever have been thought that Flaubert was anything but painfully engaged? We see that he entered into Emma's limited, dissatisfied and finally self-destructive soul because he felt a kinship. He once even said 'Emma Bovary, c'est moi' and we can see the truth of that. We see also, more slowly, that sometimes he is outside her, frankly delighted in her beauty and able to feel the pathos of her case; sometimes he is sorry for her because he is enraged at the people around her; but much more often he is punishing her, and in doing so, punishing himself.

This is partly why it is such a disturbing and ultimately lowering book. I think it is a great one, for all that I say against it; it has the force of any complex and disturbing personality that one dreads contact with, and the power such people have. Its poetic power is part of that aura. One is constantly amazed at the intensity with which everything passes before one's inward eye: those astonishing images which both startle and convince; the clarity with which everything is *seen*. Indeed that too is part of the horror; the eye is fixed open as in a constant crisis, and the mere circumstances of the crisis are taken in and imprinted on us as in the moments that we can never forget. There is no remission in this acuity of vision, and the amazing images make it a dream of horror we cannot escape. Dominated by that possession, we don't know whether it is Emma's nightmare we are living, or Flaubert's nightmare of her nightmare, or our nightmare of his nightmare of her nightmare.

The celebrated style *is* the point, but not in the way often thought. It does not convey detachment; it conceals the way in which Flaubert moves in and out between degrees of painful self-involvement. It comes across as a low-toned third person narrative; but it tells you what Emma sees and feels in ways which Flaubert notes, or notes with pain, or notes with rage and disgust; and there are moments when he is, as we say, simply 'laying it on' in an access which is self-lacerating. James Joyce's Stephen Dedalus, in love with the literary ideal represented by the stereotypal Flaubertian ironist, talked of the novelist simply presenting 'what happened', and standing aside, paring his fingernails, making no comment. But the nails aren't pared; they are bitten down to the quick in Flaubert's case.

Consider Flaubert's odd relationship with Charles Bovary, the simple unskilful unambitious uncultivated country doctor who marries Emma, and deeply loves her. If you think of his case as it might be presented by another novelist, you are struck by the mere negativeness of Flaubert's presentation. Charles loves Emma unselfishly; his love is the only human feeling of any depth or continuance in the book, apart from Emma's unfocused dissatisfaction with life. But he is seen mostly as through Emma's eyes – Flaubert's eyes for this particular purpose being usually the same.

He 'frames' the story. He is introduced on the first page as a new boy entering a class in which Flaubert is apparently a member. He is here seen with the eyes of heartless collective childhood, as ludicrous and awkward. He is shy and far from bright, and he is mocked. He wears an ill-advised hat, chosen by his doting mother, and Flaubert gives it a whole paragraph of startled wit, fixing on it with the callous joy which is the obverse of adolescent self-consciousness. It is described in its complicated anomaly as a symbol of all that is infuriating, comic and shaming in its pathetic unsuitability and humble but exasperating pretentiousness. The vigour with which Flaubert sets up complicated feelings about this piece of 'bourgeois' tastelessness ushers us into the world of feeling of the book. One supposes it is also what Emma would notice, despise, be hurt by, and make altogether too much of, like her creator. The fixation is fundamentally immature, and it reminds us that one kind of romantic self-consciousness is directly related to the feeling of the sensitive child at the stage of realizing that his father's laugh is too loud, and his mother's dress an unsuccessful gesture towards being fashionable. Loving them, he is hurt at the thought that other people may be laughing at them. So he is angry with them for being, as he fears, ridiculous; and angry with himself for being angry with them; and hostile to the world which he thinks merely hostile, or alternatively ready in a placatory way to accept its judgement. That perpetually wincing kind of anguish has not got to the point of making mature judgements, and accepting people as people with normal failings. Nor has Emma Bovary, nor does she ever. Nor, it seems to me, has Gustave Flaubert. It is complicated for him by the fact that he is an artist, feeling things at moments through his characters, at other moments through his own eyes, and never sure which judgement is true because he has no secure ground of judgement of his own. Particularly with Charles, Flaubert is not sure whether he is repulsive, as Emma in her revulsion sometimes finds him, or merely ordinary–which she cannot forgive him for being–or admirable. This extreme duality of sharply split feelings is the material of hysteria: the bitter irony which sometimes comes to the surface is a tightly controlled alternative never far away from it.

If Charles had been a peasant, Flaubert might have presented him as admirable: coarse but strong; insensitive but therefore not febrile like Emma; unintelligent but dogged; faithful, suffering, and uncomplaining. Because he is middle-class the peasant virtues are no compensation in Emma's eyes or Flaubert's for his lack of refinement, exaltation, imagination.

> She was watching the disc of the sun, far off, irradiating the dazzling pallor of the mist; but she turned her head: Charles was there. His cap was pulled down to his eyebrows, and his two thick lips were trembling a little, and this gave his expression a peculiar stupidity; his very back, his placid back was irritating to watch, and she saw all the ordinariness of his nature as if it were displayed across his overcoat.

Emma works herself into this kind of exasperation as she watches him, and that is 'her' reaction, conveyed as personally hers. But no firm alternative view is offered. At the end of the book the widowed Charles discovers the full depth of her unfaithfulness, and it breaks his heart. But the vibrations are the same here, though Emma is dead. With cold violence Flaubert writes:

Sometimes however an inquisitive passerby would pull himself
up to look over the garden hedge, and would see with amazement
this man with his long beard, dressed in filthy old clothes, wild,
and walking about weeping out loud.

It's like seeing the gorilla at the zoo, watched by laughing people
eating ice-cream: same horrifying pathos, same separating chasm
of mysterious difference.

This strangeness pervades the book: this is the celebrated irony
which records the telling detail and stands aside, withholding
comment. But the telling detail is always Flaubert's invention; and
that it is so often what we should choose to notice in order to
nourish a dislike makes it the reverse of disinterested. Indeed it is,
I have suggested, much more often a near-hysterical sarcasm, a
self-wounding. Of the great scenes which are representative of
Flaubert's contribution to the Art of the Novel, two at least
illustrate this.

Emma, at her wits' end for understanding and sympathy,
approaches the village priest, Bournisien. She wants to convey her
anguish and frustration, hoping for some consolation or strength.
Bournisien gives her a little distracted attention, being taken up
with his duties as catechist to a crowd of unruly boys. At the end
he does just discern that something is troubling her, and asks if it
is her digestion. The crudity of the irony there is repeated in the
scene at the agricultural show, at which Emma's first lover,
Rodolphe, pays court to her. (Rodolphe himself is a problem for
the reader, since he is portrayed entirely as a cynical predatory
womanizer, who thinks it would simply be rather fun to have
Emma–though getting rid of her afterwards may be difficult. He is
that nineteenth century literary phenomenon, the cad. It would be,
as always, a mistake to dismiss him as merely conventional, and to say
people don't behave with that crude simplicity. People are capable
of everything; but the more interesting question *why* Rodolphe
behaves like that is ignored. A Shakespeare–and for that matter a
Dickens–gives his villains an internal life or at least a situation
which accounts for some of their actions. But Flaubert just wanted
a device for humiliating Emma.)

Rodolphe's grossly insincere words of courtship at the show are
wounding to the reader who has acquired some regard for Emma;
all the more so in that Flaubert had the brilliant idea of alternating

snatches of his flattery with snatches of the speeches made by the local bigwigs acting as judges on the platform. (These, of course, are pompous, self-congratulatory and foolishly 'progressive', as befits the Flaubertian bourgeoisie). The device is ingenious; the parent of a million sequences of clever cutting in the Art-Film. The tempo increases, and at the moment when Rodolphe says he has wanted to leave the town a hundred times but the thought of Emma has kept him there, the voice from the platform says 'manure'. It has been held to be exquisitely ironical. It seems to me harsh and crude, serving the characteristic desire to do violence all round: to the characters, to the reader, to Flaubert himself. For this distancing, the so-called detachment, is both a self-protecting and self-punishing tactic. It half-protects Flaubert from his involvement with his characters, which would be painful if it were profound. But the inability to be wholly involved is also painful, so he punishes himself. We now call this dissociation, and it is a defect of the personality, and nothing to do with the impersonality of art.

Dissociation is what Emma suffers from too, and that way her nature and Flaubert's are linked, and he has that basic sympathy with her—is in love with her, in the kind of love where you can't finally respect the person concerned but can't cut away from them. She feels that 'life' is inadequate, that the people around her are crude, petty and dull. She looks for a salvation from without, and from love. She doesn't get it from marriage with Charles, and assumes this is because he is ordinary, and an extraordinary person would somehow fulfil her need more. But love isn't in the first place something she feels, comes to understand, and learns to develop. It is something she has heard of, the wonder ingredient.

> She said it to herself again and again: 'I have a lover. A lover!' luxuriating in the idea as if it were another puberty which had overtaken her. Now at last she was going to know fully those delights of love, that fever of happiness she had despaired of having. She was entering on something wonderful where all would be passion, ecstasy, delirium; an immense blue distance swam around her; the peaks of feeling sparkled in her imagination, and ordinary life was just visible somewhere down there, far away in the obscurity between the high places.

Then she remembered the heroines of the books she had read,
and the lyrical legion of adulteresses began to sing in her memory
with the siren voice of sister-spirits, luring her. . . .

She makes it all present to herself in her consciousness; something
to be gloated over, or sucked like a comforter.

Here we come on a peculiarly modern kind of inauthenticity.
European literature since the medieval romances has taken the
splendour of passion as one of its main themes. A debasing process
has taken place: the great works which dealt with the tragedy of
passion have been supplemented by the thousands of minor works
which lead up to the happily-ever-after or manage to have it all
ways. There is a journalism, a kitsch, of romantic love, catering for
a market. This has filled the minds of readers with expectations
about being swept off their feet (but ever so happily); the first
choice being inevitably the right one. Life is more or less over as
you leave the church. Emma discovers that this is not so, and
Flaubert anticipates her disenchantment in his most perfidious
prose:

> She sometimes thought that those were, nonetheless, the happiest
> days of her life, the honeymoon, as it is called. To taste the
> sweetness to the full they should no doubt have left for those
> countries with resonant names where the days after marriage have
> a suaver languour. In one post-chaise after another, the blue silk
> blinds drawn, driving up the rocky mountain roads, listening to
> the song of the postilion echoing round the mountain side with the
> bells of the goats and the hollow sound of the torrent. At sunset
> you would breathe in the scent of lemon trees, rising from the bay;
> then at night, on the terrace of some villa, alone together, your
> fingers intertwined, you look up at the stars and plan your life.
> It seemed to her that there were some places on earth where
> happiness grew naturally, like a plant suited to that earth and
> growing less well elsewhere. Why could she not lean out on the
> balcony of some Swiss chalet, or hide her sadness in some Scottish
> croft, with a husband dressed in a black velvet suit with long
> coat-tails, soft boots, a pointed hat, and lace cuffs!

The operatic costume or the illustration from Scott may be a neat
satiric touch, but you can see how Flaubert slips from a habit of
identifying himself with Emma's dream, entering it and giving it a

kind of poetry, to the end where he slips out of the dream and starts to guy it.

Emma wants to know 'exactly what was meant in real life by the words felicity, passion and intoxication, which had seemed so fine to her in books'. She needs that intense involvement which will make the world come alive; and she sees this as a kind of tribute to her. The world exists in order to do that for her; if she doesn't have it she is cheated. The grim thing is, of course, that the poor woman has to work the machine herself. It's a treadmill. Her passions are seized at, and *made* to do the magic for her, until finally they break down.

Her very sharp limitation as a person is her egoism. This has moments of hideous ignobility. There is a moment for instance—straight after the interview with Bournisien—where Emma in her agony strikes her child:

> Little Berthe was there, tottering around in her knitted bootees, trying to reach her mother and to snatch at the ends of her apron strings.
>
> 'Leave me alone!' she said, pushing her off with one hand. But soon the little girl came back, closer still, right up to her knees; and leaning against them with her arms up, raised her big blue eyes, while a filament of glistening saliva dripped from her mouth on to the silken apron.
>
> 'Do leave me alone!' said the young woman again, exasperated. Her face frightened the child, and it began to cry.
>
> 'Oh, for heaven's sake, get away!' she said, and pushed her with her elbow.

The fixed eye of disgust notes that string of saliva, its shine, its purity; the child's big blue eye. The child falls down and cuts its face; the mother faces Charles when he comes in and says, quite calmly, that the poor little thing fell down while playing. The child goes to sleep, and Emma convinces herself that she was very silly and very goodnatured to have been upset for so little:

> Indeed, Berthe was no longer sobbing. Her breathing scarcely lifted the cotton coverlet. Two large tears were held in the corners of her eyes; they were not quite shut, and between the lashes you could see two pale upturned pupils; the plaster, stuck on her cheek, pulled the skin obliquely askew.
>
> 'Strange,' thought Emma. 'How ugly the child is!'

The relationship with the child comes through again in those details: the cold noticing of the things which prompt or feed dislike—or more exactly dissociation. Many parents—most, perhaps—have given way to irritation and slapped a child, and then been ashamed. But Emma is only momentarily anxious; since the child isn't physically seriously hurt, that's all right, and she convinces herself that she was foolishly good-natured to have worried. It's a bleak moment for the reader, since he cannot ignore that he is in the presence of a desperately small, tight egoism, all demands, and quite heartless.

Because of that limitation Emma can't be taken as a personification of the total commitment outward to self-fulfilment in passionate love, or only so taken if you put all the emphasis on 'self'. The point, in her world as in Phèdre's, is the inability to meet the other person in the relationship, even to realize that he is there, another self, someone to be reached. The two linked characteristics which typify Emma's state are her habit of dreaming, and her using the other person as a means to a self-regarding ecstasy. In a way, it is a profound point Flaubert is making. The modern mind is stocked with clichés about love and life, derived in his time from second-rate books (and now magazines, films and television). The simple mind or the immature mind, and especially the mind that treats the world as a great breast which is just there to give it familiar comfort, has this false pap offered it, and takes it as indistinguishable from real nourishment. The tendency to want the world to be a comforting thing, ministering to the ego, or at any rate an interesting thing, highly coloured and strongly flavoured, is joined to the identification of that comfort with pre-packaged passion of the widely advertised kind.

So Emma does not even notice that her lovers are ignoble; they are only the means to her self-induced satisfaction, the drug of her addiction. And that is what Flaubert portrays: at the end of her life she is locked within an intoxication that must be continually renewed. The world doesn't exist for her; she needs money to be adulterous in style; she ruins Charles; and when the world at last threatens to break the illusion, she cannot face it, and she kills herself. The horror of her death is insisted on; Flaubert renders exactly the stages and symptoms of arsenical poisoning; and almost the last dream-horror the reader has to bear is this death, poetically clinical. But there are further horrors: the body is assaulted. Charles wants a lock of that smooth heavy black hair, divided and tightly drawn back, which has been throughout the book a symbol of her sexuality; he can't bear to cut it himself. The apothecary Homais, himself horrified and attracted in the universal way, lunges at her with the scissors and makes a botch of it. After her funeral Homais' apprentice Justin, a child at puberty who is an abyss of love for the remote and beautiful and pathetic Emma, creeps into the churchyard and weeps on her grave. Flaubert's own conflicting impulses there finally split and separate: one outrages the corpse, one abandons itself to pure grief. The reader who has responded to every emotional pull in the book ends it in a state of exhaustion, requiring a kind of convalescence.

What does he make of it in the end? One thing is certain: he can't simply see the world, love, marriage, through Emma's eyes, and isn't meant to. But what does he feel for her? An unresolved conflict of feelings, which he has to sort out for himself. It couldn't be mere blame or withdrawal: she is, at the least, pathetic. She is beautiful, intense, unhappy, and in a way courageous. She does not protect herself from her feelings: she sharpens them and throws herself upon them as if they were bayonets. At the end she bursts out of life in a way which demonstrates her strength of will. But it is a will not to accept reality, especially the reality of people. She is locked in an illusion about what life ought to be like and what it ought to do for her, and what she wants is the intensity of a passion shut out from the world, in a hotel bedroom; a universe of two people: herself and the tributary person whose function it is to arouse, stoke, intensify and gratify her will to be intoxicated by love. She comes to the point where the addiction becomes banal, a platitude—a kind of reality, you might say—and she won't come through on the other side. In other words, she won't grow on and change.

This is odd, in a sense. A woman who has a husband, then a lover, then another lover, over a period of years might be said to represent growth and change, and the painful thought that relationships are not immutable. But Emma wants all her relationships to do the same thing for her, and if the last one didn't bring it off, perhaps this one will, or perhaps the next one. It is a desperate search. What is to be realized is a fantasy; and while the dream remains intense, reality is constantly disappointing. It cannot be accepted, or the dream would have to be dismissed; so it is reality that is dismissed.

Towards the end of the book she looks back on her life. She feels dimly, as Flaubert felt more desperately, that the peasant simplicities she was born into and became too refined for may have been a reality and a comfort, but are lost. She finds herself standing before the convent where she went to school, and thinks of the emotional security it gave her—because she was able to form and indulge her adolescent dreams there. She is startled to find that Léon, her present lover, seems to have slipped back into the same lost world, like an old dream.

> 'But I love him!' she said to herself. But it was no good; she was not happy, never had been. But where did it come from, that unsatisfactoriness of life, that instant crumbling of the things she leaned on? . . . But if there were, somewhere, some being, strong and beautiful, a courageous spirit, at once full of exaltation and delicacy, with the heart of a poet in the body of an angel, a lyre with cords of bronze, always sounding elegiac epithalamia up to the heavens, why should she not stumble upon him?

That is characteristic. It shows, at first finely, a moment in which Emma almost rises out of her dream, almost sees what a fantasy she lives in. Then she drops back into the comfort of the fantasizing habit. And Flaubert gets angry with her again, and turns it into caricature once more.

The great set-piece of fantasizing is the double dream where Charles's decent humdrum clichés are set against Emma's. He comes home once, late at night, sees her and the baby in bed, and thinks she is asleep. Touched, he slips into a little dream of his own. He imagines the child growing, going to school, coming home in the evening with ink on her sleeves. She must go to boarding-school; be refined and have elegant accomplishments. He must find the money, save, invest. When she is fifteen and pretty she will wear big straw hats in summer, like Emma's; in the distance they will look like sisters. And so on; it is simple and touching and not sneered at. But Emma is not asleep; she is lost in her own dream, which is thematically linked with the passage quoted on p. 73 about enchanted honeymoons. She has decided to elope with Rodolphe, has even made quite practical arrangements:

> For a week already, to the gallop of a four-in-hand, she had been carried along towards a new country, from which they would not return. They were travelling, travelling, arm in arm, not needing to speak. Often from a mountaintop they suddenly glimpsed some shining city, with its domes, bridges, ships, forests of lemon trees and white marble cathedrals, with storks' nests on their spiky steeples. They dropped to walking pace over the great flagstones, and the ground was strewn with bunches of flowers which women in tight red bodices tried to sell you. You could hear the bells ring, hear the mules bray, and the murmuring of guitars, and the sound of fountains; their cool spray drifted over the piles of fruit, arranged in pyramids at the foot of the pale statues, smiling among the water-jets. And then they would arrive one evening at a fishing-village, with its brown nets drying in the wind along the cliff, among the huts. And there they would stop and live; they would have a long low house, with a flat roof, shaded by a palm, at the head of the bay, at the edge of the shore. They would go about in gondolas, they would sway in hammocks; and their life would be ample and easy like their silken clothes, all warm and star-laden like the night-skies they would look up at. And yet, on the great expanse of this future that she imagined, nothing very much would happen: the days, all splendid, would follow each other alike as waves; and it would roll away to the horizon, endless, harmonious, a haze of blue, ablaze with sunlight.

I hesitated over the translation 'a haze . . . ablaze'. Flaubert would have found the rhyme too obvious. I don't think an Emma Bovary would. The point here is that her dream has been taken up by Flaubert, transcended, turned into something vivid and personal. It's quite unlike the tour-de-force of this kind which Joyce brought off in *Ulysses*. His Gerty MacDowell is presented as a mind which can only function in the ready-made terms of the woman's magazine and the cheap novel. It is pure cliché, and comic in its heartless way. Here Flaubert is right inside Emma's dream for once, and giving it a power over us which is his own power. Flaubert did know what lay beneath the cliché in people who cannot find their own language and are therefore in danger of not knowing what their feelings are. For once, here, he has not pushed himself in with his scorn; so the irony is truer and deeper. It rests simply on the contrast between the dream and reality, events as they turn out. For a moment Emma has her exact stature, not sarcastically diminished. Essentially, it is no great height.

When her due has been given her, she remains a 'case'. It is an immature, limited temperament, absolutely without self-knowledge, at odds with reality. She is bound to be defeated, and there is tragedy in it. It is related to Othello's – the tragedy of that character in a situation where its limitations destroy it. What is terrible in both cases is the sense that those natures were incapable of anything else, because the self was incapable of knowledge or growth – is set against both, because they require a new self. The implication is that many people are like that, that life is hard in consequence, for these people damage others as well as themselves, and it is inevitable, a predestined and vain expenditure. Pity is called for, but it is almost wasted. Our clear sense that Emma is such a small, tight, unyielding and demanding ego – that we may know some things she doesn't and mostly manage better in consequence – limits our involvement and makes the book itself limited. Our sympathy with Emma is reduced in a way that it isn't with Phèdre, or Anna Karenina, or even Cathy Earnshaw-Linton. We don't have, with them, that reasonable assurance that we are mostly more mature and know better.

What *Madame Bovary* tells us about the self is not shallow, but it isn't very wide in its application. It is no advance on what Racine had to say, and is complicated by Flaubert's ambiguous and exasperating half-involvement. There is a sense in which the book is finally mean and reductive, because it is so willed, so deeply at the service of the nausea. Flaubert's unwillingness or inability either to enter totally and continuously into Emma's situation, or to remain firmly and critically outside it is not just an aesthetic or technical concern. It means that we find it difficult to come to a conclusion about Emma's situation, not only in the sense that it is always humanly difficult to reach a settled judgement about the nature and conduct of other people, but because we aren't allowed either to see her passion from within as a total and heroic commit-ment – even commitment to an error of judgement about the people concerned or an illusion about herself – or from without as a disastrous course of conduct. We are impressed with the horror of her death and the energy of her feeling. We could be willing to give a full and sympathetic hearing even to her–to face imaginatively what it might be to be a discontented young woman, beautiful, 'sensitive' but self-centred; betrayed by her need, her sense of dissatisfaction into a sequence of disastrous relationships. But our sympathy is circumscribed by Flaubert's, and in the end we almost want to say to him 'Make up your mind. Is she just a rather shallow, rather sad person? But why can't you *forgive* her for being that? If she is more than that, show it, and we'll give more sympathy. Don't suppose that you remove any difficulties or prove anything by going on about middle-class provincial life and its shallowness and narrowness'.

Flaubert deliberately manipulates these small characters, as if to prove points about the bourgeoisie, about false consciousness, or cliché romanticism, the articles of his anti-faith, his rage. But they are merely insisted on; they aren't the kind of thing you can 'prove'. He has nothing to set up positively against Emma's dissatisfaction with 'life'–her illusion of disillusionment. He gestures once or twice towards his peasants, as if their supposed simplicity was more real or more admirable than middle class false-sensitivity; but that's merely *his* illusion, the thing which counterbalances his instinct towards 'the great nausea'. Something both in Emma and in Charles, a distinctly human intensity of feeling, makes them potentially bigger and more disturbing than one half of him wants them to be or will allow them to be. But because Emma is not adult enough or conscious enough to feel responsibility or even know what it is, her state of being ego-bound is written off by the reader as a commonplace immaturity. About marriage Charles tells us something: he represents what it is to be simple, loving, faithful and hurt; but he can't take us further than that (it's a fair way, heaven knows). Emma tells us nothing about marriage from her side: she is never involved in her marriage. Like everything else, it is part of the dream–the bad part. About obsessive passion, passion as drug, she tells us more; but the other person is merely a strummed accompaniment to the obsessive melody of her ego. About need she tells us something; her marriage did not meet her need, but then the need is too much like that of the baby-ego which wants the world serving it and is furious when it won't oblige. She tells us therefore very little about mis-marriage and thwarted growth. She can tell us nothing about what happens when a responsible woman deeply involved in marriage falls in love with another man. She cannot raise the fundamental questions about self-fulfilment which *David Copper-field* and *Anna Karenina* raise.

7

David Copperfield: Self, childhood and growth

The possibility of growth is a crucial issue in all this. With Othello, Phèdre and Emma Bovary we have come up against the moral blank wall implied in the statement: people are what they are, and so they do what they do. Social life is impossible on those terms, except as a gamble that you may be fortunate enough to be thrown among good or peaceable or undemanding people. The law and morality cannot recognize the assertion as an excuse: to understand all is not to forgive all. To those who say 'I am as I am, therefore I must do as I do' the answer must be 'Then change'.

The self will of course reply that it can't. It will have an interest in resisting change because it is unyielding, self-protecting and closed. It will feel that change is annihilation. It will resist any interpretation of the outside world that puts it in the wrong; it will justify itself endlessly, in that protracted range of inner experience from the infant's sulk through the adult's depression to full-scale neurosis.

The alternative to growth and change is control, either repression by the group, or self-repression by the conscience: what we sum up as puritanism. In seventeenth-century France there was a good deal of hopelessness about the possibility of change from within: the main hope was self-knowledge leading to precarious self-discipline. It may be no coincidence that the drama of the time dealt exclusively in crises: the concern with Aristotle's Unity of Time, in which a play ideally dealt with the events of twenty-four hours, led naturally to the sort of drama where some final event triggers off a moral avalanche, and, suddenly, long-held-back pressures prove too much. In Racine's kind of tragedy, this leads to death.

But in much of life crises build up, last perhaps for years, and are then–perhaps–over, and we are not quite the same people as before. It is a fact of experience that we feel ourselves to be basically one person with a continuity of feeling and that at distant parts of our lives we were 'different'. Hence the feeling I touched on p. 33; when we look back and say something like 'if I knew then what I know now' the knowledge is usually something we have glimpsed about ourselves. We did not know it then, and our not having known may account for the fatality of our experience; but if we know it now it is because we have moved on and changed, and see ourselves as other. That too is a source of pain; if what we clung to then is of less or no value to us now, we ask if we were deluded then or are cynical now. People wish to be faithful to their own best feelings; but their best feelings, usually love in some form, enable the self to distort both the relationship and the course of events. Is this good or bad? One wishes to be faithful to a commitment; if your heart is invested in someone or something, that is a deep meaning for you. The cynicism which says everything passes, you come out on the other side, is not only an affront to seriousness, it can seem to deprive life of meaning. To be without meanings is to be in an automatic life where one thing simply follows another; it is only distinguished from chaos by being sequential and calm. Nobody will willingly settle for that; yet the wish to be committed and to believe that one's emotional commitments are the supreme thing in life brings into play the capacity of the self both to lock on to the other self and to become hardened round that union.

If there is a deep lesson in *Madame Bovary* it is that the self can, over many years, insist that the world must be what the self needs it to be, and that other people must minister to that need as well. The novel, we also see, can take a lifetime or a large part of one as its time-scale; the possibility of growth is entertained in a way not easy for the drama.

David Copperfield takes the form of autobiography: it follows the life of its hero literally from birth to something like his thirtieth year, through a traumatic childhood full of loss and active deprivation, through a first marriage to a second. It is a record of growth, from total innocence to a maturity which looks back on that innocence and sees how it was conditioned, so that lack of self-knowledge led to a wrong emotional choice. The great triumph of the book lies precisely where Flaubert failed: in the author's ability to maintain an attitude towards his characters which has a balance of involvement and judgement which strikes us as mature. Dickens is not David Copperfield, but there is a lot of him in David Copperfield, just as Flaubert felt at times there was a lot of him in Emma Bovary. What Dickens manages is a sympathy with the 'I' who is telling the story, and the earlier, related 'I' that David Copperfield looks back on, himself now wiser. Dickens is, we judge, a larger spirit even than the mature David Copperfield, who is beautifully caught as another consciousness, engaged in an effort of self-consciousness, and inevitably not seeing himself, even when mature, as he is seen by others–by Dickens and by us. He is sympathetic; we feel that he is good; indeed we feel that he still has a lot of the innocence of his childish self, and it is that which distinguishes him most from Charles Dickens, who comprehends the mature self, still innocent, and creates it for us from without. As a result we are not as readers harried by all the self-laceration and laceration of others that goes on in Flaubert. Both Dickens and David Copperfield have a better relationship with the world and each other. There is a lot of love in it, in various senses of the word.

Think for instance how many of the characters we are invited to *enjoy*. There is plenty of horror in Dickens's world: he knew all about lovelessness, cruelty, crime, and violence; the London he presents is a nightmare for an unprotected child, and that is one emblem of his total world. But the secure character–secure, that is, in the knowledge of loving and being loved–knows how to judge people. It can distinguish between the beasts of prey and the others, and the others delight it with their uniqueness. Flaubert's world is relatively poverty-stricken in terms of vitality and variety, and he is hampered by the wish to find the petty bourgeoisie contemptible. His apothecary Homais and the abbé Bournisien, like Emma, arouse his anger and contempt, but unlike Emma, offer nothing to his alienated consciousness that he can feel kinship with. They are the kind of people Dickens delighted in, and that he was able to see more in. For him they were comically likeable like Wilkins Micawber or grotesquely horrible like Uriah Heep. His humour has this moral element, that it is an instrument for discriminating between those he managed to hold in his love and those he knew he feared and hated. He was always clear where he stood in relation to them, as Flaubert wasn't. Almost to the end of *Madame Bovary*, you aren't quite sure whether Homais is not really rather a likeable sort of man; Flaubert uses his last few paragraphs to make your mind up for you, if you are willing to have it clinched: Homais is made contemptible. From the start Dickens would have known whether Homais' complacency, his rationalism, his professional pride were to be taken as the sign of a good nature, and exaggerated humorously; or whether he was one of society's jackals, and to be made sinister and grotesque. The world, for Dickens, is full of strange natures with pronounced characteristics, like a human zoo, and he delights in them like a child. I say that as a compliment, as he would have taken it: he says himself very early in *David Copperfield*

> . . . I believe the power of observation in numbers of very young children to be quite wonderful for its closeness and accuracy. Indeed, I think that most grown men who are remarkable in this respect, may with greater propriety be said not to have lost the faculty, than to have acquired it; the rather, as I generally observe such men to retain a certain freshness, and gentleness, and capacity of being pleased, which are also an inheritance they have preserved from their childhood.

This too is something to do with the self: the clarity of the unmoving vision which sees things as they are (like Tolstoy) or the positive outgoingness which will embrace things in their strangeness (like Dickens) contrast with the sourness which so often interposes itself in sarcastic natures like Flaubert, and yellows their vision like a moral jaundice.

Something about children, about being childlike and preserving that into later life, lies at the heart of *David Copperfield*. It is not presented as pure angelic gain: it is seen in its human complexity. Two basic truths are touched on, fifty years after Blake and fifty years before Freud. One is that being as a little child when you are an adult among adults is a very two-edged business; the other is that what happens to us as children may have a disastrous—at any rate a crucial—effect on our later emotional life. That is why *David Copperfield* takes the form it does: not because it was agreeable for Dickens to write a disguised autobiography; but because he could, in following through a whole developing human emotional life, start at the very source; and he could also follow other lives, some of them in what sociologists would call David's 'peer-group', and show related causes having related effects. He could do this through the medium of a nature which was itself more innocent than his own, and he could maintain a friendly warmth towards that innocence. He could give it some experiences which he knew from his own life to be crucial. The whole thing was to be a masterly deployment of the relationship between parental love or its opposite, deprivation, and the later success or failure in the sexual love-relationship. It could oppose the principles of free spontaneous development and self-control; of domination or repression as against selfless supportiveness. It shows again, more clearly even than *Lear*, that the parent-child relationship is as relevant as passion is to the whole question of the relationship between selves.

The plot can be displayed schematically, to make the point. David is a posthumous child of a father he never knew: the first David Copperfield. They have the same name, and it suggests the same nature. The first David was an elderly innocent who married a child-wife, loving her for her child-likeness, and dying before he could get through loving it. That child-like mother, still in her twenties, David remembers for her charm and beauty. Innocently she marries a dominating second husband, Mr Murdstone. He is attracted to her as to a natural victim; his drive being to form pliable natures. Something in her, perhaps, was an easy, if not consciously willing victim. He attacks her through David, being wantonly cruel. She dies in a childbirth-induced consumption, and David is completely orphaned, having been exposed to the cruelty of other rapaciously dominant adult animals at a hideous school. The trauma of a childhood almost without love or security or even a basic relationship to a family—except for surrogates—is completed when the child is sent to London to do menial work at Murdstone and Grinby's warehouse. His mere innocence protects him from knowledge of the corruption of Dickens's London. He runs away and after a nightmare walk to Dover casts himself upon his eccentric great-aunt Betsy Trotwood. His grief, his need, his appeal as basic human animal in need of love and care to preserve it as more than an animal, break through her own shell, which has been self-induced as a protection against her disappointment in marriage and her childlessness. Hitherto his former nurse, Clara Peggotty, also childless, has offered him the needed kindness and love, and so kept him from total emotional deprivation and disaster. Now Betsy Trotwood takes over as mother-surrogate, takes him in, and sends him to school. There he lodges with the widowed Mr Wickfield, who has an intense fixation on his daughter Agnes. The school is run by the elderly Dr Strong, married to a wife young enough to be his daughter.

Betsy Trotwood, having learnt wisdom from her own thwarted life, wishes to allow David to develop freely into a responsible adult: she offers him a financial security which gives him also a moral freedom. What does he do? He falls in love with a motherless child (like himself, like Agnes Wickfield) damaged by a father's indulgence (as Agnes is not)—who is, above all, the mirror-image of the mother he lost as a child. To Betsy's horror, he marries Dora Spenlow, his child wife.

Meanwhile his childhood hero, the older, stronger, more handsome charmer James Steerforth, fatherless, and ruined by his mother's insane indulgence, has seduced little Em'ly, the orphan child whom the childless Daniel Peggotty has reared, and who was to marry the orphan Ham, also reared by Peggotty. The relationship between David and Steerforth is a profound one: David loves him as D. H. Lawrence's Birkin loves Gerald Crich in *Women in Love*.

There is a theatrical sub-plot in which it is suggested that Mrs Strong, young, beautiful and presumably sexually unfulfilled, may be adulterously in love with her cousin, Jack Maldon, whom Dr Strong selflessly assists in his idleness. There is a dramatic set-piece in which, with onlookers picturesquely grouped, Mrs Strong falls to her knees and delivers a very effective self-explanation, revealing her innocence. The main structural effect is to deploy, and leave in the observing David's mind, some phrases which link with obscure dissatisfactions he feels about his marriage to Dora.

The heart of the novel is in the pages in which this marriage is described. Dora dies, like his mother, in a consumption following a miscarriage. Steerforth's liaison with Em'ly ends with his casting her off, a Victorian ruined woman. The selfless Peggotty tramps all over Europe to find her before she can lapse into prostitution. In a cataclysmic storm, which also symbolizes some upheaval within David, Steerforth is drowned. Recovering from the two deaths, David realizes that he has, all along, loved Agnes Wickfield. He is at last able to overcome his scruple and reveal this; he finds she has loved *him* all along. They enter on a mature marriage as adults, and are blessed with children to whom they can give a prosperous home and the example of a loving relationship.

The two most vital parts of the book are the searing account of David's dereliction in childhood, told without histrionic fervour but hitting the reader in all its cruelty, both deliberate and casual: and the account of David's marriage, told with a painful but delicately just self-irony. That the two experiences are related and complementary, who can doubt? They bring into this whole account a fresh kind of determinism. We saw it before as the helplessness of 'I do as I do because I am what I am'. Now is added 'I am what I am because of my heredity and my early environment'. Dickens does not opt for that further abandonment of responsibility, precisely because his hero develops a consciousness, which becomes a self-consciousness, which becomes a conscience directing a will. In other words he becomes a self, but not a closed self; he goes on growing all the way through the book—growing into an identity, an adult self-consciousness. Therefore he grows away from the innocence and spontaneity he had as a child, but he never loses it entirely. His final self, for us, is the writer of the book, who looks back on and recreates his childhood and youth, and is so far at one with his former self that he does not repudiate it even though he now feels a poignant distance from it. The tenderness with which he looks back on that child, the tact with which he refuses to rush in categorically with his adult knowledge or judgement, means also that 'the story' is not spoilt for us by premature later wisdom or hindsight. It is a triumph of art beyond the artist Flaubert, and is linked with the ability to consider childhood as a lost state from which one must move forward, and as a moral condition an adult cannot afford to be entirely severed from.

Hence the poignancy of the treatment of Clara Copperfield and Dora Spenlow, the child-mother and the child-wife. From one point of view they are just silly and tiresome, from another they are entitled to endless devotion. How they fare depends on who loves them, with what kind of love. Clara finds Mr Murdstone; Dora finds David Copperfield, who values her because he lost Clara.

With Mr Murdstone the issues become more complicated. In David's eyes he is just the cruel man who destroyed his mother by 'forming her character'. The reader grasps that there is more to

him than that: there is evidence that he is genuinely attached to
Clara and she to him–hence his power over her. After her death
he mourns her; there are also signs that he is aware of his cruelty to
David and it is a painful memory to him. In short, he is a man of
some conscience; necessarily so, since what he represents is a kind
of puritanism.

One of Dickens's great intellectual or moral distinctions is his
insight into malignant puritanism and its emotional effects. At its
crudest, puritanism is self-repressive, unremitting and harsh. It is
no surprise that what people do so painfully to themselves they do
in heightened form to other people. The successful self-scourger
is reproached, and perhaps proved wrong, by easy-going people all
around him, and by a natural operation of what one might call the
Iago-effect, he has a double interest in making other people like
him, so confirming his faith in himself. If it can be represented
also as the will of God (or for that matter the will of Mammon,
since money-pride was closely associated with rectitude by
Victorian puritans) the whole thing becomes a parody of true
puritanism. Moreover, and this is a cardinal point, one of the main
operations of the self locked on to another self, especially in an
insecure relationship or a blocked one, is to repress the flow of
natural feeling, or to divert it into a complimentary channel like
anger or disapproval or sarcasm. So the ordinary outgoings of love
are thwarted or transformed. There is an obvious and natural
relationship with the dogmatic puritanism which sets itself up in a
dominant or quasi-parental relationship; and so we have the
patriarchal husband ruling his wife with iron Old Testament hand.

Clara Copperfield, the child in need of guidance, likely even to
seek a semi-parental relationship, is a natural victim, almost predestined. The Murdstones, brother and sister, settle on her like an
ancestral curse, and set about teaching her 'firmness'–with herself,
with David, with Peggotty–with everyone but them. Of herself
Miss Murdstone says 'I belong to a family remarkable, I believe,
for some firmness; and I am not the creature of circumstance or
change'. Indeed not. It was Clara who had to change, but not to
grow naturally; she had to be bent to a human will, belonging to
another; and it is an epitome of all that is horrible in Victorian
education, marriage, and economic and social life.

The Murdstones, he portrayed with some subtlety, she a deft
Dickensian caricature, exemplify a theme, a kind of relationship

which runs through the book. They represent the self as unbending will, operating on a more or less pliant, more or less helpless victim. The most repulsive examples are the vicious headmaster Mr Creakle, and Uriah Heep. Of Mr Creakle Dickens says 'He had a delight in cutting at the boys, which was like the satisfaction of a craving appetite. I am confident that he couldn't resist a chubby boy, especially; that there was a fascination in such a subject, which made him restless in his mind, until he had scored and marked him for the day. I was chubby myself, and ought to know.' It is the pure infliction of self on another, in a kind of ideal abstraction of violence. Uriah Heep, like David, was by his own account (and we believe him) deprived and repressed as a poor child, where he learned to be umble. He demonstrates that familiar tendency of sufferers once they are in the position where they can do it, to make other people suffer what they had to–simply to turn the tables on life. He wants to be transformed from umbleness to supreme power, and the symbol and goal is Agnes Wickfield on whom he wishes to inflict himself in another but related way. He bays for her like a dog at the moon, he calls her 'my Agnes' at one stage to David, and the evident gloating possessiveness is made abundantly loathsome.

More strange and more interesting is the case of James Steerforth. Dickens's charmer and cad is far deeper than Flaubert's Rodolphe, because he is understood. He is fatherless, and his distorted power springs from the intense support of his egoism given him by his mother. She wants to live through him; wants him to be an extension of her personality, has brought him up as a powerful will to dominate others; yet she is tragically thwarted when he turns that will in directions she hadn't foreseen and can't approve. It is not that she is against his turning women into victims; what offends her is that he should get more deeply involved with a victim than she thinks fit, as that upsets her primacy in his heart, her imagined control over him, her social pride and her plans of a career for him. Over little Em'ly, whom he seduces, there is a rift between these two insanely strong wills. There is a suggestion that Steerforth having compulsively thrown off Em'ly is horrified at his own power and his own defect. He wanders about aimlessly and is drowned. His earlier conquest, the willing victim Rosa Dartle, his mother's companion, faces the old woman after his death with an annihilating summation of her relationship with her son. It is magnificently theatrical, in Dickens's way:

> 'Look at me, I say, proud mother of a proud false son! Moan for your nurture of him, moan for your corruption of him, moan for your loss of him, moan for mine.' She clenched her hand, and trembled through her spare, worn figure, as if her passion were killing her by inches. 'YOU, resent his self-will!' she exclaimed. 'YOU, injured by his haughty temper! YOU, who opposed to both when your hair was grey, the qualities which made both when you gave him birth! YOU, who from his cradle reared him to be what he was, and stunted what he should have been!' . . .

That's exact, if not the whole truth. Rosa's interest is as exactly revealed when she goes on

> 'I loved him better than you ever loved him! . . . I could have loved him and asked no return. If I had been his wife, I could have been the slave of his caprices for a word of love a year. I should have been. Who knows it better than I? You were exacting, proud, punctilious, selfish. My love would have been devoted—would have trod your paltry whimpering under foot.'

It's an extraordinary imagination that gives us all this. Rosa is the creation of genius. Consider her statement as ideal of selflessness, for instance. It poses as that, but it isn't at all; it is another perversion of puritan self-punishment, becoming self-abasing victim where in Murdstone it became victimizer. She has characteristic bodily reactions: a livid scar that lights up when her passionate self is engaged. Steerforth gave it her, adding a bodily injury to the spiritual one, and its strange kind of sympathetic life expresses both what has been done to her and what she has done to herself, to convert herself into willing victim. It links with Uriah Heep's writhing and hand-rubbing, which are also the bodily expression of a mad will of self-hood, with the same ambiguity of meaning. Uriah's body is both insinuating itself with others—literally—and writhing with self-disgust, in impotent rebellion at being unnaturally will-driven. It links self-disgust with the world's disgust: umbleness is both a weapon, a placatory stance, and censored self-loathing. Rosa's attachment bursts out as violence to others when she discovers that Em'ly was not a scheming little monster who entrapped Steerforth, but that he was genuinely attracted to her and she loved him: that brings on an access of mad raging jealousy.

Steerforth is as genuinely complex. His power over people is demonstrated: he can will to charm them by concentrating his attention on them in a temporarily self-forgetful interest. He can enter into their concerns; and this, coming from a man of birth, wealth, evident talent, and good looks–a superior being–constitutes a bewitching charm. But it *is* an effort of the will; it flags; and he returns to a fundamental self-centredness to which the attachment of 'lesser' people is both necessary and tiresome. He can't in the end be bothered with them when they have served his turn and flattered his ego, so he casts them off. He can't, that is, enter into a sustained relatedness with other people, and yet this final solitude is a torture to him, and so he has to exert the charm again on some-one else. His snobbery, in which he is fortified by his mother, is at bottom a feeling that other people don't matter. The poor and the low are there to be used, to be victimized; but it's all right to do this because they don't have feelings; a conscience is not required with people who are not one's equals. He knows enough about himself to want better for himself; to feel that his charm is potentially a good thing if he could use it better. But in the end, everyone is a victim. The best he can hope for is that some victims truly love him. David does; and that is an odd and interesting thing.

When they first meet, he makes a revealing remark. David– younger, smaller, less handsome, not rich, emotionally craving some support–throws himself on Steerforth's patronage. Steer-forth is half-touched, half-flattered, and cheerfully exploits the situation. There is this curious exchange:

> 'Goodnight, young Copperfield,' said Steerforth. 'I'll take care of you.'
>
> 'You're very kind,' I gratefully returned, 'I am very much obliged to you.'
>
> 'You haven't got a sister, have you?' said Steerforth, yawning.
>
> 'No,' I answered.
>
> 'That's a pity,' said Steerforth. 'If you had had one, I should think she would have been a pretty, timid, little bright-eyed sort of girl. I should have liked to know her. Goodnight, young Copperfield.'

How should we take that? The imagined sister is like some little pet animal, who could be taken over and both indulged and cruelly treated, as spoilt children treat their pets: almost gobbled up, with an appetite like Creakle's. And of course little Em'ly fills that role in due course. I am more struck by the sexual transformation of David himself in imagination. It is the case that Steerforth is constitutionally unable to love a woman; his mother has done that to him; the nearest thing to a mutual equal love in his life *is* his relationship with David which Dickens presents as deep, genuine and troubled. It is not an accident that Steerforth calls David 'Daisy', yet I am not talking of covert homosexuality, but of something perhaps more general: a deep man-man relationship between people who do not have, or have difficulty in reaching, an adequate sexual relationship. It is an essential part of the relationship that it is not sexual. Since David is not a woman, Steerforth does not feel obliged to gobble him up like his sexual conquests, and then to cast him off. He can, with a man, hope for a lasting relationship, if only the man will forgive him his failings. So, at their farewell, he throws out a challenge—a plea—which is met:

> 'Daisy, if anything should ever separate us, you must think of me at my best, old boy. Come! Let us make that bargain. Think of me at my best, if circumstances should ever part us!'
> 'You have no best to me, Steerforth,' said I, 'and no worst. You are always equally loved, and cherished in my heart.'

Let us not dodge the force and reality of that by calling it sentimental. The impulse arises often enough in reading Dickens, and he answers it in this book, when he says of a tearful meeting between Peggotty and David: 'I was troubled with no misgiving that it was young in me to respond to her emotions.' That puts it exactly. The emotion offered here is seriously meant, offered with thought. Love is felt for other people, regardless of sex or age; and a whole-hearted love is a commitment, necessarily implying acceptance of failings and the hurt that failings cause. That maxim, which David here puts to Steerforth, Dolly Oblonsky puts to Anna Karenina in Tolstoy's novel; and Rupert Birkin has that feeling for Gerald Crich. David does not move back from that feeling when he knows all that Steerforth has done. It is an outgoing of the heart which has the whole personality behind it: a tragic absolute. There is no change *there*.

A last little point about Steerforth. He takes up Em'ly and goes off to Italy with her. His man-servant Littimer later reports that 'the young woman' (Em'ly) 'was very improvable'. Before being abandoned she is therefore worked on by the will of others. The 'improvement' she wanted, however, was marriage, and that was not on offer. It would have implied social equality and loving commitment: the refusal of the one is the excuse for the refusal of the other.

'Improving' the person you are involved with or married to links Em'ly with Clara Copperfield married to Murdstone, and Dora Spenlow married to David. Miss Murdstone provides a choric link. Her 'firmness' is the equal of her brother's: indeed it is greater, since she does not unbend to the extent of having any feelings for anyone, though we deduce that she would have been jealous of her brother's attachment to Clara Copperfield if she could have had a feeling; as it is, she merely manifests a distant lugubrious interest in the strange relationship. When it is over, she feels confirmed (if that, too, were possible): 'I consider our lamented Clara to have been, in all essential respects, a mere child', she says, and is promptly devastated by Betsy Trotwood:

> 'It is a comfort to you and me, ma'am,' said my aunt, 'who are getting on in life, and are not likely to be made unhappy by our personal attractions, that nobody can say the same of us.'
>
> 'No doubt!' returned Miss Murdstone, though, I thought, not with a very ready or gracious assent. 'And it certainly might have been, as you say, a better and happier thing for my brother if he had never entered into such a marriage. I have always been of that opinion.'
>
> 'I have no doubt you have,' said my aunt.

Miss Murdstone turns up again as Dora Spenlow's 'confidential friend'—an ironic term meaning 'paid companion and spy'. She links the two relationships: she is again engaged in being companion to someone 'in all essential respects a mere child'. Having followed David's own childhood, we are now prepared to see that being a child constitutes a claim on those who are older and wiser. The child has its own qualities which make it lovable, which give it its own truth of vision. They also attract predators, whether they are brutal teachers, or seducers, or confidence tricksters; so that the child is, as Betsy points out 'likely to be made unhappy by its personal attractions'—pre-eminently in marriage to a person who cannot offer support, or who wants to 'improve' the child, moulding it to his 'firmness'.

David is infatuated with Dora, and marries her. He then discovers that she *is* a child, and is taken aback. He had been very tactfully warned by Betsy Trotwood:

'Oh, Trot, Trot! And so you fancy yourself in love! Do you?'

'Fancy, aunt!' I exclaimed, as red as I could be. 'I adore her with my whole soul!'

'Dora, indeed!' returned my aunt. 'And you mean to say the little thing is very fascinating, I suppose?'

'My dear aunt,' I replied, 'no one can form the least idea what she is!'

'Ah! And not silly?' said my aunt.

'Silly, aunt!'

I seriously believe it had never once entered my head for a single moment whether she was or not. I resented the idea, of course; but I was in a manner struck by it, as a new one altogether.

'Not light-headed?' said my aunt.

'Light-headed, aunt!' I could only repeat this daring speculation with the same kind of feeling with which I had repeated the preceding question.

'Well, well!' said my aunt. 'I only ask. I don't depreciate her. Poor little couple! And so you think you were formed for one another, and are to go through a party-supper-table kind of life, like two pretty pieces of confectionery, do you, Trot?' She asked me this so kindly, and with such a gentle air, half playful and half sorrowful, that I was quite touched.

'We are young and inexperienced, aunt, I know,' I replied; 'and I dare say we say and think a good deal that is rather foolish. But we love one another truly, I am sure. If I thought Dora could ever love anybody else, or cease to love me; or that I could ever love anybody else, or cease to love her; I don't know what I should do—go out of my mind, I think!'

'Ah, Trot!' said my aunt, shaking her head, and smiling gravely; 'blind, blind, blind!'

'Someone that I know, Trot,' my aunt pursued, after a pause, 'though of a very pliant disposition, has an earnestness of affection

in him that reminds me of poor Baby. Earnestness is what that
Somebody must look for, to sustain him and improve him, Trot.
Deep, downright, faithful earnestness.'

'If you only knew the earnestness of Dora, aunt!' I cried.

'Oh, Trot!' she said again; 'blind, blind!' and without knowing
why, I felt a vague unhappy loss or want of something overshadow
me like a cloud.

Very striking here is the way in which Dickens conveys David's
resistance to reality, yet its power also to make a subconscious
impression on him: 'resented the idea, of course; but I was in a
manner struck by it, as a new one altogether'; and '. . . without
knowing why, I felt a vague unhappy loss or want of something
overshadow me like a cloud.' His self is set on marriage to Dora,
because, among other things, she is the lost mother restored to him
as a child. He has a tendency to identify himself with the young—
to offer them a child's love: Steerforth was an elder brother, and
here is his mother returning as a doll dream-sister ('like two pretty
pieces of confectionery'). What he has, like his mother, is a gentle
overflowing heart looking for objects to go out towards, to confide
in and to lean on. Neither Steerforth in his kind of self-centredness
nor Dora in her total unformedness can offer any returning support:
they don't have the 'earnestness' which can go out to him in an
equal return of affection.

He finds, married to Dora, that he has to do all the work of
sustaining the relationship. He too is on a kind of treadmill and
he has to mature for both of them, since she can't grow. It's
delicately done: the comedy of Dora's not being able to keep
house, look after money, stop dishonest servants cheating them, or
even see that the oysters are opened before anyone tries to eat
them, doesn't mask the basic and growing misery of David's
essential solitude. He is simultaneously embarking on a career and
working himself to death, and there is a moment of desperation
when he turns to Betsy for help, and she has again to put the
essential truths to him, more plainly this time. He is told, in
relation to Dora, something that he had known from within himself in relation to Steerforth:

> 'Don't you think, aunt,' said I, after some further contemplation
> of the fire, 'that you could advise and counsel Dora a little, for
> our mutual advantage, now, and then?'

'Trot,' returned my aunt, with some emotion, 'no! Don't ask me such a thing.'

Her tone was so very earnest that I raised my eyes in surprise.

'I look back on my life, child,' said my aunt, 'and I think of some who are in their graves, with whom I might have been on kinder terms. If I judged harshly of other people's mistakes in marriage, it may have been because I had bitter reason to judge harshly of my own. Let that pass. I have been a grumpy, frumpy, wayward sort of a woman, a good many years. I am still, and I always shall be. But you and I have done one another some good, Trot,—at all events, you have done me good, my dear; and division must not come between us, at this time of day.'

'Division between *us*!' cried I.

'Child, child!' said my aunt, smoothing her dress, 'how soon it might come between us, or how unhappy I might make our Little Blossom, if I meddled in anything, a prophet couldn't say. I want your pet to like me, and be as gay as a butterfly. Remember your own home, in that second marriage; and never do both me and her the injury you have hinted at!'

I comprehended, at once, that my aunt was right; and I comprehended the full extent of her generous feeling towards my dear wife.

'These are early days, Trot,' she pursued, 'and Rome was not built in a day, nor in a year. You have chosen freely for yourself'; a cloud passed over her face for a moment, I thought; 'and you have chosen a very pretty and a very affectionate creature. It will be your duty, and it will be your pleasure too—of course I know that; I am not delivering a lecture—to estimate her (as you chose her) by the qualities she has, and not by the qualities she may not have. The latter you must develop in her, if you can. And if you cannot, child,' here my aunt rubbed her nose, 'you must just accustom yourself to do without 'em. But remember, my dear, your future is between you two. No one can assist you; you are to work it out for yourselves. This is marriage, Trot; and Heaven bless you both, in it, for a pair of babes in the wood as you are!'

Indeed Dora is gifted with a related kind of wisdom in respect to herself—either she has a sense of her own limitations, or she is

G

determined not to move beyond them, which is a kind of perverse self-will:

> 'When you are going to be angry with me, say to yourself, "it's only my child-wife!" When I am very disappointing, say "I knew, a long time ago, that she would make but a child-wife!" When you miss what I should like to be, and I think can never be, say "still my foolish child-wife loves me!" For indeed I do.'

Perhaps that *is* sentimental—not in the sense that it is a strong feeling to which we respond strongly and are then frightened or ashamed of our response (Dickens's usual form, which is not *falsely* sentimental)—but in the sense that Dora is here made touchingly half-honest in a way one can't really imagine in such a nature. The child does not have that insight into itself. The self may have ploys to protect itself against anticipated reproaches, but not such disarming ones; they usually reinforce the offence and intensify the reaction. Or perhaps Dora *is* warding off criticism by conceding it, and so being less honest than she seems?

The heartfelt truth of David's situation is expressed in phrases like 'The old unhappy loss or want of something had, I am conscious, some place in my heart; but not to the embitterment of life.' Or, more grimly, 'Thus it was that I took upon myself the toils and cares of our life, and had no partner in them.' The things which have lodged at the back of his mind, like Betsy Trotwood's 'Blind, blind, blind', are suddenly given a conscious reality by Annie Strong's theatrical set-piece declamation to her husband-father Doctor Strong. It turns out that she has an unblemished affection for the Doctor—needs that fatherly relationship, however perverse it looks to others. The Doctor has saved her from light-mindedness of a kind like David's. Two sentences are like a knell to him: 'There can be no disparity in marriage like unsuitability of mind and purpose'; and 'I should be thankful to him for having saved me from the first mistaken impulse of my undisciplined heart'.

That is, David and Dora are alike in years and outward-seeming temperament as Annie Strong and the Doctor aren't: but that is superficial: it is suitability of mind and purpose that matters more. As for 'the undisciplined heart', we touch there on the deep issues of the book. How does a heart get disciplined, and by whom? Not by being improved by Murdstones, nor by Steerforths, where the discipline expresses the defects of the teacher. David here reaches one stage of maturity: that is to say, he understands his predicament, or has a glimpse of it. To learn to cope with it is the later stage of maturity. But what to do? The novel shows several false solutions. Rosa Dartle is the victim who embraces her fate: but the violence of her nature shows how something inside rebels against that. Mrs Steerforth opposes the inflexibility of her nature to the related inflexibility of James's nature, and there is a straightforward impasse. No answer there.

Strangely, it is the Peggottys who offer the answer, unless it is offered by David himself. Clara Peggotty's unobstructed flow of warm good feeling, her love for Clara Copperfield and David, is an obvious and positive good, but then Clara is not in any predicament which tests that feeling or threatens to block the flow. Daniel Peggotty, the childless parent, who had selflessly taken in Mrs Gummidge, Ham and Em'ly, sheltered and supported them, and raised Ham and Em'ly to love each other, in hope that they would marry each other, has his idyll shattered by Steerforth, who makes off with Em'ly. In his way, Peggotty who sets off to tramp over Europe like some successful wandering Jew, while James Steerforth skulks about in boats like a failed Flying Dutchman, is a very schematic answer. He offers a faithful and unchanging love which Em'ly finds she can count on and return to. But then in *her* equally schematic way, she is redeemed, changed, made solid and good—mature in a sense. One wants to respond to the Peggotty story; it has its power. But it is too like a myth or a fairy story to fit the context of the rest of the book. It is also unreal in a moral way—an unreality one finds elsewhere in Dickens. He had this ideal of 'selflessness', and it is always embodied in people you can't quite believe in—just because of the selflessness. Peggotty makes the ideal as impressive as it can be made, and is clearly offered as something to be endorsed, indeed revered, as in this passage. Em'ly has been found, and for a moment his joy is mixed with a pang; he repines at her fate. But

> 'It warn't for long as I felt that; for she was found. I had on'y to think as she was found, and it was gone. I doen't know why I do so much as mention of it now, I'm sure. I didn't have it in my mind a minute ago, to say a word about myself; but it come up so nat'ral that I yielded to it afore I was aweer.'

'You are a self-denying soul,' said my aunt, 'and will have your reward.'

Peggotty momentarily taken aback to discover that he is capable of a natural resentment, but able in his selflessness to accept that tiny speck of ordinary humanity–it's a bit much. He is an impressive creation, but as a myth or allegorical figure. He doesn't begin to be human, or real. The myth of utter selflessness is like the myth of virgin purity and other Victorian moral furniture, and the two together blight Dickens's good women. Tolstoy buried that myth by showing that 'selflessness' is a kind of crippled state (p. 116). (I don't mean that there is not 'selfless' behaviour, but that it is the action, either willed or spontaneous, of a self capable of other impulses. Agnes Wickfield has no such impulses, and we have just boggled at Peggotty's sole moment of moral struggle.)

The reality of the book is David's marriage to Dora, his discovery that it was a bad choice; that Dora is locked in her immaturity (even if it is the immaturity of a sweet child rather than a spoiled one), that his marriage offers him no support, doesn't answer his own needs. In that situation to be merely selfless and forgiving, like Daniel Peggotty, is to offer the response of a father. That may suit Peggotty's situation, whose child grows up and returns to him from her prodigal adventure; it may suit the Dr Strongs and Annies who *need* a father-child relationship. It doesn't help a young man who needs an equal partner, a sexual partner.

Dickens releases David by having Dora die. Of course, a lot of young women did die of consumption in the nineteenth century; so if you made a mismarriage nature offered you better odds of release than she does now. None the less the knot is cut in a way it wasn't for Dickens himself (he left his wife). To be able to weep farewell to your child-wife just before the moment when you might have to admit that the alternatives are a superhuman self-discipline or an inexorably unhappy and possibly sordid middle-age is a fortunate dispensation. On the other hand, Dora's death is the one really imaginable *resolution* of the situation (as distinct from false solutions or failures to find one). David Copperfield has throughout a long book established himself in our minds as earnest, innocent, good and kind. He has therefore the capacity–a necessary capacity –to see things in human terms in the best sense. He knows his love for Dora, hers for him. He is not the person to cancel out those feelings, to say at a certain stage 'This is all a mistake. I must break free.' Nor is he the person to say 'I can go on if I have a therapeutic adultery', though he might find himself in an adultery through his own need and his lack of self-knowledge. But that would be a torture to him, a source of self-reproach, not a second life. He is the incarnation of earnest faithfulness, concealing from itself its own unhappiness. We suppose that he would have gone on, using work as an anodyne, or finding allowable consolation where he could beyond his marriage–in friendship, in writing, in good works: anything which gave him an outward flow of sub-limated feeling. If we have any temptation to say, now, that that is all wasteful and wrong, he could cut free in our time, and thank heaven for the new divorce laws, we are being crude. It is his nature to be kind, therefore faithful and self-abnegating. It would be a violence to that nature, and a source of lifelong guilt, to take the way out. We have no later wisdom, no wisdom of any sort, to offer him in what is a tragic situation, cut short in the only natural way, the only way acceptable to that nature. He is not Dickens, in a way that Dickens must have been painfully aware of.

David has Dora's and Steerforth's deaths to contend with almost simultaneously: his mother-sister-wife and his elder-brother-friend in both of whom he had placed all his deepest feeling, leave him alone in the world in a repetition of his original orphan state. He undergoes a kind of breakdown, naturally enough, and in the after-math it is borne in on him that Agnes Wickfield, whom he had thought of as a sister because he always felt a kind of friendly equality with her, an easy relationship founded on liking and respect, is the person he truly loves. There is a rightness about this discovery which makes us willing not to worry too much about Dora's elimination. This is the kind of relationship David *ought* to have managed in the beginning, and we are glad he finds it in the end; we want it for him; and so we are not tempted to think that if Dora hadn't died he might have had to face leaving her, or want an adulterous relationship which Agnes herself in her purity and goodness would not contemplate–so it would have to be where he could find it. Like other Dickens heroines, Agnes is incapable of wrong–has no blemishes at all. We don't believe in her for that reason. The fact is that a person so incapable of self-assertion is not only incapable of doing wrong but virtually incapable of doing anything at all. Tolstoy, I have hinted, put Dickens right about that sort of heroine in his portrayal of Varenka in *Anna Karenina*.

But he may have taken a tip from Dickens even here. David says to Agnes, by way of password to her love: 'You have not taught me quite in vain. There is no alloy of self in what I feel for you.' A page later, quite inconsistently but much more sensibly, he says: 'If you had been more mindful of yourself, and less of me, when we grew up here together, I think my heedless fancy never would have wandered from you.'

It is idle to imagine the book Dickens would have written 'if his public had let him'. One very powerful part of him had no wish to offend that public because he needed its love and esteem and would not dream of forfeiting it. He was not therefore concerned to write another book, in which a David Copperfield is not released from a mistaken marriage and has to find how to live with the consequences of the first mistaken impulse of his undisciplined heart. He has in any case suggested the range of possibilities: to be a Murdstone, a Mrs Steerforth, a Rosa Dartle, a Steerforth, a Doctor Strong, a Peggotty. Of those possibilities the one which strikes us as most real is being a Murdstone. It's no accident that Murdstone's kind of puritanism, where the self turns its disciplinary powers, its will, outwards onto another, is the temptation which David finds in himself, and shrinks from, in relation to Dora. How long he could have deflected himself from that course, how long he could have resisted the temptation to 'help' Dora to become what he needed her to be, how long he could simply have rejoiced in her being a child, how he could have lived with a middle-aged child (who would for most purposes be an imbecile or a monster)– the questions may be 'improper' in that the novel as we have it is the novel we are supposed to be content with. But we aren't, entirely, and so we do ask questions. An absolute commitment to marriage as a social institution, and itself an absolute commitment, can only answer 'adapt yourself to it'. Unadaptability produces the only other answer–'Bear it'. David Copperfield would have borne it, or tried to. What it would have done to him–that is what we are left thinking about.

8

Anna Karenina and the cost of self-fulfilment

We know that Tolstoy read *David Copperfield* and was impressed by it. Perhaps it was a matter, for him, of seeing that both he and Dickens understood certain things–about the self in particular. This, for instance: a very small touch, but Tolstoy would have recognized the interest and relevance:

> A figure appeared in the distance before long, and I soon knew it to be Em'ly, who was a little creature still in stature, though she was grown. But when she drew nearer, and I saw her blue eyes looking bluer, and her dimpled face looking brighter, and her whole self prettier and gayer, a curious feeling came over me that made me pretend not to know her, and pass by as if I were looking at something a long way off. I have done such a thing since in later life, or I am mistaken.

Tolstoy even borrowed in *Childhood* the profound moment in which the death of his mother turns David from an unconscious self into a self-conscious self (a crucial stage, and Dickens both identified it and knew what kind of thing caused it):

> I stood upon a chair when I was left alone, and looked into the glass to see how red my eyes were, and how sorrowful my face. I considered, after some hours were gone, if my tears were really hard to flow now, as they seemed to be; what, in connexion with my loss, it would affect me most to think of when I drew near home–for I was going home to the funeral. I am sensible of having felt that a dignity attached to me among the rest of the boys, and that I was important in my affliction.
>
> If ever child were stricken with sincere grief, I was. But I remember that this importance was a kind of satisfaction to me, when I walked in the playground that afternoon while the boys were in school. When I saw them glancing at me out of the

windows, as they went up to their classes, I felt distinguished, and looked more melancholy, and walked slower. When school was over, and they came out and spoke to me, I felt it rather good in myself not to be proud to any of them, and to take exactly the same notice of them all, as before.

A more important link between the Dickens of *David Copperfield* and the Tolstoy of *Anna Karenina* is rather general, and not easy to define: something about seeking, seeking for something to rest in. Looking back on David's account of his marriage to Dora, one is most impressed by his sense of something not there, the unease of unconscious disappointment–'without knowing why, I felt a vague unhappy loss or want of something overshadow me like a cloud'. The consciousness is just aware of this, but will not grasp it, partly because it does not fully understand, has not advanced to the point where it knows what is wrong, but much more because it cannot afford to. The knowledge would dislodge something very deep (David's impulse to rediscover and possess someone like his mother) and that something cannot be identified or it would be contested and perhaps annihilated. The daylight knowledge would also become a conscious unhappiness that would either call for action or emphasize that action was impossible, and life would then become intolerable.

We may think in this connection of Levin, early on in *Anna Karenina*, rejected by Kitty Schcherbatsky, whom he loves. He has gone back to his estate, the other deep thing in his life, and is there partly consoled by his sense of belonging to it (rather than it to him). It stands for what bears him up, but he also sees how he needs completion–how if he doesn't grow on he and his life are stagnant:

He went into his study, which was gradually lit up by the candle. The familiar objects in the room were revealed: the antlers, the bookshelves, the tiled stove with the ventilator which had long been in need of repair, his father's sofa, the big table with an open book, a broken ash tray, and a notebook with his writing. When he saw all this, he was for a moment overcome by a feeling of doubt of the possibility of starting the new life he had been dreaming of during his drive home. All these traces of his old life seemed to seize hold of him, saying: 'No, you won't get away from us, and you're not going to be different; you're going to be just the same as you've always been with your doubts, your everlasting dissatisfaction with yourself, your vain attempts at reform, your falling from grace, and *the constant expectation of the happiness you have missed and which is not possible for you.*' (*My italics.*)

It is that last thought which eats the heart away. Tolstoy shows with his own kind of intensity, and then by his own kind of humour (not a muscle of his face moving in either mood) how Levin reacts against it. First it is a desperate rush of resistance:

But this was what the things said to him. Another voice inside him was saying that one must not submit to the past and one can make what one likes of oneself.

Then Tolstoy sees that that is comic:

And obeying this voice, he went to the corner where his two eighty-pound dumbbells lay, and started exercising with them, raising and lowering them, trying to put heart into himself.

('Heart' turns out to be an important word.) Then a final touch of humour:

There was a sound of creaking footsteps behind the door. He hastily put down the dumbbells.

Two things stand out about that characteristic paragraph. One is that Tolstoy's art is his power to enter with amazing adaptability and insight into the consciousness of each of his characters successively. That is his 'narrative method'. He is fully but neutrally inside first this self, and then that other quite different self, and the book moves on by presenting the world as seen by one centre of consciousness after another. Inevitably there is a profound irony in this, but it is unlike Flaubert's because Tolstoy is so calmly separate from each centre. This does not mean that he has no judgement of his own, but that he trusts his art to do its job. He has the sympathy implied by his power to project himself entirely within the character and for a moment to see the world and others through the eyes of that character, and he has the detachment to let these subjectivities work against each other. The element of mere narration, the novelist's framework, is equally neutral, since it consists in showing how this character or that character felt, and therefore why they did this or that. That makes the novel a world of fully autonomous separate selves, like the world we live in. Each of these selves is dedicated to the task of self-fulfilment.

That leads to the second point. These are all selves, but they are not seen as merely engaged in Racine's terrible struggle. Most of them have a profound need not merely to be fulfilled, but to be in a right relationship with the world as well, meaning other people in the first place, and something which transcends personal need in the second. They want to be comfortable with themselves because they are concentrated on what is *for them* the right aim in life. Indissolubly linked with the right aim in life, is life with the right person. Being happy, they learn, is not, as it was for Emma Bovary, the world as big breast giving the baby ego endless support and automatic comfort. Happiness is not given on demand; it is something harder, something earned–that consciousness of a right overall relationship with something beyond the ego. In that deeper sense people have a right to want to be happy, or at any rate to try. They don't all manage; in the nature of the case, they can't, Tolstoy shows; the part of the novel which deals with Anna is a tragedy; the part which deals with Levin ends with an open question.

Any reader of *Anna Karenina* can spontaneously recall scene after scene when the sense of momentary happiness or the possibility of happiness is expressed as an intense moment of individual physical life, or when the sense of tragedy is turned into ineluctable conflict between selves. This is how the moral and social life is actually lived and felt.

Emma Bovary thought of the possibility of endless happiness as the blue haze of an exotic distance: somewhere else, strange and new. Or she had the sense of being intensely alive, but essentially in some private place where two lovers are shut off in a world of their own. Tolstoy's people do feel love as being intensely alive at other times too. And the world is not hazy, or a daydream, or imagined as some part of it one hasn't been to and which is therefore more satisfying: it is this place now, in its immediate clarity, with me quite naturally feeling I am at the centre of it because I see it, but reminded that I don't matter particularly to *it*. The great scenes of haymaking, shooting, racing and so on, are not set-piece descriptive interludes affording indulgent relief from the human intensities and griefs; they are reminders that we are in the world and of it, and at best intensely at home in it, and always amazed at its perfectly ordinary and natural beauty, which goes on and on whatever happens to us–and that is a comfort to the mature person, though it is an affront to the mere ego. It is one of the foundations of religious feeling, and this is clearly related to the overall sense of *vocation* which lies at the heart of the book. Marriage to this person; dedication to this job or social function; bearing and bringing up these children; life in this place among these people – these are the normal possibilities of life, and if we are to find meaning it is in those things, and in our ability to turn them into something more than a mere set of circumstances, or a predicament.

As one of the moments of physical content, think of Vronsky in his carriage, smiling involuntarily, crossing one leg over another, taking it in his hand, feeling the springy muscle of his calf, throwing himself back and taking in great breaths of cold air. He is deep in trouble: his adultery with Anna is about to be an open scandal and to enter a period of crisis; but the relationship has given his life its meaning. He is intensely aware at this moment of the goodness of life – indeed he is identified with life; and so he is comfortably at home in the world, however dangerous it is, pleased to be himself, in his body, in his carriage, now. It is happiness; and feeling it he is aware of the cold clear air, and the smell of the brilliantine on his moustache. Yet it is the same light, the same air in which Anna, looking from the terrace of her country cottage at the aspens glittering in the cold sunshine, is aware of a threat to her existence. Neither of them is wrong.

Or we remember Levin, at last accepted by Kitty. He drifts about in a transformed world, where his body, unlike the more 'physical' Vronsky's, is almost annihilated. He can't be bothered to eat or sleep. Again we see things in Tolstoy's limpid atmosphere – the marvellousness of the ordinary, the ordinariness of the marvellous.

And what he saw then, he never saw again. He was moved particularly by the children going to school, the grayish-blue pigeons flying from the roofs to the pavement, and the little loaves of bread, sprinkled with flour, that some invisible hand had put outside a baker's shop. These loaves, the pigeons, and the boys were not of this world. It all happened at the same time: one of the boys ran up to a pigeon and, smiling, looked at Levin; the pigeon fluttered its wings and flew away, glittering in the sunshine among the quivering specks of snow in the air; and from the window of the baker's shop came the smell of hot bread and the loaves were put out. All this together was so extraordinarily nice that Levin laughed and cried with joy . . . He told his cabby to drive to the Schcherbatsky's. The cabby looked marvellous with the white band of his shirt showing from under his coat and fitting tightly round his thick, red, sturdy neck. His sledge was high and comfortable, and never after did Levin drive in one like it, and the horse was wonderful too, and tried its best to go fast but did not move from its place. The cabby knew the Schcherbatskys' house, and rounding his elbows in a way that was meant to be especially respectful to his fare, and crying 'Whoa!', he drove up to the front door.

That is the happiness of returned love, turning outwards to embrace the world; it is related to the mystic state. It is a thing which passes, and it is intensely personal, but it is not an illusion. Though there is something comic in Levin's intoxication, it is also moving, and enviable. It has to do with seeing clearly one's goal in life, finding it attainable, and finding (in this case) that the friendly world gives it to you as something natural and right.

If this feeling is principally associated with the 'seeker' Levin, who is growing into the right relationship with the world which he needs in order to live at peace with himself, he is joined in that by all the important characters. The world is crucially represented by the person one loves. Of all the emblematic scenes perhaps the one which makes the deepest impression, where Levin again grasps the sense that the world converges, for him, in one person, is that earlier scene where he stands alone in the meadows at dawn after a night of solemn and naïf self-examination. He has just come to a wrong decision—to form or join a commune of peasants and lose his identity among them. He notices that while he has been thinking a pattern has formed in the clouds above him. With a touching and gentle irony he sees a significance here: he joyfully takes the instability, the tenuousness, the essential meaninglessness of the onward drift of vapours as replicating the crystallization of his own consciousness and will. At that moment Kitty drives past, and his decision is instantly annulled. He knows at once what he really wants: life with her:

> Bright and thoughtful, full of an exquisite complex inner life to which Levin was a stranger, she gazed beyond him at the glow of the sunrise.
>
> At the very moment when the vision was about to disappear,

a pair of truthful eyes glanced at him. She recognized him, and a
look of amazement and joy lit up her face.

He could not be mistaken. There were no other eyes in the
world like those. There was only one being in the world who was
able to concentrate for him the whole world and the meaning of
life. It was she. It was Kitty, . . . the only possible solution to the
riddle of his life. . . .

Looking up at the sky again, he sees his cloud-pattern has dis-
appeared. But for him that is as significant as the first 'meaning'.
It turns out later that Kitty hadn't even seen him, either—and that
is another of Tolstoy's gentle ironies. Flaubert would have been
sardonic about this, not allowing that the wish to find meanings
and to read them from the world around is a deep and right
instinct. After all, Levin *has* found his meaning.

Kitty comes to have the same sense of him: 'All her life, all her
desires and hopes, were concentrated on this one man, whom she
still did not understand, to whom she was bound by a feeling she
understood even less than the man himself.' She knows that her
life with him is something to enter upon in a kind of dread,
because of its possibilities for fulfilment or of deep unhappiness.

The point is made structurally. At the very centre of this huge
novel, Anna leaves Karenin and her son, and goes off to live with
Vronsky, at the same time as Levin marries Kitty, who had once
been in love with Vronsky. There is a parallel between the two
relationships, and a link, in that the two women have both loved
(in some sense of the word) two men, one of whom was—as it
turned out—the wrong man, the other being perhaps the right man.
But Kitty is entering, Anna leaving, marriage. Up to this central
point the book follows the characters through a carefully plotted
process. The first relationships are indicated: Anna and Kitty are
shown as intolerably placed—the one married to Karenin and in
love with Vronsky, the other jilted by Vronsky, humiliated, and
feeling that Levin, whom she had refused, is lost to her. Levin
is equally humiliated by Kitty's refusal of him, while Karenin
begins to fear but resists the knowledge that he is indeed deceived
and must be unhappy. This is put in portentous terms:

Karenin was face to face with life; he was confronted with the possibility that she might be in love with some other person besides

himself, and that seemed quite absurd and incomprehensible to him because it was life itself.

Levin and Vronsky grow towards certitude about their love and how it must be fulfilled; so do Kitty and Anna. For all of them it is a lonely process full of doubt and slow self-discovery, following on self-conflict and self-deception. The second half of the book follows the two exceptional couples – Vronsky and Anna, Kitty and Levin – and shows the one relationship disintegrating and the other establishing itself.

But of course there is the third couple: Stiva Oblonsky, who is Anna's brother, and Dolly, Kitty's sister. One would say that they are the 'ordinary' couple with whom the extraordinary couples are contrasted, but it isn't quite true. They are, however, some sort of foil. They are long-married, and point to a possible future: to disenchantment and unfaithfulness on one side, and mature love on the other. But Tolstoy is never merely schematic; we can't simply react away from Stiva, who has Anna's charm and life-delight, if not her depth. His unfaithfulness is something more than mere fickleness, and in its odd way is not sordid, is even rather daunting. For he too is at home in the world all the time. Life is a succession of genuine pleasures: a pretty woman, a good meal, a cigar, a shooting-expedition, a party. He relishes them all, in the order in which they arrive, and with no shame. If it is a pleasure, why not? And since *he* can enjoy it, why can't others take it as lightly? It's a life-stance; Lawrence's Birkin and Gerald Crich in *Women in Love* at one point solemnly and theoretically agree that 'one should enjoy what is given'. Stiva lives that out, except that he doesn't greatly enjoy his marriage now that his wife has lost her looks, and he doesn't enjoy the worries of family life. Rather too much of an unselective kind gets 'given' in the course of a lifetime. His position may not be all-embracing, but it is logical, so far as it goes, and certainly not hypocritical, and since he is (when allowed to be) so comfortable with himself, others enjoy him as a phenomenon. Only for Dolly is he a problem, but for her it's real enough. She loves him; she is committed to holding her family together; and she has to cope with his apparent weak will, which is really a very economical way of enjoying the benefits of a strong will.

It sounds comic, and in a way it is. Stiva is an instinctive example of Princess Betsy Tverskoy's maxim that 'one can look at a thing tragically and turn it into a torment, or one can look at it simply and even gaily.' There isn't really that choice; Stiva and Betsy Tverskoy are made one way and Anna and Dolly another. When Anna thinks of Betsy

> She was wondering why for others, Betsy for instance (whose secret liaison with Tushkevich she knew about) it was all so easy, while for her it was so agonizing.

Dolly has the same depth, which is one reason why she and Anna are so close to each other: they respect a gravity in each other even if it takes them in different directions. Indeed, if one was playing the 'real hero' game, one could make a good case for Dolly's being the real heroine of the book. If you reflect that it is among other things an exploration of growth and limitation, then Dolly is one of the few characters who shows real growth and maintains the position she wins.

We see her at the start of the novel in a passion of grief and anger, made jealous and hurt by Stiva's first infidelity. She knows what she feels: she is divided between the wish to punish and the wish to forgive and go on loving. She knows that to leave him may not deeply injure him, but it would deeply injure *her*; it would gratify her angry self but undo everything that matters to her. So she is in an exasperation of feelings which frustrate each other. Anna arrives, and shows instinctive wisdom by asking Dolly the question she needs to be asked—whether she loves Stiva enough to forgive him. She helps Dolly to give way to that feeling rather than the other, and it comes out wholeheartedly. Both women have an instinctive depth of feeling which creates and defines values.

Dolly goes on having these pure and piercing insights. She maintains a centre of love in herself for the essential Stiva, the universal charmer with his Micawber-like belief that 'everything will come right' (for him it does). She finds a beautifully evoked fulfilment in her children. Think of the scene in which she takes them to church and to bathe in the river. This family feeling turns out to be the meaning of her life, what she has given herself to; and at moments when she is aware that it is a meaningful self-surrender, she embraces it whole-heartedly:

> Dolly had done her hair and dressed, feeling anxious and excited. There was a time when she used to dress for her own sake, to look

beautiful and be admired; later on, the older she grew, the less and less pleasure she took in dressing up; she saw she was losing her good looks. But now she was beginning to feel pleasure and excitement again in dressing. Now she was not dressing for her own sake, not to look beautiful, but so that, as the mother of all those charming children, she should not spoil the general effect. And looking at herself for the last time in the glass, she was satisfied with herself. She looked beautiful. Not as beautiful as she had wished to look when going to a ball, but beautiful enough for the purpose she had now in mind.

Later, at the river

To hold in her hands all those plump little legs, to pull on their stockings, to take the naked little bodies in their arms and dip them in the water and to hear their happy frightened squeals, to see her little cherubs with their wide-open frightened and merry eyes, gasping and splashing, was a great joy to her.

Levin sees her in this glory, and is moved by it. Tolstoy shows with humour and compassion that such moments pass; they are the shafts of light between clouds. The children commit childish enormities in the raspberry beds, and she is shocked and worried and thinks they may turn out badly. That is an equally real and much more frequent feeling; but it doesn't cancel out the first one. At Levin's wedding, the other women tend naturally to think what *theirs* was like. Characteristically, Dolly goes on to think of all the marriages she has seen, to think of herself as part of a generation, only a drop in the wave, and is touched with awe at the vastness and strangeness of it. She may worry, or repine, or fantasize (as on her journey to see Anna and Vronsky, when she imagines herself turning the tables on Stiva by having a lover), but she stands for the truth of commitment to the natural human order. She is *there*, at a point some of the other characters reach, especially Levin and Kitty. When her centrality has been established, she makes that journey to visit Anna, who is living with Vronsky in disconcertingly unreal and not very comfortable luxury, with a few strange dependents, amongst objects which are foreign and new and expensive. Dolly is the only 'respectable' woman who will acknowledge them socially, because she is kind, and her troubles have made her kinder. She says one essential thing and notices another. Asked what she thinks of Anna's life with Vronsky, she says, in her kindness, 'I don't think anything. I've always loved you, and when you love someone you love the whole person just as he or she is, and not as you would like them to be.' That is part of the wisdom she has grown into, won from her hurt, her unselfishness, and her vocation for creating a family and holding it together, and if it seems a good-hearted commonplace to say such things, it costs a good deal to live them out. David Copperfield knew the same thing instinctively about his feeling for Steerforth. It is the only kind of feeling which can withstand change in the other person, or full knowledge of them. It is as near as can be got to a pure selflessness, and it can stand the recognition of another's self. It is a tough attitude, only a short distance from cynicism, and with tragic recognition just as close.

But there is more. Dolly doesn't really 'not think anything'. She thinks to a good deal of purpose, though she has the heart to keep the thought to herself. She finds herself going back to her ordinary life and her unsatisfactory marriage as something better, for all its dissatisfactions, than what Anna and Vronsky have so far managed. Their life is 'wrong' not in the sense that they are public sinners, but because their relationship is not related to the world and supported by it. Each has the other, but that other does not put each in relationship with the world; just the opposite. Their love is therefore related only to the two selves, is turned back on itself, and in the end becomes malignant.

Throughout the book the love relationship is shown engaging the deepest impulses of the self, and Tolstoy shows himself to be subtly aware of their powers for harm, especially self-harm. This is shown at first in the consequences for Levin of being refused by Kitty, for Kitty of being jilted by Vronsky. Both rebound, deeply hurt; and Tolstoy shows how rejected love turns to wounded pride, so that it is very difficult for the two to return to their underlying love for each other. They have to go by a long route, through distorted or false feelings: the urge to deny what is there, or to turn it into something complementary like religion or a passion for identifying oneself with some way of life arbitrarily chosen; the impulse to take satisfaction in the other's hurt (Levin is not exempt from that smallness); the wish to dissociate oneself and just be at peace, unrelated to others and therefore not hurt by them.

H

Kitty's self-discovery is traced with care and exactitude. Most striking is her extraordinary conversation with Dolly in which her own hurt makes her hurt Dolly when she flashes out,

> 'I've nothing to be distressed or comforted about. I've enough pride never to let myself love a man who does not love me.'

Of course, the suppressed reference to Vronsky shows that what she says isn't true. She *did* love him. Dolly replies gently

> 'But I'm not saying . . . Only tell me the truth . . . Tell me, has Levin proposed to you?'
>
> The mention of Levin's name seemed to deprive Kitty of the last traces of self-control; she leaped up from her chair, and flinging the buckle on the floor and rapidly gesticulating with her hands, began
>
> 'What has Levin to do with it? I can't understand why you want to torment me. I've said and I repeat that I have some pride, and that I shall never, *never* do what you're doing–go back to a man who has been unfaithful to you, who fell in love with another woman–I simply can't understand that! You may do it, but I can't.'
>
> And having said that, she looked at her sister, and seeing that Dolly was silent, her head bowed sadly, Kitty did not leave the room as she had intended to do, but sat down by the door and, burying her face in her handkerchief, hung her head.

Kitty then throws herself into Dolly's arms and is forgiven. The conversation resumes, and a little later Kitty says another odd thing, about the disgusting thoughts she has. She's somewhere near Othello here, but it is strangely transmuted:

> Kitty faltered. She was going to say that since this change had come over her, Oblonsky had become unbearable and loathsome to her, and she could not see him without imagining the coarsest and most disgusting things.

The subterranean workings of the injured ego, its self-defences, its hysterical morbidity, are deftly caught. The reader thinks, 'Good heavens, why should she think *that*?' In tracing the complex silent impulses which make her think it, he is aware, as in the greatest drama, of the pressures of an inner life determining speech and behaviour; another self. The perverted logic behind Kitty's outburst is 'you may go back to the man who deceived you, but I am too proud to go back to the man I disappointed'. She has obviously been brooding on this; her wounded love for Vronsky stands in the way of her underlying love for Levin, and her pride won't let her do what she now knows had been the right thing all along. This has been proved now; Levin loved and loves her, but she turned him down and her pride won't let her turn back to him. Vronsky didn't really love her, and has let her down. So her second outburst transfers to the unfaithful Oblonsky the hate she feels for Vronsky now that he has fallen in love with Anna and actually become her lover. Her sexual jealousy is transformed into disapproving Oblonsky, and being disgusted by him.

Kitty has to go through a stage of pious exaltation and devotion to the needs of others before self-confrontation, induced by watching the self-less (indeed burnt-out, and almost annihilated) Varenka, brings her back to a robust self-knowledge and an instinctively wise acceptance of her limits. Varenka too loved and lost the man she loved; she has since moved to a plane of self-less devotion where nothing agitates her. But she isn't really alive, and Kitty, even though she loves her, moves back from that false ideal. Varenka lacks what Tolstoy calls 'the suppressed fire of life and the consciousness of her own attractiveness'. This is what gives Kitty her spontaneous charm, her liveliness; what makes Levin love her. It makes her a self, of course, with needs and a capacity to be hurt when they are not fulfilled. She won't admit, and she is right not to admit, that these things are, as Varenka says, not important, since they relate only to her. She comes to a full recognition of herself, her needs, and her limitations, and from then on she lives spontaneously and fully from that central impulse. She sees that her pious self-abnegation 'was all a sham, because it was all pretence and did not come from my heart'. She refuses to pretend any more. 'I can't live except as my heart dictates', she says. She embraces her self-hood, the need for fulfilment. She has used that word, 'heart', again. She ranges herself with Levin, and with Anna and Vronsky, as a person who will follow where her 'heart', where 'life', leads. Dolly expresses it for them all when she acknowledges that Anna is following 'the need to live which God has put in all our hearts'.

It's no accident that at the end of the book Varenka and Koznyshev, Levin's half-brother, almost fall in love, and almost say it to each other, but shrink back. They haven't that force of self which will know where its happiness lies and will reach out for it, taking a risk both of self-exposure and of refusal. They play safe, don't dare; they don't in consequence live. Of Koznyshev Levin had thought shrewdly—and this is in the very next chapter after the Kitty-Varenka episode—

> Levin regarded his brother as a man of great intellect and vast knowledge, noble in the highest sense of the word and endowed with the faculty [like Varenka] of working for the general good. But in his heart of hearts, the older he grew and the more intimately he knew his brother, the more and more often it occurred to him that this faculty of working for the general good . . . was perhaps not so much a faculty as a lack of something, not a lack of kindly, honest and noble desires and tastes, but a lack of the life-force, of what is called heart, the impulse which drives a man to choose one out of all the innumerable paths of life open to him, and to desire that one only.

Varenka's sort of selflessness is a denial of the self in the same way as leglessness is a denial of the legs. That is to say, something has been cut off or burnt out which is necessary to getting around in life. It looks like a splendid theoretical ideal, but practically it is an invalid state. (This reflects back on the perfect selflessness of Dickens's heroines, like Agnes Wickfield). If you are like that, you are more likely to be one of life's walking wounded than a saint. And Koznyshev's kind of selflessness is perhaps the ultimate self-protecting device of the timid self that won't be put at risk by going out and committing itself to this particular person or that.

The walking symbol of the disguised and perverted impulses of the self is Karenin, that hideous and pitiful triumph of Tolstoy's imagination. A sensitive and lonely man, he has always had to protect himself against the world; he fears its strength against his smallness and loneliness; he also fears and inhibits his own powerful feelings which give the world a hold on him. He has hidden himself behind the carapace of a dégagé manner that implies condescension and uninvolvement, for he needs to feel that he is on a safe eminence, not in need of pity, above contempt, and not at the mercy of his own feelings. It is pure self-protection, and one of the things it protects him from is love, since love puts the self at

risk. Anna has a latent sense of the unprotected being behind the
shell and the self-satisfaction. But their life together has been an
evasion, a denial of something essential in Anna–the life, the
'heart'.

But in a related sense she has heart enough to want to feel for
him. At the beginning of the book their relationship is deftly
sketched. Anna comes back home on the train with Vronsky;
Karenin meets them. Vronsky has already made a profound impression on Anna; so seeing Karenin again, she sees him as for the
first time, and the odd thought strikes her 'Goodness, why are his
ears like that?' Her dissatisfaction is censored into this little oddity
of appearance. A few pages on

> 'All the same, he's a good man; upright, kind and remarkable in
> his own sphere,' Anna said to herself when she had returned to
> her room, as though defending him against someone who was
> accusing him and maintaining that one could not love him. 'But
> why do his ears stick out so oddly? Has he had a haircut?'

Compare with that Emma Bovary's revulsion from Charles (p. 70).
Anna is a more complex character, aware of other people and their
claim on her, wanting to be just, and wanting to be in the right
relationship with the world in a way Emma simply doesn't know
or care about. Necessarily this comes out as regard for other people,
a wish to think well of them, undermined by unconscious dissatisfaction. Anna's troubled defence of Karenin is like David Copperfield's painful involvement with Dora, his sense of loss.

In giving way to her love for Vronsky Anna is committed to a
new life–or indeed to life for the first time. She has fully grasped
that her life with Karenin was a falsehood–'that he has never once
thought I was a live woman who was in need of love', as she puts it.
That's not entirely just to Karenin, but what is clear is that she
'cannot repent that I breathe, that I love'. She puts this plainly to
Karenin. She 'cannot change', she says; meaning that her new love
is an absolute commitment, and the meaning of life for her. To
give that up would be a betrayal. Yet leaving Karenin, and finding
that she cannot take her son with her, does a deep injury to the
part of herself which is represented by her affinity with Dolly. So
one of the scenes most expressive of inner states, and most poignant,
is the moment, the morning after the uncontrollable outburst of
self in which she had told Karenin of her adultery in peculiarly

wounding words, when she finds herself standing alone, in a dream, holding her hair at the temples, pulling it so hard that it hurts, bringing her back to consciousness and the pain of the things which are pulling her apart internally.

The falseness of her relationship with Karenin is shown in their early conversations with each other, especially the one where he first taxes her with imprudence in her relationship with Vronsky. She finds to her astonishment that she can match him; the self will carry it off. She can put on a bright air of unconcern to trump his air of disinterested concern. He feels shut out by this smooth surface, and loses control; his own mask slips, and he once says something urgent and almost true: 'I am your husband, and I love you'. For an instant that gets through her armour; but she is able to readjust it, for she knows that he has as yet no right to use the word 'love': he is too self-absorbed. Karenin finds himself at this stage unable to talk in his 'normal' voice because it is parodied by Anna; his own defect is turned against him.

When he learns about Vronsky, his outer self turns vicious at first. He is self-righteous and pharisaical, and he tries to punish her by being unyielding, demanding concealment, and attacking her through her child. He is withdrawn deep into his ego-shell, from which he makes mean little forays. But then at a climactic moment Anna is near death after the delivery of Vronsky's child. She wants to clear her moral account, and in this state she has the grace to see good in Karenin. She feels instinctively that there is a heart there. Weeping, she begs his forgiveness. All his defences are swept away by her own defencelessness; his whole social self, the manufactured carapace, splits right open, and for a time his real unprotected self is delivered into the world, tender and open, capable now of intense spontaneous feeling, of a direct relationship. He manages a real love for her, a dignified forgiveness of Vronsky; he even loves the new child, responding to its innocence and vulnerability. So what Anna feared is confirmed; there is a human being there, and when she recovers, is forced back into life, part of her has to hurt him and she moves into a state where she is actively revolted by him, is horrified at herself, and has to hate him both so that she may do what she must do to him, and because she is doing it to him. We recognize the painful truth of that.

In that turmoil of almost hysterical self-conflict, she refuses a divorce, because she won't profit by another's unhappiness. She doesn't want, for a time, to be happy because she feels she has no right to be. She wants to live without hurting anybody but herself. At that stage she thinks of denying herself the chance of marriage and of happiness through her own scrupulousness, so moving from one intolerable situation to another. The essential element in her which wants to 'live' is in conflict with the other essential element which wants to be in the right relationship with the world. By a tragic irony, when events force her back into wanting a divorce, Karenin has moved back into his social shell, reinforced by a hideous religiosity. He had felt that his tender feelings exposed him—and indeed they did; but he is frightened of that exposure. His basic insecurity makes him feel that other people think him ridiculous, and he externalizes that self-consciousness into a stern social force which, he thinks, will not let him remain in that state. He senses contempt in the people he meets, and has no self-belief with which to meet the feeling. So he channels his emotions into the safe social form of pietism, and moves back into the shell, becoming credulous and petty, a whited sepulchre. The repulsiveness of this degeneration is transformed by the delicacy of the treatment: Karenin is understandable as a case, but he is fully human, and therefore not wholly predictable. It is important also to see that his false piety is like Kitty's phase of the same thing; and it makes one look narrowly at Levin's final religious state. Is that equally a device of the compensating self?

Anna's life with Vronsky is thus from the start under a fatal constraint of insecurity. He is bound to her by his love, but only by that. She finds herself having to exert her power over him, to keep him in love with her, and so the possessive impulses of the self are set in play. He finds himself reacting against that domination: asserting his right to a measure of freedom, a normal life which gives him a role of his own in the world—as progressive landowner and politician, as member of a social group—making a space between them that a marriage will allow, but a possessive liaison won't. And so his self reacts against hers; it becomes a conflict of wills.

But at the same time, to indicate that marriage isn't an automatic solution or a windless harbour, Kitty and Levin are experiencing their own first quarrels, and the first jealousies of marriage. They too have a war of selves; Levin too feels at one moment that the relationship is making him a slave, and rebels. He is also ludicrously jealous of a foolish young visitor who pays a little superficial court to Kitty. Levin finds that what he is troubled by is partly something in him; if he can master it he will be free. He finds that when he hurts Kitty he hurts himself. This is expressed as his not knowing where his personality ends and hers begins; that may sound romantic, but it is also the dangerous ground of a possessive relationship where the other person is merely the extension of oneself (like Mrs Steerforth and James). But Levin is spared the perverse impulse to punish himself by punishing Kitty. This is something Anna doesn't see.

She and Vronsky tear each other down. They have no sure external footing in their relationship with each other. The freedom Anna won from Karenin is now, horrifyingly, what she most fears, and what she cannot give Vronsky. In the last chapters of their story we see, dismayed, all the perversions of the self in a possessive love: again the urge to own turning into the urge to control, turning then into the urge to punish if one can't control; chronic unjustified jealousy; verbal fencing expressing the lack of trust; the impulse to provoke the feared crisis and have it all out to the death; the self-blindness and self-justification; the obsessive self-pity and histrionic role-playing; the final urge to punish the other by punishing oneself, with the childish underthought that he'll be sorry when I'm dead, and serve him right. Anna is not the person (many are) just to go on rehearsing that part indefinitely, always funking the last act. She plays it right through once, to the end, and kills herself. That too is an aspect of her vitality.

Her inability to find a secure commitment, a resting place, with Vronsky, safe from these demands of the insecure self, follows tragically from the damage she did to her own integrity in amputating her relationships with her son and husband, and refusing to allow herself to replace them. It was the family relationship she needed, as well as love. As it is, with Vronsky, she can only be as mistress to him as lover.

What is terrible in her visible moral decline and death is our sense that she has responded sensitively to two incompatible pulls, each as strong as life. She could not deny her need for self-fulfilment in love, which was an obligation to herself and to life; but she could not without loss of integrity seek that fulfilment. The other things she needed were also 'life'. She is not destroyed because she offends against the world's public morality. She destroys herself because she offends against moral allegiances which she discovers in herself.

Self-fulfilment is a deeper matter than appears. The self which demands fulfilment is not appeased at the simple level of its own demands. It needs to be at peace with itself in a deeper way, by being at peace with the world: that is, to feel itself rightly at peace as a moral being. We glimpse again the possibility of two kinds of self: the mere self which makes demands–the ego–and a socialized self which needs a relationship with others which is open to *their* needs. We can call the one the 'self' *tout court*, and we can call the other the identity, and it may be useful to do so. But the danger in using the two terms is that we may think of them as implying exclusive states. You start as mere baby ego; you grow up to be a self-conscious identity. Ideally you do, but the notion that you leave behind all impulses from the old closed ego is an illusion which few people hold. The 'heart' whose dictates Kitty and Dolly and Anna and Levin must all follow is also the self, the thing which makes demands. Tolstoy's genius is in part his gift of showing this, especially showing how all his characters are akin. 'Transcendence' of the self is not an effortless ascent to a higher level of behaviour; it is strikingly clear that all his best characters have to fight with a self-centredness which is normal, insidious and permanent. It is also necessary, and if you are fortunate in your temperament and circumstances, beneficial. Kitty and Anna are the same kind of person; for Kitty, spontaneity brings fulfilment; for Anna it brings disaster. They both follow 'life'. Neither is simply egotistical. Indeed the one really selfish person in the main plot, Stiva, suffers nothing because his selfishness is a shell against suffering. The one truly unselfish person, Varenka, has extirpated her self and is visibly burnt-out. This places her beyond normal relationships; she has come full circle to the state where, as for Stiva, nothing is important because she is above involvement with it. That is evidently, in her, the self-defence of someone who has been hurt and wants to stop being hurt. In the end life escapes her for that reason. All the other characters are fully engaged in their own selves with other selves. It is a matter of self-struggle and conflict. None escapes hurt, and Anna kills herself.

The things which are affirmed by the book–'life', 'heart',– contain irreducible elements of conflict. One must seek the right path in life; one must accept one's limitations. Love is essential; it cannot be forced. It is a condition of some kinds of growth; but one cannot grow beyond a certain point. As Karenin shows, ground won is not always held. Love involves being open to other people, therefore being hurt by them; it also brings the self into play, and the self will resist the demands of other people. One must be fulfilled; fulfilment is often at someone else's expense, and in other cases at one's own unexpected expense. Some kinds of commitment won't permit others; but to deny them is death in life. As in *King Lear* the characters in moments of stress cry out limited truths which contradict each other. Kitty realizes 'she was deceiving herself in imagining that she could be what she wanted to be.' Just before, the far-distant Levin had concluded that 'one must not submit to the past, and one can make what one likes of oneself.' Anna sees that 'however much she tried, she could not be stronger than herself.' But that is what she has to try to do. In the crisis with Karenin, Anna asks herself in despair 'what can I be sure of, what do I want, what do I love?' At the end of the book Levin echoes her: 'What then am I? Where am I? Why am I here?' The questions have been turned from those of love and morality into those of religion and vocation.

The women, as a group, offer an answer which has an instinctive wisdom. Whether joyfully or regretfully, they acquiesce, they join the stream. Dolly finds she is in it, and submits. Kitty jumps in gladly. Anna finds in despair that she is swimming against it. I mean that Dolly discovers it is her vocation to rear her family, to be its anchor and support. Kitty opts for the same vocation and finds she has the emotional gift for it. Anna would have wanted to give herself to that life, but was not – married to Karenin – linked to the right man and is not – linked to Vronsky – in the relationship with the world which she needs.

Vronsky and Levin have a male limitation. Vronsky cannot afford to see what Anna had, needs and has lost in losing her son. So he is cut off from Anna's deepest need. Levin is also curiously blind. He is self-centred in dangerous ways. He is not meanly self-absorbed, indeed he is attractively unselfconscious, but he has therefore a limited self-knowledge. He cannot see his affinity with Anna. His vitality and spontaneity mean that he will follow where life leads him, as she did. But he learns nothing from her history.

He has a conversation with Oblonsky early in the book in which he expresses a callow contempt for 'fallen women'. They are by definition people for whom one has trivial feelings. He meets Anna towards the end of the book, is charmed by her, even falls a little in love with her, but sees the charm as evidence of her 'fall'. He cannot see that she has been engaged in the same search as himself, and that her courage has lessons for him.

Apart from showing that Levin is not Tolstoy—he obviously couldn't have written *Anna Karenina* if he can't understand the heroine—it casts an important light on Levin's religious conversion at the end of the book. His religion is not explicitly Christian: it springs from the feeling that man must not live for himself only, but for something else that Levin is prepared to call God, but cannot define. He has been impressed by a conversation with a peasant, who convinces him that he is naturally religious. 'Now take you, sir' he says, 'You wouldn't wrong a man, either, would you?' 'No, of course not', says Levin. Well, he is like Anna, and she *did* wrong a man. Levin simply hasn't been tested as she has. Her life presents her with a choice of evils; she opts for the one which her 'heart', or 'life', dictates. She would have wanted not to injure another person, and finds that that is not possible. Life does not permit it, or she does not ultimately choose it, whichever way you prefer to put it.

More satisfying as an expression of Levin's religion is the parable-figure used of him in VIII, 10. 'Now, as though against his own will, he cut deeper and deeper into the earth, so that, like a ploughshare, he could not get out without turning up the furrow.' It fits his desperate search for meaning, his eager nature, and any peace he may win in life. It implies purposiveness, and also compulsion. Some of the compulsions come from within. We end the book thinking that there is no reason to believe that nothing more is ever going to happen to Kitty and Levin, two passionate natures. They are not exempt from universal selfhood, and it is Tolstoy's realism that tells us this.

There is a superbly rendered quarrel between Vronsky and Anna in which at one moment Vronsky is touched with grace. In the middle of the fight

'Anna, why? Why?' he added after a moment's pause, bending over towards her and opening his hand in the hope that she would put hers in it.

She was glad of this appeal to tenderness. But some kind of strange evil power prevented her from giving in to her impulse, as if the rules of the fight did not permit her to give in ... She felt that side by side with the love that bound them together, there had grown up some evil spirit of strife, which she could not cast out of his heart, and still less out of her own.

'As if the rules of the fight did not permit her to give in.' Who does not recognize that insight? 'The evil spirit of strife' is lodged in the self; it is universal and indestructible, and means that life is tragic.

9

Wuthering Heights: Romantic self-commitment

Wuthering Heights was written before *Madame Bovary, David Copperfield* and *Anna Karenina*. I write about it after them because they help to give the reader some slight handholds on this strange book. They manage to get some things clear and established in their own worlds, as if a part of life could be pinned down and a lasting insight gained: perhaps that momentary security – that feeling that we have a piece of usable wisdom – will help us with *Wuthering Heights*? Perhaps; but it is a deeply subversive novel. Some things in it can be grasped and held; but overall its effect is to go on disturbing the reader, leaving him with questions, not answers, and the feeling that if we reach a formulated 'truth' in it, it is a painful one. And especially our hard-headedness, our conventionality, any consequent inability to feel things deeply or long are shown to be smallness, not wisdom.

The other reason why the book can be placed here, or anywhere, is that it is timeless. It was published in 1847, and scarcely noticed. Already it referred to the past: the events take place between 1770 and 1802. But there is no sense of that period: American Independence, the French Revolution, the Napoleonic Wars have no bearing on this world; they are mere passing external events, not noticed because not relevant. Jane Austen's un-interest in the great world, often commented on, is as nothing to Emily Brontë's. You are perfectly aware with Jane Austen that you are in the Bath, Hampshire, or London that she knew, at the time she knew it. It is a social world where people take colour and tone from their surroundings; and so is Flaubert's Normandy, Dickens's London and Suffolk, Tolstoy's St Petersburg and Moscow. These are actual societies, watched at a particular moment, and the people belong to them. The people of Thrushcross Grange and Wuthering

Heights belong in quite a different sense to those minute spots on the map. The Heights are intensely seen and felt as a place; but the house is already a hundred years old when the action unfurls; it represents something ancestral, and the moors represent something primeval and eternal. Equally, the chief characters don't belong to 1770 and Yorkshire so much as to the human race and all time. By the end of the book things have taken place between heroic characters which the surviving inhabitants, smaller people, look back on with dread and doubtful understanding. The obsessions, the violences, the occasional births and the more frequent deaths, have been a prolonged struggle like something in an epic. In thirty years a convulsive energy has worked itself out. The people who die and are looked back on by Nelly Dean and the little boy at the very end, who sees Heathcliff and 'a woman' as ghosts, are so large in their capacity to feel one or two things, and they live out their lives with such commitment to those bare feelings, which are their personal meaning, that those who are left, not fully understanding something which transcends them, turn it into myth, or ballad or folk-tale, which are the tribute of the ordinary limited person to the men and women who go beyond those limits.

It is that tribute of the awestruck narrators (Nelly Dean, Mr Lockwood, the other characters to whom it falls to tell a chapter or two) which turns Heathcliff into a demon king, a goblin, a were-wolf, an ogre or any other of the devices by which ordinariness holds off its sense of failure: failure in this case to reach a lonely, suffering and violent man. That incomprehension of Heathcliff is one of the things which the book does allow *us* to grasp and understand. Heathcliff's flashing eyes and sharp grinding teeth, the diabolic poses and gestures, are all in the reporting: they are a convention which turns misunderstanding into a more familiar kind of mystery, a romantic cliché: one that people can thrill to, which fortifies them in their sense of being normal, and enables them to write Heathcliff off as demonic, therefore not to be understood, therefore another kind of being, not akin.

Heathcliff *is* demonic, but in a way which is specifically human, and therefore fundamentally akin to us even if he is larger in scale. Nelly Dean is sometimes wiser than she knows, as well as being quite often less wise than she thinks. There is a moment in the book when Mr Lockwood, whose main function is to be told the story, be amazed by it and confirmed in his smallness, begins to ruminate over what he has been told so far. Of the people of the Heights and the Grange, he says solemnly:

> They do live more in earnest, more in themselves, and less in surface change, and frivolous external things. I could fancy a love for life here almost possible . . .

So much is true, but he makes the mistake of thinking they are for that reason, 'different' as a total group. Mrs Dean knows better than this, and replies 'Oh! here we are the same as anywhere else, when you get to know us'. She is right: the fundamental differences are not between people here and townees like Lockwood who think they have stumbled on interesting local fauna with unusually long-lasting feelings (as if the rustic crudity gave strength). It is the difference between the Heathcliffs and Catherines and people like Nelly Dean herself, who goes on to describe herself quite rightly as 'a steady reasonable kind of body'. One pattern which recurs in the book is the failure of the 'steady reasonable kind of body' to understand those who are otherwise, and the compulsion of the 'unreasonable' to bring each other down. An overall result is to cast doubt on that kind of 'reason' as a guide to the truth. The intensely-feeling are by definition beyond reason. But that does not throw us into the world of the totally incomprehensible; there is no act in *Wuthering Heights* which is gratuitous. Indeed the inevitability, the comprehensibility of it in one sense, may leave us saying we should prefer not to understand, and that our reasonableness is a device for not seeing what we prefer not to face.

Heathcliff can be understood, if we ever understand anybody. So far from being a mysterious semi-mythical psychic force, he is presented with some care as a humanly conceivable evolution. Indeed he reflects a *reality* onto Dickens. It was Dickens's nightmare recurrently to imagine a small child, sensitive and totally alone, orphaned in a hideous world symbolized as a London given over almost entirely to monstrous criminals (think of *Oliver Twist*). The threat is that first you will be degraded socially, then corrupted morally, then destroyed. That nightmare is approached in *David Copperfield*, in the Murdstone and Grinby warehouse episode, followed by David's fearful journey on foot to Dover, penniless, exhausted, menaced by madmen and violent outcasts, and ignored by uncomprehending nice people. At the end of the nightmare is an equivalent heaven; you are taken in by a lovable, eccentric, middle-aged and above all rich person, who adopts you, lavishes affection on you, and leaves you a lot of money, or starts you off in life as a gentleman, and therefore secure. Evidently that is also a fantasy, but it is a powerful one, like the first. It speaks to a deep wish as the first appeals to a deep fear.

Emily Brontë deals in reality. Old Mr Earnshaw, in Liverpool one day, finds the abandoned Heathcliff; small, ugly, dirty, as repulsive as he is pathetic. He takes the child home, not to a Dickensian world of red-cheeked loving retainers and gentle eccentrics, but to an actual family capable of shock and jealousy. The result is inevitable. The adoption looks like a monstrous whim; most of the family are alienated. The old man has to stand by his action: he insists on carrying it through–hence further alienation. He is then *committed* to an affection for the foundling, to justify himself; and the conflict becomes violent. His son Hindley feels his position has been usurped, hates the newcomer and persecutes him. Apart from the old man, only his daughter Catherine and the servant Nelly Dean show any kindness to Heathcliff: Catherine because she discovers an intense affinity, Nelly because she is decent, is not involved in the family conflict, and can afford to show ordinary kindness where others can't because they are affronted or threatened.

Heathcliff is the victim in all this. He has to submit to the old man's puzzled and mostly will-driven affection, and finds himself exerting his will over him in return: his 'spoilt' behaviour as a child is a continual test of the old man's love. He is grateful to Nelly for average good nature and occasional real kindness and sympathy. He hates Hindley and anyone else who offers him hate. He responds to Catherine for giving him the only equal love, strong, unforced and natural, as from child to related child, that he has in the world–it is his only firm hold on human life. Without it he would be an animal; having strong passions and an energetic nature, he would be a wolf–something Catherine comes to realize later when the process is almost completed and she has become responsible for part of it. Describing Heathcliff to Isabella Linton, who has fallen romantically in love with him, she calls him

an unreclaimed creature, without refinement, without cultivation;
an arid wilderness of furze and whinstone.

In other words, he is like the Heights. She goes on:

> Pray don't imagine that he conceals depths of benevolence and
> affection beneath a stern exterior! He's not a rough diamond–a
> pearl-containing oyster of a rustic; he's a fierce, pitiless, wolfish
> man. I never say to him let this or that enemy alone, because it
> would be ungenerous or cruel to harm them, I say–'Let them
> alone, because *I* should hate them to be wronged.'

We can't accept what Catherine says as the whole truth, because
Catherine is involved with Heathcliff, but also because she can't
admit to herself, or doesn't yet realize, what she did at a certain
moment to make him like that. Her power over him she realizes:
it is displayed in that last boast: just as she could, as a child, make
him 'behave', so now *she* can make him stay his hand, because he
will not hurt her, and so will not hurt those dear to her. What she
has not fully grasped is the reason why he is as he is.

Old Mr Earnshaw died, leaving Heathcliff and Catherine still
children, and in the power of the elder child Hindley Earnshaw.
Hindley persecutes Heathcliff, setting out to turn him back into
the abandoned asocial unregarded being that the old man tried to
save him from remaining. It's striking that Hindley doesn't turn
him out; we deduce an operation of the self: that he actually wants
Heathcliff in his power, wants to get a revenge, to degrade and
subvert him, to make him like the trees up at the Heights–the
'range of gaunt thorns all stretching their limbs one way as if
craving alms of the sun'. Hindley is the cruel wind that will work
this long distortion, as naturally and without conscience as the real
wind. He simply expresses his nature, his will, his sense of injury
in childhood, his power to revenge it now. The sun, on the other
hand, is Catherine herself. As long as Heathcliff can 'stretch his
arms' to her, as long as they are all in all to each other, as they were
in their unconscious childhood state, Heathcliff has a human hope
and purpose, and a human nature. When the sun is removed, he
becomes 'the arid wilderness'. She removes the sun by denying
her love for him, by assuming he has a smaller and undemanding
love for her, and by marrying Edgar Linton, the gentle, overbred,

I

fairhaired delicate lad who lives down in the valley at Thrushcross Grange.

Catherine is less comprehensible than Heathcliff, and for that reason may be more frightening. What she seems to represent is either an immature unconsciousness, or a very tough power of the will, a thornlike hardness, a separate selfhood, a determination quite equal to Heathcliff's, far more self-confident, and far less clear about its own need. And, from first to last, he *is* clear about his one need: union with Catherine, alive or dead. She wavers, and that causes the tragedy.

Hindley's persecution merely toughens Heathcliff's exterior, his bark, and sharpens his thorns. It causes him to consecrate himself to his subsidiary aim in life: an ordinary revenge on Hindley's family. He decides to do this at a specific moment, noted by Nelly Dean. There has been a Christmas party, with the Lintons coming to the Heights. Heathcliff, conscious of his gracelessness, the uncouthness he has wilfully adopted just because it is forced upon him, but still sensitive and suffering, makes an effort to be accepted, and cleans himself up, saying 'Nelly, make me decent, I'm going to be good'. He appears; Hindley rebuffs him, and Edgar Linton in mere complacent self-superiority slights him. Heathcliff assaults Edgar, being already jealous of his attraction for Catherine, and Hindley has the pleasure of beating him pitilessly. Heathcliff vows himself to revenge:

> 'I'm trying to settle how I shall pay Hindley back. I don't care how long I wait, if I can only do it, at last. I hope he will not die before I do!'
>
> 'For shame, Heathcliff!' said I. 'It is for God to punish wicked people; we should learn to forgive.'
>
> 'No, God won't have the satisfaction that I shall,' he returned. 'I only wish I knew the best way.'

He hits on the best way. Hindley's wife dies, and Hindley is in his own way of the true Heights stock:

> His sorrow was of that kind that will not lament, he neither wept nor prayed – he cursed and defied – execrated God and man, and gave himself up to reckless dissipation.

So in due course Heathcliff aims at revenge by letting the drunken

Hindley gamble away the house and land, winning them from him, and by taking Hareton, Hindley's son, and inciting Hareton to the loutish degradation Hindley had tried to bring Heathcliff to earlier. But this ambition, almost realized, becomes unreal at the end of the book, and this is because what Hindley had done to Heathcliff was merely an external – merely unkindness, so to speak. What Catherine did to him was worse because it went to the root of his being, what Othello called 'the fountain from the whence my current springs'. Trying to hold himself together in face of that deprivation, trying finally to win back what he had lost, becomes the true meaning of his life.

Catherine is in some sense in love with Edgar Linton; it is a somewhat conventional feeling, but there is no reason to think it is not real. He represents an opposite: graceful, gentle, pliable, cultivated. Her roots are intermingled with Heathcliff's, but that is below the surface, hard to account for, and hard to be fully conscious of. She is to some degree aware of it, but she under-estimates its importance for her, and in an almost incomprehensible way takes no account of what she may be doing to him. She assumes that she can manage everything; that both Heathcliff and Edgar will be easy to manipulate, or will not even need manipu-lating – they will just fall in with her all-disposing will. None of the three can in fact master their variously strong natures, so this is a crucial miscalculation.

This is skilfully demonstrated, as a kind of warning prelude, on one occasion when, Hindley being away, Edgar calls. Heathcliff had hoped to have Catherine's company to himself, and says so. She is embarrassed, she wants to get rid of him so as to be with Edgar, and finally has to tell him that Edgar is coming. She is by now upset at herself for having to try to bundle Heathcliff out of the way, upset at him for being *in* the way. He makes a direct claim on her ('Don't turn me out for those pitiful silly friends of yours'), and she is further surprised and upset to find out in what degree he cares and is demanding. He has actually marked on a calendar the times she has spent with him, and those with the Lintons. Her troubled sense of being in a conflict of irreconcilable demands made on her makes her merely peevish; she snubs Heathcliff in a wounding way; he is genuinely hurt, and leaves. Edgar comes, and finds her in this turmoil, and so quite soon she pinches Nelly Dean for spying on her and Edgar, is loudly accused of doing so by Nelly, tells a lie in denying the act and boxes Nelly's ears.

'Catherine, love! Catherine!' interposed Linton, greatly shocked at the double fault of falsehood and violence which his idol had committed.

'Leave the room, Ellen!' she repeated, trembling all over. Little Hareton [Hindley's son] who followed me everywhere, and was sitting near me on the floor, at seeing my tears commenced crying himself, and sobbed out complaints against 'wicked Aunt Cathy', which drew her fury on to his unlucky head: she seized his shoulders and shook him till the poor child waxed livid, and Edgar thoughtlessly laid hold of her hands to deliver him. In an instant one was wrung free, and the astounded young man felt it applied over his own ear in a way that could not be mistaken for jest.

He drew back in consternation—I lifted Hareton in my arms, and walked off to the kitchen with him; leaving the door of communication open, for I was curious to watch how they should settle their disagreement.

The insulted visitor moved to the spot where he had laid his hat, pale and with a quivering lip.

'That's right!' I said to myself. 'Take warning and begone! It's a kindness to let you have a glimpse of her genuine disposition.'

'Where are you going?' demanded Catherine, advancing to the door.

He swerved aside and attempted to pass.

'You must not go!' she exclaimed energetically.

'I must and shall!' he replied in a subdued voice.

'No,' she persisted, grasping the handle; 'not yet. Edgar Linton —sit down, you shall not leave me in that temper. I should be miserable all night, and I won't be miserable for you!'

'Can I stay after you have struck me?' asked Linton.

Catherine was mute.

'You've made me afraid and ashamed of you,' he continued; 'I'll not come here again!'

Her eyes began to glisten and her lids to twinkle.

'And you told a deliberate untruth!' he said.

'I didn't!' she cried, recovering her speech. 'I did nothing deliberately–Well, go, if you please–get away! And now I'll cry –I'll cry myself sick.'

She dropped down on her knees by a chair and set to weeping in serious earnest.

Edgar persevered in his resolution as far as the court; there he lingered. I resolved to encourage him.

'Miss is dreadfully wayward, sir!' I called out. 'As bad as any marred child–you'd better be riding home, or else she'll be sick only to grieve us.'

The soft thing looked askance through the window–he possessed the power to depart, as much as the cat possesses the power to leave a mouse half-killed, or a bird half-eaten.

Ah, I thought, there will be no saving him–He's doomed, and flies to his fate!

And so it was; he turned abruptly, hastened into the house again, shut the door behind him . . .

Compare the assault on the child with Emma Bovary's (p. 74). It is much more in good hot blood. It is equally a violent outburst of self, but is not followed by Emma's repulsive re-establishment of her self-esteem. What Catherine says here–'I did nothing deliberately'–is a powerful and disturbing truth. She flew out in that way because of the succession of pressures she had just undergone with Heathcliff and Edgar, and because she is herself. She was expressing her nature in the direct and uninhibited way which characterizes the people on the Heights. It makes them naturally powerful and dangerous people, and when they conflict with each other it leads to a fight to the death. That is the element of unconsciousness in her, of spontaneity and directness. It is bound up with her vitality and attraction. But her 'I won't be miserable for you' is bound up with her hardness.

There is something childish about it, as in 'And now I'll cry– I'll cry myself sick!' It looks like a piece of infantile blackmail, and it puts Nelly Dean's back up. She sees only the 'marred child' in that behaviour. Like *David Copperfield*, this raises questions about 'being a child' and 'being an adult' that one never gets to the end of. Perhaps the truth is that the self, directly expressing itself, is seen at its purest in the child. We say of some unacceptable behaviour that it is 'childish', meaning so to diminish it, make it seem petty, and ultimately manageable (we learn to manage naughty children by distracting their attention and other dodges. We dare not engage in the direct conflict of wills or we'd murder them. Every year a number of simple enraged people murder or brutally assault their children–usually for crying–because they don't think of side-stepping and using patience and deceit as an acceptable middle course between surrender and violence). Psychology has told us how much adults are like children, when it might be as much to the point and more salutary to show how much children are like uninhibited adults. Adults are not manageable, least of all by themselves. Nelly Dean misunderstands Catherine here, and–fatally–later. She assumes both times that Catherine is 'trying it on', when she is really at the mercy of her self and its conflicting needs in a situation she cannot manage. In the end this becomes intolerable, after she has married Edgar.

Heathcliff under Hindley's persecution has become ignoble in his overt behaviour and appearance. Catherine isn't much more than a child, nor is Heathcliff; so he has no adult pride which pulls him back from that degradation; he pushes wilfully into it in the spirit of 'I'll show them I can outdo them at their own game'; or 'it shall be *my* will that I am like this'. That inevitably disgusts her at the surface level, and she hasn't the adult judgement to see beyond. Offered Edgar Linton, handsome, rich and charming, in contrast with Heathcliff, rough, destitute and unsupported by family or wealth, there's little that she can do but accept him. She has a terrible inkling that she is wrong, but it is subdued by her youthful confidence that she can somehow manage, and that in any case it is her will to take the situation on.

In her long exchange with Nelly in chapter 9 she moves steadily away from her deep sense that in marrying Edgar she is on a false path. To Nelly's question 'where is the obstacle?' she at first replies

> 'Here! and here!' . . . striking one hand on her forehead, and the other on her breast. 'In whichever place the soul lives–in my soul and in my heart, I'm convinced I'm wrong.'

She explains herself to the listening Nelly in mysterious terms. I say 'mysterious' because the reader cannot accept them neutrally: he will either think them deeply true or dangerous self-delusion, so far as he does understand them; there is in any case an element of ambiguity in them; and the whole of the rest of the book is a commentary on them–and although at the end it is not clear whether they are endorsed or proved an illusion, our impulse is to feel them proved, or her stance vindicated.

She begins with her thematic dream about 'being in heaven':

> '. . . heaven did not seem to be my home; and I broke my heart with weeping to come back to earth; and the angels were so angry that they flung me out, into the middle of the heath on the top of Wuthering Heights, where I woke sobbing for joy.'

'Heaven' may offer itself as Thrushcross Grange, or marriage to Edgar, or a domesticated kind of virtuous married life of the ordinary sort; but she is bound at the roots to the Heights, and to Heathcliff. She makes the connection herself:

> That will do to explain my secret, as well as the other. I've no more business to marry Edgar Linton than I have to be in heaven; and if the wicked man in there [Hindley] had not brought Heathcliff so low, I shouldn't have thought of it. It would degrade me to marry Heathcliff, now . . .

(and Heathcliff, who has been eavesdropping, creeps out, cut to the heart, and disappears for three years)

> . . . so he shall never know how I love him; and that, not because he's handsome, Nelly, but because he's more myself than I am. Whatever our souls are made of, his and mine are the same, and Linton's is as different as a moonbeam from lightning, or frost from fire.'

She goes on to show that she wants to be convinced that Heathcliff 'has no notion of these things. . . . He does not know what being in love is'. Nelly does not let her off:

> 'I see no reason that he should not know, as well as you,' I returned; 'and if you are his choice, he'll be the most unfortunate creature that was ever born! As soon as you become Mrs Linton, he loses *friend*, and love, and all! Have you considered how you'll bear the separation, and how he'll bear to be quite deserted in the world?' (*my italics*).

That is Nelly's truth, and it is here that Catherine takes off into a kind of self-deception. Or is it?

> He quite deserted! we separated! . . . Who is to separate us, pray? . . . Every Linton on the face of the earth might melt into nothing, before I could consent to forsake Heathcliff.

She goes on to say what she means, or what she has failed to grasp as a real meaning that demands she act differently:

> He'll be as much to me as he has been all his lifetime. Edgar must shake off his antipathy, and tolerate him, at least. He will when he learns my true feelings towards him.

And then she offers as bright after-thought:

> . . . if Heathcliff and I married, we should be beggars, whereas if I marry Linton, I can aid Heathcliff to rise . . .

We have a sense here that Catherine is struggling with things she can't fully realize; that she is making partly hopeful, partly wild remarks, half talking herself round into the belief that what she is doing is right, half imagining some kind of ideal relationship in which Edgars are not jealous of Heathcliffs and vice versa. Edgar shall have formal possession, and that should be good enough for him; and she will go on loving Heathcliff in the profound, wordless—perhaps actionless, gestureless—way; for words and actions and gestures are not needed when you 'are' the other person. She is struggling with an idea which comes out as a poetic utterance:

> I cannot express it; but surely you and everybody have a notion that there is, or should be an existence beyond you. What were the use of my creation if I were entirely contained here? My great miseries in this world have been Heathcliff's miseries, and I watched and felt each from the beginning; my great thought in living is himself. If all else perished and *he* remained, I should still continue to be; and if all else remained and he were annihilated, the universe would turn to a mighty stranger. I should not seem a part of it. My love for Linton is like the foliage in the woods. Time will change it, I'm well aware, as winter changes the trees. My love for Heathcliff resembles the eternal rocks beneath—a source of little visible delight, but necessary. Nelly, I *am* Heathcliff—he's always, always in my mind—not as a pleasure, any more than I am always a pleasure to myself—but as my own being . . .

The question which the book poses for us, is—do we feel that as a profound insight or as an egoistic illusion? Does Catherine's unhappy marriage and death disprove it, or does the ultimate course of the book, especially the end, validate it?

One can't dismiss it; at any rate Catherine believes it as an ultimate or higher truth. She goes on believing it even when Heathcliff instantly disappears–thus in a practical way proving that he is *not* her, and that he has no automatic sense of her love for him. He is deeply wounded by her marrying Linton in preference to him; yet the trauma also has the effect of shocking him into being his possible social self. He comes back later, educated, self-possessed, suave, rich and dangerous. He has, we infer, to prove to her what he could be, what she has thrown away: something stronger than Linton and as marriageable. His plan, he reveals in an aside, was to reappear briefly, be seen and recognized by her, to kill Hindley and to commit suicide. This would be a simple vengeance on Hindley and a complicated revenge on Catherine, who is (as usual) to be sorry when he's dead, and serve her right. We recognize that need from *Anna Karenina*: it's one of 'the rules of the game', as Tolstoy put it.

But in any case Heathcliff's disappearance for that long time is already a blow and a grievance to Catherine. This sign of a separate existence is like the one James Steerforth gave to his mother: it was Mrs Steerforth who said of her son that he had been

the object of my life, to whom its every thought has been devoted, whom I have gratified from a child in every wish, *from whom I have had no separate existence since his birth*–to take up in a moment with a miserable girl, and avoid me! (*my italics*).

Catherine and Heathcliff do later make similar jealous charges against each other: she that he left her without a word, to sorrow alone; he that she married Linton, forcing him away. They offer these reproaches in all bitterness; and we wonder, are these merely two powerful simple predatory egos, with an equal jealous hold on each other and an equal proud independent will? Or is that the mere accident of their surface selfhood, incident to humanity, and *do* they finally strike on the something deeper, the thing that Catherine expresses as 'the eternal rocks beneath'?

On Heathcliff's disappearance, Catherine has the first of her mysterious illnesses. This has been prepared for in the incident where she said she would 'cry herself sick', but also explained that she did nothing deliberately. She now spends all night outside in the rain, watching and calling for Heathcliff and weeping like a child; and when he doesn't return, has a collapse which is like a breakdown, and is also the onset of epilepsy or consumption or both. Thereafter she must not be crossed, or she will have a fit, the doctor says. Again, it is a curiously childish notion, misunderstood by Nelly at the key moment, misunderstood even by Catherine. For in the end she dies, having willed herself to die. But the odd thing is that though she wills it, and it happens, it doesn't necessarily happen solely because she wills it. The root of her life is cut through (at the level of the rocks), and her death happens to coincide with her will.

The core of the book, the lacerating part, is the succession of violent exchanges when Heathcliff returns to find her married, and he, she and Edgar find themselves in the classic triangle. She and Edgar have what seems to be a workable relationship though it is founded on his giving way to her:

> She seemed almost over fond of Mr Linton; and even to his sister she showed plenty of affection. They were both very attentive to her comfort certainly. It was not the thorn bending to the honeysuckles, but the honeysuckles embracing the thorn. There were no mutual concessions; one stood erect and the others yielded; and who *can* be ill-natured, and bad tempered, when they encounter neither opposition nor indifference?

That is Nelly's summing up, spiced with malice. Catherine later lets fall that her placidity and fondness is an effort of will: underneath she was grieving for Heathcliff. Nelly goes on to say, with some grimness:

> It ended. Well, we *must* be for ourselves in the long run; the mild and generous are only more justly selfish than the domineering— and it ended when circumstances caused each to feel that the one's interest was not the chief consideration in the other's thoughts.

The 'circumstances' were those following Heathcliff's return. He calls at the Grange, meaning not to do more than let her see him and realize what a mistake she made, and be off to murder Hindley:

> He took a seat opposite Catherine, who kept her gaze fixed on him as if she feared he would vanish were she to remove it. He did not raise his to her, often; a quick glance now and then sufficed; but it flashed back, each time more confidently, the undisguised delight he drank from hers.

It's very economically stated. No more need be said. The consequences are immediate:

> They were too much absorbed in their mutual joy to suffer embarrassment; not so Mr Edgar, he grew pale with pure annoyance, a feeling that reached its climax when his lady rose – and stepping across the rug, seized Heathcliff's hands again, and laughed like one beside herself.

She does nothing deliberately, we remember. It is the natural expression of a true deep feeling that goes right back into her childhood and is now suddenly maturing into something else.

Edgar sees it at once. That night, according to Catherine, he is 'childish':

> He always contrives to be sick at the least cross! I gave a few sentences of commendation to Heathcliff, and he, either for a head-ache or a pang of envy, began to cry: so I got up and left him.

Her fatal unconsciousness, or her unwillingness to see that people are people, and therefore perhaps as 'childish' as she, or less fearless, or more sensitive, or clearer-sighted about consequences, is both her strength and her limitation. She goes on 'But does it not show great weakness? . . . I'm not envious'. She has nothing to be envious of, since she is, in the world's eyes, about to try to have her cake and eat it, or some such envious phrase. She becomes hard about Isabella and Edgar in a way which reflects back on herself:

> . . . they are spoiled children, and fancy the world was made for their accommodation; and though I humour both, I think a smart chastisement might improve them all the same.

Nelly makes the obvious retort, going on

> 'You may however, fall out at last, over something of equal consequence to both sides; and then those you term weak are very capable of being as obstinate as you.'
>
> 'And then we shall fight to the death, shan't we, Nelly?' she returned, laughing. 'No, I tell you, I have such faith in Linton's love that I believe I might kill him, and he wouldn't wish to retaliate.'

It is a grim prediction, for she kills herself (or 'it' kills her that she is in the situation she finds herself in) and in due course both Linton and Heathcliff appease their longing for her by following her to the grave, after eighteen and twenty years of grieving and restlessness.

It would cut the discussion unhelpfully short to say Catherine is a spoilt bitch; that she enjoys exerting her power over two men; that she cannot see why they should not be willing to be both there, in love with her, and getting from her what she is willing to grant to each of them; and that she is destroyed when they decline to accept the situation docilely but make ever-increasing jealous demands on her and fall out violently with each other. It is near enough to the truth to be disturbing, but it doesn't fully cover the case. It is a kind of innocence in her, even a purity, which insists that what she feels for the two men comes from her quite spontaneously; what she feels for each is the due of each, so what is wrong? And 'she does nothing deliberately'. Equally, though she can be made, and is made, to suffer by them, it is, she thinks, fundamentally not right that she should be 'miserable for you'. This may be the innocence of childhood, in which case our reaction, as with Emma Bovary, is to say that people who won't grow up suffer for it. Alternatively it is the glimpse of a possibility, an ideal, that people ought to be able to manage: a forbearing maturity that would permit people to accept the reality of their feelings and the feelings of those they love, and learn to make no demands. But she is the last person to be able to manage that herself, since it requires a maturity she doesn't have; indeed her charm depends on her not having it. And the last-but-one person to attempt it with is Edgar, and the last-but-two is Heathcliff.

There is a certain contrast in the behaviour of the two men. There is a moment when Edgar forces the issue in the classic terms:

'Will you give up Heathcliff hereafter, or will you give up me? It is impossible for you to be *my* friend, and *his* at the same time; and I absolutely *require* to know which you choose.'

The conventionality of that—apart from the strange use once more of the word 'friend'—may blind us to its unreality. The world, in the person of the spouse exerting his or her 'rights', says 'which of these two limbs are you going to cut off?', and the victim is merely

aware that she wants them both, or that even if a choice is possible
it remains a violence, as any amputation must be.

It is Heathcliff who shows a gleam of realism here, even though
it hardly amounts to a forbearing sympathy:

> Had he been in my place, and I in his, though I hated him with
> a hatred that turned my life to gall, I never would have raised a
> hand against him. . . . I never would have banished him from her
> society, as long as she desired his.

Catherine is aware of this as her *power* over Heathcliff; he is aware
of it as part of his regard for her as a being with an independent
existence and freedom to bestow her love on other people. It is
part of his peculiar strength; and an indication of the depth of his
love.

An odd reflection is cast on this capacity by Catherine's earlier
asking him, more or less, whether he would like to have Isabella
Linton as a kind of consolation prize ('If you like Isabella, you
shall marry her'). He takes it as a profound insult, and perhaps it
is. Catherine's hope is that if he will have Isabella he can live near
by in his wedded bliss; and there will Catherine and Edgar be in
their wedded bliss; and Catherine and Heathcliff can also have
their wordless communion of spirit, which is satisfied by 'being'
each other. But Heathcliff is profoundly faithful to his love for
Catherine which for him excludes other loves; he wants her and
only her. Her marriage to Edgar was a grief and a deprival, and he
won't pretend otherwise. He will accept it since he must–she has
done it because she wanted to, and her will is paramount. But he
will not accept substitutes, or diversions or palliatives for himself,
and is offended at the offer. If he then marries Isabella, it is purely
because she delivers herself into his hands. He detests her, but she
offers a path to his revenge and a lever on Edgar.

'The tyrant grinds down his slaves', he says to Catherine (the
tyrant) '–and they don't turn against him, they crush those beneath
them' (Isabella). 'You are welcome to torture me to death for your
amusement, only, allow me to amuse myself in the same style–And
refrain from insult as much as you are able. Having levelled my
palace, don't erect a hovel and complacently admire your own
charity in giving me that for a home.' We hear the real anger and
bitterness there, and the violence brewing.

It is at this moment that Catherine begins to realize that she is lost. Heathcliff's violence–his urge to be revenged on those who have deprived him–threatens to be uncontrollable; Edgar's more commonplace but real jealousy is equally a threat. It turns out that people have wills as strong as hers, and the people who love her pull against her, make conflicting demands on her. Her resource is to make an even wilder, a truly childish, demand on them:

> Well, if I cannot keep Heathcliff for *my friend* – if Edgar will be mean and jealous, I'll try to break their hearts by breaking my own (*my italics*).

The threat is made to Nelly, who is resistant to that blackmail and looks stolid. She has heard it before. It is a fine touch of insight that Catherine, seeing that stolidity, is frightened. She may have to carry out her threat if she can't make people believe her and pull her back. It's in the rules of the game that you have to do it when dared:

> 'I wish you could dismiss that apathy out of your countenance, and look rather more anxious about me!'

It sounds spoilt and self-deceiving, but is a desperate cry for help, from a child. Nelly ignores it. She understands children, but not grown-up children. Anyway, the rules of the game apply to her too, and she is convinced that she is the only sensible person in the house. If only they would all be sensible! She is the solid extrovert who tells the depressive, the neurotic, to snap out of it, to pull herself together, to make the effort of will. That too is a self-regarding role, enclosing in its limitations. But it makes Nelly a real person. Compare Dickens's Clara Peggotty, who is just a projection of David Copperfield's need for a surrogate mother, and who does nothing but radiate uncritical love for him. Nelly has a mind of her own, and a will, which she uses. She offers all the main characters affection, but also a critical judgement, and she takes decisive and sometimes disastrous steps of her own–as when she refuses to take Catherine's threat seriously.

Catherine has her fit, but doesn't die–not then. Giving up is a deeper business, prolonged, and from the whole person including the body, not the conscious will alone. This delay permits the final interview with Heathcliff, where they have their last clash, above the deep agony of their separation. It is like seeing some flayed creature still active, all the muscles moving.

What the reader remembers about this scene is how at this supreme moment the two still torture each other: each strong will reproaching the other. It symbolizes the relationship that she softens at one moment, but he cannot easily make the physical gesture which bridges the divide between them:

> 'I'm not wishing you greater torment than I have, Heathcliff. I only wish us never to be parted–and should a word of mine distress you hereafter, think I feel the same distress underground, and for my own sake, forgive me! Come here and kneel down again! You never harmed me in your life. Nay, if you nurse anger, that will be worse to remember than my harsh words! Won't you come here again? Do!'

However that touches the heart, it is still the expression of a will; a wish to have, and a wish to be knelt to. Heathcliff can't submit to it, and turns his back. Catherine lets out a torrent of possessive reproach, ending

> '*That* is how I am loved! Well, never mind! That is not my Heathcliff. I shall love mine yet; and take him with me–he's in my soul.'

It reflects back on her thought that she *was* Heathcliff. Only it seems, 'her' Heathcliff: but there is a real one outside her, with a will of his own. This Heathcliff at last manages to cross over to her:

> 'Do come to me, Heathcliff.'
>
> In her eagerness she rose, and supported herself on the arm of the chair. At that earnest appeal, he turned to her, looking absolutely desperate. His eyes wide, and wet, at last, flashed fiercely on her; his breast heaved convulsively. An instant they held asunder; and then how they met I hardly saw, but Catherine made a spring, and he caught her, and they were locked in an embrace from which I thought my mistress would never be released alive.

The undertones would have been familiar to Racine; the spring of the predatory animal. Indeed Nelly goes on expressly, and rather luridly, to say

> . . . on my approaching hurriedly to ascertain if she had fainted, he gnashed at me, and foamed like a mad dog, and gathered her to him with greedy jealousy.

That is the myth-making tendency at work; expressing Nelly's smallness. These feelings are too big for her and too savage:

> I did not feel as if I were in the company of a creature of my own species.

But she *is* of that species; Racine knew we all were, and Nelly in her reflective moments knows it too.

That leap together, and the convulsive clinging together, express physically one kind of love, as other gestures we have seen in other books express different kinds: the prodigal's father running towards him; Lear and Cordelia kneeling to each other; Vronsky putting out an open hand which Anna will not put her hand into. Those moments and gestures are great things, and speak at the deepest level–this one among them. It is softened in its animal desperation by a specifically human touch. At the very end, Catherine holds on to Heathcliff like a child in fear of the dark, unwilling to let its father go from the bedside:

> He would have risen, and unfixed her fingers by the act–she clung fast, gasping: there was mad resolution in her face.
> 'No!' she shrieked, 'Oh, don't, don't go. It is the last time! Edgar will not hurt us. Heathcliff, I shall die! I shall die!'

Recurrently all the characters move into these implacably child-like postures. His response is fatherly: 'Hush, my darling! Hush, hush, Catherine! I'll stay.' They are the only humanly consoling words he speaks in the book. She needs him; he responds, glad to meet her last need. This meeting in her fear and desolation–she terrified of being alone, he comforting her in her dread–is as near as they get to a union before the end of the book. It gives them their relative stature, he larger and potentially kinder than she.

After that, the difficulty for Emily Brontë was to prevent the rest of the book being an anti-climax. It isn't one, but I don't find it strikes with the same strength partly because it moves into an equivocal kind of reality. It is meant to be a working out, an appeasement, or a laying to rest of the forces aroused in the first half. Catherine Earnshaw, who forsakes Heathcliff and marries Edgar Linton, gives birth at this mid-point to Catherine Linton, who first marries Heathcliff's son Linton Heathcliff, who dies, and then Hareton Earnshaw. She has much of her mother in her, but goes through a maturing process induced by Heathcliff. The

Catherine Earnshaw we see at the end of the book is like an exorcized version of the Catherine Earnshaw we see at the beginning, and she is united to a young man who is like an exorcized Heathcliff. For Heathcliff had wanted to brutalize Hareton as Hareton's father brutalized him. He finds to his puzzlement that this has an unintended effect: Hareton does not resent it; he is not ultimately brutalized at all, nor vengeful, since he has reserves of goodness; and the isolated Catherine comes to love him as the other Catherine had loved Heathcliff. But this time the love is not self-thwarted: the second Catherine learns to subdue her will; in the process she discovers that Hareton is a separate person unlike her projected image of him, and lovable.

The searing thing in the second half of the book is Catherine's forced marriage to the weak, consumptive and dying Linton Heathcliff. She is trapped into the marriage, having never had more than childish playmate feelings for him in the first place, or protective motherly or elder-sisterly feelings in the second. But she sees him through to his death.

It is important that in a moment of clarity about himself he says to her

You are so much happier than I am, you ought to be better . . . I *am* worthless, and bad in temper, and bad in spirit, almost always – and if you choose you may say goodbye – you'll get rid of an annoyance – Only, Catherine, do me this justice; believe that if I might be as sweet, and as kind, and as good as you are, I would be, as willingly, and more so, than as happy and as healthy. And believe that your kindness has made me love you deeper than if I deserved your love, and though I couldn't, and cannot help showing my nature to you, I regret it and repent it, and shall regret it and repent it, till I die.

That insight shines back towards the young Heathcliff, who is to some extent made what he is by what has happened to him from the beginning. The degree to which we are what we have in native strength, or are what life, especially early life, has twisted us into, like the thorns praying to the sun but twisted by the wind, is one of the mysterious issues of the book and it raises the other old question – do we do things 'deliberately'? Linton Heathcliff is a sickly child, conceived in hate, brought up by a strong-willed mother without a father, taken over by the father in scorn and

K

hate, and used to further a will to power. He is evidently entirely twisted, and it is a question which defines the nature of the on-looker whether he is more pitiful or contemptible. Catherine finds pity, and the beginnings of wisdom. It enables her to begin to see Heathcliff; she says to him:

I know he [Linton] has a bad nature . . . he's your son. But I'm glad I've a better, to forgive it; and I know he loves me and for that reason I love him. Mr Heathcliff, *you* have *nobody* to love you, and, however miserable you make us, we shall still have the revenge of thinking that your cruelty arises from your greater misery! You *are* miserable, are you not? Lonely, like the devil, and envious like him? *Nobody* loves you–nobody will cry for you when you die! I wouldn't be you!

Even here, though, there is spite and enmity and the desire for revenge amongst the truths, which are therefore incomplete. Nobody understands Heathcliff in the novel. In the second half of the book he is working out an allotted span, bringing about the things which release him from the world, to be reunited with the first Catherine. What he is to find with her is, in the first place, peace; and that is probably all, but it may be enough. The union of two beings is achieved when, laid side by side in earth, their bodies both become part of it, their separate natures annihilated. Emily Brontë is quite carefully specific about this in a level-headed way reminiscent of the seventeenth century. She points out very early that the chapel graveyard 'lies in a hollow, between two hills– an elevated hollow–near a swamp, whose peaty moisture is said to answer all the purposes of embalming on the few corpses deposited there'. Catherine is buried there; when Edgar Linton is buried beside her, Heathcliff opens her coffin and is appeased to see that she is, so to speak, waiting for him:

'Disturbed her? No! she has disturbed me, night and day, through eighteen years–incessantly–remorselessly–till yesternight–and yesternight, I was tranquil. I dreamt I was sleeping the last sleep, by that sleeper, with my heart stopped, and my cheek frozen against hers.'

'And if she had been dissolved into earth, or worse, what would you have dreamt of then?' I said.

'Of dissolving with her and being more happy still!' he answered. 'Do you suppose I dread any change of that sort? I expected such a transformation on raising the lid, but I'm better pleased that it should not commence until I share it.'

The little patch of green, which is the graveyard in the hills, is constantly invaded by the bracken of the Heights. In due course that silent taking-over will be accomplished. Lockwood's last three paragraphs, the last in the book, envisage in sober wisdom the natural intransigence that takes over when human intransigence is stilled, the chapel dropping back to earth, the three headstones, side by side, being worked into the texture of the place by lichen, the 'sleepers in that quiet earth' reconciled by being taken into it. It is in that sense too that Catherine *is* finally Heathcliff. They become the world to each other, having always been so.

Before Heathcliff can enter that sleep he has to be formally released, to feel that Catherine's will is no longer exerted on him. It happens in the end, and, rationalizing (or perhaps I mean irrationalizing) the occurrence, we say that Catherine's spirit approves the union of the younger Catherine and Hareton and is put to rest, so releasing Heathcliff. The marriage of the young people unites the Heights and the Grange; it also unites a purified Catherine and a humanized Heathcliff; so that those two could see in this final love a happy resolution of their own unhappy love. They can let go, and leave.

So it falls out. Catherine and Hareton are at first at odds, all will and ego and pride. Both learn to subdue their pride, and so are able to give way to their tender feelings. It is a question of getting one part of oneself subdued, so that the other part may flourish (a truth young Linton Heathcliff saw, except that he also saw that it was not in *his* nature to manage that). Hareton's pride makes him gloomy and awkward, and prevents Catherine seeing what is underneath. In sheer anger he at one moment explains he has defended her to Heathcliff, and regrets it as a waste of good nature:

> 'I didn't know you took my part,' she answered, drying her eyes;
> 'and I was miserable and bitter at everybody; but now I thank
> you, and beg you to forgive me; what can I do besides?'
> She returned to the hearth, and frankly extended her hand. He
> blackened and scowled like a thundercloud, and kept his fists
> resolutely clenched, and his gaze fixed on the ground.
> Catherine, by instinct, must have divined it was obdurate

perversity and not dislike that prompted this dogged conduct; for, after remaining an instant, undecided, she stooped, and impressed on his cheek a gentle kiss.

We recognize the gesture. It is touching, but pretty small in scale after the first half of the book. It is in any case overshadowed by the presence of Heathcliff still, approaching his deliverance; and his final release returns us to the people of that first half, and their unappeased longings, which are set at rest in the only possible way –by his death.

The extraordinary utterance Lockwood had overheard at the beginning of the book is, we sense, answered at the end:

'Come in! come in!' he sobbed. 'Cathy do come. Oh do–*once* more! Oh my heart's darling! hear me *this* time–Catherine, at last!'

We take that at the fairy-tale level by agreeing that throughout the second half of the book Catherine's ghost is awaited by Heathcliff. When she returns to him, a kind of half-compact, half-curse is fulfilled; he will be released; they will both be at peace. Emily Brontë equivocates brilliantly here; Heathcliff is clearly under the power of that obsession, and it is real for *him*. What it means for us is left to us. At the literal level we can say we don't believe in ghosts. The last sentence of the book may mean that the narrator Lockwood never *has* believed in ghosts; or that he is convinced that they are *now* both laid. But our response to the narrative is to feel both Heathcliff's agonized expectation and the profound relaxation of his deliverance.

Miss Murdstone may help us a little. The late lamented Catherine, she would give it as her opinion, was in all essential respects a child. Dickens helps us, by preventing us from taking that in the sense of 'only' a child. What the child has pre-eminently is an undulled power of feeling, an unchecked sense of will as the prime source of its identity, and a capacity to say 'why not?' where adults say 'of course not'. That goes with egoism, of course; why shouldn't I, since I want to? The first Catherine is introduced to us as a child with the power to ask such questions. Old Mr Earnshaw, being charmed by her, on one occasion, asks, 'Why can't thou not always be a good lass?' She answers his question by making it unanswerable, saying, 'Why cannot you always be a good man, father?' It's cheeky as well as unanswerable; he's annoyed; she kisses his hand and sings him to sleep. He dies in a few minutes. It's the kind of heart-stopping Shakespearian effect Emily Brontë naturally rose to. It is one of the things which make us unwilling to write Catherine off as hard and spoilt. She is hard, she is spoilt, from the point of view of the mediocre ego that sees a less mediocre ego as excessively demanding. But we must all be for ourselves in the end, as Nelly Dean says, and Catherine is in the end an innocent and a power of nature. She has a glimpse of the possibilities that only a kind of intransigence can see or secure. She is not, that is to say, a Stiva Oblonsky. He too says 'why not?' and he too is surprised that the world won't let him have this *and* that, but only this *or* that. But he is, however charmingly, a closed surface: nothing can hurt him. How fortunate, perhaps. Catherine has an endless power of being hurt, and it comes from a trait which looks egoistic. Stiva is under no illusion that other people 'are' him. It is because they are not him that *they* can be hurt and he can not care. For Catherine, to learn that Heathcliff is not herself is a deep childish grief and a threat to her power, which is the source of her life. But she will not let go, for that reason, of what he is to her. Her sense that they were one being has to be redefined; and the conviction of affinity–that they are, to a miraculous power, what the child calls 'friends' is a deep truth. That Edgar, who has something else, is jealous of her 'friendship', that Heathcliff may want to turn 'being friends' into something like Edgar's formal possession in legal marriage, is a crisis she can't manage, because these are adults using their conventional language for conventional relationships and explaining 'why not'. It can never make sense to her.

Heathcliff's feeling for her is as surely grounded in their having been 'friends' at a time when he needed 'friends' and she was the only one. He seems to me an adult in a way she is not, but to love her none the less for being what she is–except that as he sees it, she betrayed her feeling for him. This is one of the lingering questions: did she fundamentally betray her true straightforward inclination, as Heathcliff insists; or was it her nature to attempt what the conventional world thinks impossible?

What one glimpses in both her and him–in Edgar too–is fidelity–faithfulness to one's best feelings, regardless of convention. Indeed Catherine turns the conventions upside down. The world

says that if you love two men you must be 'unfaithful', by definition. The person with the feelings in question is bound to reply
that they *are* feelings, and it is feelings one is faithful to. If you
annihilate one feeling, you are unfaithful to it. Anna Karenina
knew that. It was in her case her feelings that forced a choice on
her, not the world; but even so the choice was destructive. There
is a moment when she thinks Karenin is going to make some unreal
demand on her, and she feels that he must himself be immune to
feeling and cannot therefore understand her position:

'I cannot change anything,' she whispered.

Commitment to a feeling means that you cannot *want* it to change;
that would be a betrayal. And so one finds that one is saying
something horrifyingly like Miss Murdstone, to whom it was a
satisfaction to find that she was not a creature subject to chance
and change. Here are irreconcilables: our need for growth and
change; our need for commitment and stability. One's certainties
vanish here, except that Miss Murdstone's self-congratulation is
certainly odious–she offers something hard and dried-up, a
mummy-self, and expects to be congratulated as if it were living.
But if life means growth and change, there are some things one
does not wish to 'grow out of' because one has put one's faith in
them, one's self in them: they are meanings which cannot be
allowed to be meaningless. Dolly Oblonsky is witness to that.

But that is our problem, not Catherine's or Heathcliff's. It never
enters their minds that their feelings for each other are anything
but eternal, founded on the rock; and so, we must remember, is
Edgar's for Catherine. This is the intransigence of the self completely identified with its passion, which comes out at last as
untrammelled direct feeling, all flowing one way. Hence inevitable
conflict between selves–life seen as a very fierce fight to the death
between wills. Racine saw the same vision, and reacted with dread
and horror. Emily Brontë sees it as perfectly natural, inevitable and
potentially heroic. It is the world of epic.

Our own reaction may be more mundane. Something in most of
us is with Nelly Dean, who sighs and is disapproving sometimes,
but has some love for all these people. She is not as large as they
are, but she is of their race, and she knows that 'here we are the
same as anywhere else'. If our first instinct is to see them as
mythical, heroic or superhuman, the second thought is that though

large, they are human and reflect honour on the race. Mr Lockwood comes to that view too: at the end of the book it has been proved to him that a love for life is not just 'almost possible'; it is a natural demand on life, and he has seen it happen, even if he could not himself become large enough to make that demand and live it out.

For he has also seen the cost of sustaining it. If it is not an illusion, it is because life may have to be sacrificed to it to keep it real. The images which remain in our minds when we close the book are of Catherine and Heathcliff in each other's arms, yet struggling with each other and speaking bitterly to each other right up to the moment of death; of the three gravestones which mark a highly equivocal 'peace' and 'union'; but most of all, of Heathcliff's long ascetic discipline. His willed cruelty has all fallen away, as unreal. He has learnt that he only wants something that he has lost. It is not to be regained by exerting his will on others. So there he is, a mature unhappy man, a solitary man approaching death, waiting at his window in agonized expectation–for the ghost of a child, with whom as a child he had been 'friends', to whom as a man he had been, for a brief moment, a father.

Portrait of a Lady

Sentences like the last one may seem only to provide a graceful or an inspiriting flourish–a touch of purple–at the end of a long chapter. But it was soberly meant. A commitment of the kind Heathcliff has made has a clear meaning when the object of his love is present to him. It's a more difficult meaning when she is married to another man, but that obstacle is faced: fidelity can mean fidelity across the barriers of conventional relationship. It has its most profound meaning held as he finally holds it, the fidelity of a lonely man to something which to the world seems lost and gone. At this moment it must look at best a touching delusion to other people, or a foolish one (at one moment Nelly Dean talks slightingly of his 'monomania on the subject of his departed idol'). The second half of *Wuthering Heights* is tied to the first half by this seemingly maniac obstinacy of Heathcliff's over twenty years. It was a stroke of genius that Emily Brontë conveyed it as in the mode of a ballad: the figure of the bereaved lover waiting for the dead to return from the grave, so that they may be released together. This has the multiple meaning of poetry–the deeper truth is overlaid by the convention of form; the everyday consciousness may mock it as folly or superstition. But this note is essential to the meaning. *Wuthering Heights* is one of the great romantic works of art: it embraces the ideal of total self-surrender with far less circumspection than Tolstoy, and without Flaubert's anguish. It accepts with calmness what Racine saw with horror, that the self identified with and given up to its passion is locked on to the other self in a relationship that makes extreme demands; that it leads swiftly to conflict; that the condition of life, lived this way, is mortal combat. That is faced, almost welcomed. It gives life its dignity; it gives people a heroic stature. The large people, Catherine and Heathcliff, are from one point of view straight-forwardly antisocial, since they demand their satisfactions in ways which take no account of the claims of bystanders. People get hurt, may be killed, as a matter of course; there is no prudent accommodation. Things must be played out. For Heathcliff, his life has its natural end when his compact with Catherine is fulfilled at the end of those years of solitary waiting, in which he holds on, alone, to his sense of what his life was about and what its final fulfilment must be. He dies in an ecstasy.

Held that way it is a kind of religion, a viewpoint from which life makes sense, and people all find their place. We saw it even with the stunted and morally deformed Linton Heathcliff. The worm is given its voice; he has that moment of clarity (p. 145) in which he presents himself as he is, a warped nature, making the same demand on the younger Catherine as everyone else in the book makes on the person they love. The difference is that he is weak, contemptible and unworthy of love. But he needs to be responded to as much as the strongest; he makes his claim and it is answered. The world is not complete without inferior or damaged beings; and since we are approaching the realm of Nietzsche and Lawrence, it is worth pointing to the greater health and strength of Emily Brontë's moral feeling.

If we look back at Levin's and Anna Karenina's questions, they resolve themselves into 'Who am I? What do I know? What do I feel? What do I need? Who do I love? Why am I here?' *Wuthering Heights* presents triumphantly sure answers to them. The main characters know, and they act out of that knowledge. The answers are the purest romanticism. We have seen that there are other answers. The classical ones are 'My self-knowledge is incomplete and necessarily partial. I know that I am a social being. I know that I have obligations to others. I feel a need to be in a good relation to the world so that my self-approval corresponds with the world's approval. Love can conflict with conscience. I am here to do my duty.' These are the tenets of the puritan ethic, and if we look about for the literary representative of that ethic in modern literature our eye falls naturally on Henry James. In the particular context of this book, one turns to *The Portrait of a Lady*, at the end of which James's heroine, Isabel Archer, seems to be settling down like Heathcliff to a vigil of twenty years or even longer. The difference is that she seems to be waiting for her husband to die. She may then be able to take up her life again. We are horrified at the waste of life, but are asked to accept it as a duty, or as the expression of her nature.

Or is that the wrong interpretation? One trouble with the book is that James's delicacy of behaviour to the reader—he won't say crude things about the meaning—can mask his own failures and uncertainties. Certainly, just to be told 'think this, understand that, judge that way' is both an insult to one's intelligence and a crude short-circuiting of the interest of art. Certainly too, to have to find one's way through to a meaning, balancing this indication against that, noting that qualification, pondering the other significance, means that the art is valuably like life, where we have to make the same effort; no truth is handed to us on the way in, or on the way out either. James's books are therefore like an ideal drama; you have to judge people by what they say and do, and the author can only convey his meaning that way. He can also conceal his lack of certainty, or he can multiply ambiguities in the vain hope that they will add up to a fruitful complexity.

At the beginning of the book Isabel Archer is on the point of accepting a young man from Boston, Caspar Goodwood. Her aunt, Mrs Touchett, comes to America, offers her the chance of a stay in Europe. 'Life' in an undefined sense, but something wider and freer than marriage to a Goodwood seems to open up (or is she, rather, liberated from a fear of commitment to his uncompromising passion?). It is perhaps a duty to herself to undertake the journey, to see more of the world before devoting herself to a narrower, more conventional duty. Indeed the journey offers itself as a wider range of choice, and in a way the marriage represented an absence of choice (but we suspect that she is frightened of having to choose). She puts off Goodwood, so injuring him, and leaves. In England she is entertained by the Touchetts. Mrs Touchett's consumptive son Ralph is first delighted with, then in love with her. But since he must soon die he cannot press himself on her, so he is content to try to do something large for her. (Does she finally come to love him—in a way—*because* he makes no claim?) He persuades his father to leave her half the fortune that might otherwise have come to him. Possession of wealth will give her freedom, he thinks—not only to voyage and 'see things' but in the wider sense to choose what she shall do, where she shall freely bestow herself. She finally makes her free choice (or is she chosen?). She bestows herself on Gilbert Osmond, an emigré American aesthete

living in Italy, who seems nobly refined, exquisite in his perceptions, a fine flower of civilization. She then finds first that he is an
egoist, second that he married her for her money, third that he
was urged into marrying her by Isabel's false friend Madame
Merle, finally that Madame Merle was once his mistress, is the
mother of his daughter, and that one aim of the pair is to use
Isabel's money to find the daughter a dowry for a socially ambi-
tious marriage. The men who love Isabel–Caspar Goodwood, the
English Lord Warburton whose offer of marriage she also refuses
early in the book, Ralph Touchett himself–all come to realize that
her marriage is a disaster. Ralph dies, and her journey to his
deathbed threatens a breach with Osmond, who virtually forbids
her to go. Goodwood offers her his love a last time, is willing to
face the social consequences of their going off like Anna Karenina
and Vronsky, and living together. She refuses, and returns to
Osmond.

Why? the reader asks. The answer, 'it is her duty' is easy to
give, but begs the questions, 'is that her *real* duty, and where do
one's duties lie?' It is a merely conventional duty, and you are a
merely conventional person, if you accept such duties as imposed
on you by the world. Isabel has not shown herself merely conventional so far. Moreover the notion of merely conventional duty
is expressed in the book by the odious Osmond himself. He is
clearly using that conventional demand as a weapon, as the
instrument of his will. He wants clearly enough to strip Isabel of
what he calls her 'ideas', and chief among them is her idea of
herself.

The ideal she seems to express is that of a spontaneous freely
choosing being, seeking out the highest so that she may of her own
free will give herself to it. In that search she refuses Caspar
Goodwood and Lord Warburton–both good men and men of
moral substance–and opts for the loathsome Osmond. It's an
error, that is freely conceded; is it meant to be a noble error? And
would sticking by it be equally noble or perverse? One ends the
book disgusted. Suppose we set it alongside *Wuthering Heights*,
Anna Karenina and *David Copperfield*, how does it look?

One answer is, weakly literary. What we feel about those other
books is that they come to us with the force of a personal knowledge
behind them. There were things Emily Brontë, Dickens and
Tolstoy knew with the impact, actuality and specificity of lived

experience. In Dickens, for instance, you can distinguish quite clearly what he knew as from life and what he got ready-made from bad literary traditions, and the one tells against the other. When James came, later in life, to write the scarcely-sufferable preface to *Portrait of a Lady*, he offered as a measure of any novel's worth the amount of 'felt life' it contains. By that standard the book stands infinitely lower than the others, and the trouble is self-diagnosed.

By 'literary' I mean two specific things. First, James had like most nineteenth-century English novelists a tendency to lapse into the falsely theatrical. It provides strong crude thrills, but it is fundamentally commonplace and untrue to life. I suppose the most notable example is that where Madame Merle finally reveals her part in determining Isabel's fate (to fall into that way of speaking):

> As she went on Isabel grew pale; she clasped her hands more tightly in her lap. It was not that her visitor had at last thought it the right time to be insolent; for this was not what was most apparent. It was a worse horror than that.
>
> 'Who are you—what are you?' Isabel murmured. 'What have you to do with my husband?' It was strange that for the moment she drew as near to him as if she had loved him.
>
> 'Ah then, you take it heroically! I'm very sorry. Don't think, however, that I shall do so.'
>
> 'What have you to do with me!' Isabel went on.
>
> Madame Merle slowly got up, stroking her muff, but not removing her eyes from Isabel's face. 'Everything!' she answered.
>
> Isabel sat there looking up at her, without rising; her face was almost a prayer to be enlightened. But the light of this woman's eyes seemed only a darkness.
>
> 'Oh misery!' she murmured at last; and she fell back, covering her face with her hands. It had come over her like a high-surging wave that Mrs Touchett was right. Madame Merle had married her. Before she uncovered her face again that lady had left the room.

Strong curtain, we murmur to ourselves. We are in the world of the elegant theatre of the late nineteenth century, knowing that we are near the end of the act, thrilling to the *coup de théâtre*, watching people make histrionic gestures: they draw themselves up, cast themselves back, cover their eyes with their hands, and utter enigmatic words of power and threat. It's tosh, of course; enjoyable if you know it is tosh, but it is more damaging in Henry James than it was in Dickens and George Eliot, because there isn't anything sufficiently real and directly felt in the book to carry it off. Compare the drama in *Wuthering Heights*, which seems on the surface to be much more extravagant, even unsophisticated in its early-romantic terms, and which consistently conveys human truth.

Gilbert Osmond and Madame Merle are James's version of George Eliot's villainous pair Grandcourt and Lush, in *Daniel Deronda*. They go back even further, to Dickens's Steerforth and his servant Littimer in *David Copperfield*. Steerforth's compulsion to charm is transmuted into Osmond's ability to charm when he puts himself out. Grandcourt's brutal disregard of other people's feelings, his coldness, is taken over and turned into something a little more refined. The instrument of Steerforth's will, the cold and respectable Littimer, and the instrument of Grandcourt's will, the coarse Lush, are more changed: Madame Merle is more independent in her personality and operation, and is even given a little stagey pathos at the end, but basically the idea of a sinister subservience is taken over from Dickens and George Eliot, and left with its equivocal thrill, which is finally damaging to the meaning of the book.

For that matter Isabel Archer herself is fundamentally a literary conception. She derives from Jane Austen's Emma Woodhouse (handsome, young, independent-minded, over-confident, a little pert, but basically admirable: a really human heroine, with failings) but is crossed with George Eliot's Gwendolen Harleth (less clever, less brave, also handsome, young, more spoilt, her self-confidence falsely based, but still sympathetic, and married to the hateful Grandcourt).

It would be no grave criticism if James, seeing what Jane Austen, Dickens and George Eliot had done, had wanted to develop a neighbouring moral territory. A novelist might well say 'Suppose I take a girl, something like Emma Woodhouse in basic spirit and intelligence, something like David Copperfield and Gwendolen Harleth in that she makes a disastrous marriage – can I do something with that?' It is perhaps a damaging thought that Emma Woodhouse's sceptical intelligence is such that she would probably see through Gilbert Osmond. And Gwendolen Harleth snatched at marriage very largely as a way of saving herself from being a governess; underestimating Grandcourt's egoism, manifested at first as a languorous kind of indifference, she assumed he would be undemanding in a marriage where she herself proposed to lend only her decorative social self. She didn't even know what else she was. That terrible error made for her misery, and it sprang from her social predicament and a kind of stupidity in her. But James is positing an intelligent, sensitive, very serious girl who wishes with great earnestness to give herself to a marriage which shall be the finest thing she can do in life. Unlike Gwendolen, she is rich, and can choose. She is intelligent: she has refused two offers of marriage because the men were not adequate to her sense of what she was looking for. How, then, does *she* fall for Osmond, who in the second half of the book is very convincingly shown to be invincibly small, mean-minded, cold, malignantly conventional, and also (given his past) hypocritical to the point of corruption? And when she discovers all that, does not her own standard *demand* that she leave him?

The alternatives seem to be four. Either Isabel is a very poor judge of people after all (no answer, really); or she was tremendously deceived by a brilliant histrionic performance by Osmond (again no answer; she is not bound by a deception); or she was most cunningly manipulated by Madame Merle and Osmond together (again no answer; it frees her)—or in some deep way domination by a Gilbert is what she seeks and needs; she is a willing victim underneath. One could go into all that; perhaps one has to in order to understand the book. But, one thinks, that third answer would mean we really are in the realm of the novelettish. Fair maidens being trapped into marriage for their money by designing society women providing for their ex-lovers and their unacknowledged daughters—it is thoroughly unreal; and however hard James works at it to make it seem plausible or even interesting, one basic strand of his plot is this rather etiolated kind of melodrama. Indeed, he knows that it's a weakness to depend too much on this trap, and so he equivocates about its importance.

People are not manipulated like puppets. If they fall into traps, it is because they are inclined to do so. As Dickens knew, mistaken marriages express some kind of need in at least one party. They are disastrous; but to represent them merely as the result of a plot would be an insult to the intelligence. So Isabel's reflection, at one point, 'that she had been an applied handled hung-up tool, as senseless and convenient as mere shaped wood and iron' might be a truthful report of a moment of self-deceiving rage and shame, but as a full account of what has actually happened would be an ignoble avoidance of responsibility. It conflicts with what she herself had thought earlier:

> It was impossible to pretend that she had not acted with her eyes open; if ever a girl was a free agent she had been. A girl in love was doubtless not a free agent; but the sole source of her mistake had been within herself. There had been no plot, no snare; she had looked and considered and chosen. When a woman had made such a mistake, there was only one way to repair it – just immensely (oh, with the highest grandeur!) to accept it. One folly was enough, especially when it was to last for ever; a second one would not much set it off.

She accepts her responsibility in those terms before she learns of Osmond's relationship with Madame Merle and Madame Merle's manipulation of herself. Is James suggesting that that later knowledge cancels out this acceptance? He can hardly do that, so he keeps the factors of freedom and manipulation awkwardly balanced.

In any case, the terms of that meditation are curious. The calm recognition of a 'mistake': is that what it is to feel one is unhappily married? Compare David Copperfield's desperate (and in a way honourable) unconscious wish not to recognize that Dora is not a complete and lasting joy to him; or Anna Karenina's anguished relationship with Karenin – even Emma Bovary's petulant rage against Charles. Those people are deeply engaged, and therefore troubled; they are in the ways possible to them trying to live through their troubles. They don't make conscious resolves (oh, with the highest grandeur!) to 'accept' it; they are in it, struggling. What would 'accepting' it mean, for Isabel Archer? We hardly know. It sounds like some merely external observance of social decencies. That is to fall, precisely, and without any 'grandeur', into Gilbert Osmond's own conventionality, of which he is so complacently conscious.

Of course, if people do finally recognize 'mistakes' they must face that recognition. But if you get to that conscious state, the acceptance of the 'mistake' could then be a self-betrayal. It can hardly be a matter of the highest grandeur. It might be a bitter necessity; it might be all one could manage; or it might be a brave attempt to make things better. It might involve a recognition of one's own feelings as part of a shared fault, and a wish, by self-discipline, to manage better for one's own part. Isabel has no consciousness of failings; she remains to the end a bit of a mystery to the reader; one does ask whether her apparent strength and charm are the surface of a deep turmoil, but there's no clear sign that James meant to present her–despite some limitations–as anything but lovable, and really rather uncomplicated. And she is married to this mere monster.

James's other illusion (apart from the one about 'felt life') is that Isabel's consciousness is the focus of the book: ' "Place the centre of the subject in the young woman's own consciousness" I said to myself "and you get as interesting and as beautiful a difficulty as you could wish . . . To depend upon her and her little concerns wholly to see you through will necessitate, remember, your really 'doing' her." ' From beginning to end, one is never really inside her consciousness, as one is with Tolstoy's characters. The reason is that James was without that tragic sense of the self, either as universal or as inhering in this individual or that, that we have met in Shakespeare, Racine and the tragic writers. He was usually a comic writer, and saw things from outside.

True, there are occasions when Isabel seems massively to reflect. There is a long and crucial chapter (James pats himself on the back for it in the preface) in which Isabel spends much of a night looking back on the whole history of her marriage, and at last sees things in their 'true light' (chapter XLII). But it is not a personal meditation; it isn't felt through the medium of her consciousness; it is Henry James deploying a colossal flash-back in which all the difficulties of his plot are resolved simply by being stated to have happened, all recounted in middle-period Jacobean prose, so that James's is the only consciousness we are aware of. Gilbert Osmond had seemed to be the man Isabel was seeking in life; he has instead proved himself a monster of egoism. *How* he had first charmed her into thinking him the first thing; *how* he had revealed himself to be the second–that is dodged. We never see it happen. The first was 'the extraordinary charm that he, on his side, had taken pains to put forth . . . Ah, she had been immensely under the charm! It had not passed away; it was still there: she still knew perfectly what it was that made Osmond delightful when he chose to be.' Well, what *was* it? We scarcely see. One or two meagre moments when Osmond might be alleged to be displaying his charm are recorded; for instance, this:

> '... Do everything that's proper; I go in for that. Excuse my being so patronising. You say you don't know me, but when you do you'll discover what a worship I have for propriety.'
> 'You're not conventional?' Isabel gravely asked.
> 'I like the way you utter that word! No, I'm not conventional: I'm convention itself. You don't understand that?' And he paused a moment, smiling. 'I should like to explain it.' Then with a sudden, quick, bright naturalness, 'Do come back again,' he pleaded. 'There are so many things we might talk about.'
> She stood with lowered eyes. 'What service did you speak of just now?'
> 'Go and see my little daughter before you leave Florence. She's alone at the villa; I decided not to send her to my sister, who hasn't at all my ideas. Tell her she must love her poor father very much,' said Gilbert Osmond gently.

If that's the charm, we might think she's had fair warning of his utter fraudulence, and we are much shaken to see how little she can judge.

His nastiness is quite effectively shown, on the other hand. But even here, James has a preference for the long reflective analysis, aphoristically stated and staked out in a flowerbed of metaphor. What he is weak at is that kind of dramatic presentation of character from within, in which what people are, what they want, determines what they say, overriding a conscious intention (think again of Tolstoy's triumphs of this kind, for instance the little scene between Dolly and Kitty quoted on p. 114). This is a sad thing: James's theatricality is plain enough; his actual dramatic gift—in *The Portrait of a Lady* at any rate—is deployed only as social comedy.

This difficulty of plot (how to manoeuvre Isabel into the impossible situation without making her seem stupid) and his merely literary inspiration (neither Isabel nor Gilbert nor Madame Merle are real enough people: they are constructs put together laboriously to fit the situation) necessarily take charge of the book. It's *about* Isabel; her situation is the essential interest; if James can't bring that off, the book fails. It has led him beyond his

L

first-hand knowledge, which was always that of the spectator; it has led him out of his natural mode, which is comedy. And for that reason, if you ignore the central relationship, the book is full of charm, life and wit. The minor characters are amusing, the scene-setting is attractive, the social encounters are well managed. That's an essential point. Where James's talents, interests and gifts cohere, where his method really coincides with the ethos he wanted to convey, is in a peculiarly witty sort of drawing-room comedy. The wit is at the service of serious issues (as it never is in Wilde's comedy, for instance) which means that the exchanges are often barbed, the intentions veiled, and the elegance has a sting. The characteristic strength of a Jamesian scene is the opposite of the one between Isabel and Madame Merle quoted above: it is the exchange in which nobody sinks back and covers their eyes, and nobody makes a rash claim to power and influence for the sake of sweeping out of the room on a strong curtain line. At its best, two clever social beings fence with each other, each reading in the other's replies some knowledge the other may want to conceal. Neither gives himself or herself away. It is thus very much a matter of holding in, or holding back, of being consciously in control, of being intelligent, of being witty, conceivably of being cruel. The self, in these circumstances, is either a force which is effectively held in check, so that appearances are always saved, or it is channelled into these exchanges, so that they acquire an extra edge. The Gilbert Osmond of the monstrous phase is one exemplification of this way of feeling; he is its negative pole. There's plenty of self there, and it can fairly freely display itself as social brutality—deliberate rudeness. But he is never at risk, because he is always in command. He is not broken down by any surge from within, or attack on him; his gift is precisely for putting other people in the wrong, or putting them out of countenance. He is impenetrable and unchangeable. Compare Karenin, who is some kind of moral relative, but whom Tolstoy knows to be capable of being morally or emotionally penetrated, or being broken right down. Tolstoy knows more about Karenin than James knows about Osmond, because Tolstoy posits a universal selfhood, and can imaginatively enter it. James can't; or at any rate he doesn't. He remains outside, watching, and making the social judgement.

The only exception to this is Ralph Touchett. He is condemned by his illness to be just that kind of observer. He performs one action—he persuades his father to leave Isabel a fortune. It is generously meant but turns out disastrously, because the sharks Madame Merle and Osmond scent the money and snap up Isabel. That is a grief to Ralph, who had wanted to make Isabel free to live out her aspirations, to have a life of large-mannered motions, to be noble, generous and imaginative. It's all the more painful in that he loves her, can make no claim on her, cannot even warn her without seeming indelicate—even jealous. He is disinterested enough, however, to do that, and to anger her in consequence. When he dies they are touchingly reconciled: he speaks again of his love for her, and she at last breaks down. She confesses a kind of love for him—but implies that it is a sisterly love. That too we ponder. Are we to feel that perhaps the only real love she can feel is this sort of disinterested asexual affection: that she can love Ralph, recognize her love at the end, because he can never offer to possess her?

In any case, they come heart to heart. It is the moral centre of the book, whether it was meant to be or not. We feel that two people have given way to their real feeling, come close; that the love they recognize, which they explicitly claim to be the most valuable thing in life and the only counterpoise against its suffering, is there given the only fruition it gets in the whole book. If Ralph was Isabel's only love; if his death closes her emotional life, the ending—the return to Osmond—is more comprehensible. Life offers her nothing more, we might think.

It is a possible meaning. But Ralph may have run away with the story because he is so obviously Henry James: kind, interested, witty, permanently placed in the wings, doing his best to sympathize, not quite sure that he understands, fundamentally an invalid observer making a guess at what really goes on.

If he thought he entered Isabel's consciousness, one can only ask why he shows so little of her distress, or why he imagines it as so small. Suppose we drop the objection to the implausibility of her situation, just grant that she is in it, how can she seem so relatively phlegmatic about it? In a real sense, her life is at stake. One doesn't get to the end of that puzzlement either, and the reason can only be that it isn't adequately grasped and presented.

We can imagine—it is daily the case—that a morally sensitive person might decide that a marriage once contracted is a sacred obligation, and that it is a duty to remain in that situation. Children

are an overriding claim—many people feel that—and Isabel recognizes a duty to Osmond's daughter, who depends on her.
Equally, people feel that the other person, the husband or wife, is
someone to whom they are bound—not just by the ceremony and
the certificate, but by ties of old affection, long companionship, and
a willingness to believe that there are imperfections on both sides.
Also, people can feel they are bound at the roots; the relationship
may be painful, but separating the roots could be more painful. If
James had wanted to enter into all that, he would have been dealing
with a complex issue worth exploring. But he doesn't enter into it.
In fact the novel ends where, for serious purposes, it ought to
begin. Isabel goes back to Osmond; and all we know is that she has
chosen to do so. It looks as if she has done so for reasons connected
with her view of herself; her self-respect, her obligation to her
feeling of her own honour.

That is a kind of puritanism, but perhaps it is the ignoble part
of it—the wish to be personally saved, an elect soul, highly regarded
by the world and God for having done the right thing at whatever
expense of comfort or inclination. If you buy salvation, what does
it matter if you sacrifice self-fulfilment? You are able to approve
of yourself here below, like Miss Murdstone; you pride yourself
on your strength and resistance to change, and in the end you
enjoy the approval of a god strikingly like yourself. Here is a
conversation which seems to me very troubling. Isabel is speaking
to Henrietta Stackpole, the American journalist (who represents
simple moral penetration):

> 'Yes, I'm wretched,' she said very mildly. She hated to hear
> herself say it; she tried to say it as judicially as possible.
> 'What does he do to you?' Henrietta asked, frowning as if she
> were enquiring into the operations of a quack doctor.
> 'He does nothing. But he doesn't like me.'
> 'He's very hard to please!' cried Miss Stackpole. 'Why don't
> you leave him?'
> 'I can't change that way,' Isabel said.
> 'Why not, I should like to know? You won't confess that you've
> made a mistake. You're too proud.'
> 'I don't know whether I'm too proud. But I can't publish my
> mistake. I don't think that's decent. I'd much rather die.'
> 'You won't think so always,' said Henrietta.

'I don't know what great unhappiness might bring me to; but it seems to me I shall always be ashamed. One must accept one's deeds. I married him before all the world; I was perfectly free; it was impossible to do anything more deliberate. One can't change that way,' Isabel repeated.

'You *have* changed, in spite of the impossibility. I hope you don't mean to say you like him.'

Isabel debated. 'No, I don't like him. I can tell you, because I'm weary of my secret. But that's enough; I can't announce it on the housetops.'

Henrietta gave a laugh. 'Don't you think you're rather too considerate?'

'It's not of him that I'm considerate—it's of myself,' Isabel answered.

One is tempted to think Isabel deserves Osmond; in both cases a kind of self-regard is raised to an aesthetico-moral principle. Did James mean her to seem so like him; or was he making some subtle point about the knife-edge that separates a strenuous attempt to have a proper self-respect from self-protection or crass self-love? He must have known that his fine consciences were always in that danger. He was in a good position to know that the strictness of conscience, the attempt to live finely, to raise the simple moral principle to a less cut-and-dried matter than just knowing the rules, so that good behaviour became a matter of taste and people behaved 'beautifully'—that there are dangers in all this. One is that life is not served, that excesses of deliberation and infinite refinements of motivation simply kill spontaneity. On the one hand people may become so self-critical as to become totally without will; on the other these refinements may be merely refinements of self-deception. You can also come right through that maze to a conviction that you are finally exquisite, and behave like Gilbert Osmond. This schematic point: that either being or admiring Gilbert Osmond is a temptation to the over-refined, is no doubt part of what James wanted to convey. I suspect also that he wanted to make a rather sweeping 'tragic' point: that Isabel's earnestness in the search for 'life' would lead her in the wrong direction, so that the 'life' in her is ground in the conventional mill represented by Osmond—indeed Ralph Touchett says so on his deathbed. Hence, I fear, the schematic force of Caspar Goodwood who 'stands for' life: he has a simple passionate devoted love for Isabel, constant throughout the book. She feels his simplicity, his directness, as awkwardness or stiffness at first, and thinks this is not what she is looking for, because 'these things suggested a want of easy consciousness of the deeper rhythms of life'. That, we have seen, might just be a rationalization of her fear of commitment. Perhaps at the end, when he makes his final appeal to her, she recognizes that she was wrong; his physical contact–he takes her in his arms– is a momentary temptation. If that's what James is saying, then she finally turns her back on 'life', and his vinegary comedy is meant to sharpen and preserve a morose irony about 'life' of the Flaubertian kind.

The word is a trap. 'Life' is Gilbert Osmond too. It finds one expression in him, as it did in Linton Heathcliff. In any case Isabel's final decision to go back to Osmond is as much a free choice as her marriage to him. She does it, and she appears to do it for reasons of self-respect which are open to a sharper questioning than Henrietta Stackpole provides.

This book doesn't, finally, stand too much peering into. It is schematic; an effort by a bystander to give a surmise about things he hasn't grasped from the inside. If you want to read about the real horrors of a blocked marriage, you may get a truthful glimpse of them in Lawrence's *The Trespasser*, or the beginning of his *Aaron's Rod*. If you want to read a faithful account of how a heroic woman makes a life, wrings some kind of success, out of a 'bad' marriage, read *Sons and Lovers*. The marriage of the Morels begins in the glamour of real mutual attraction–which Lawrence could imagine and show as James can't begin to. It settles into a conflict which Mrs Morel has no way of avoiding: she is tied by her poverty and her children. It is a lifelong struggle in which there is right and wrong on both sides; the two selves, locked on to each other, are both known from the inside. The conflict is not in the end either sordid or depressing, despite Morel's decline and her painful death; nor is it merely negative, despite his limitations or the wrongs she does him and her favourite son. It is a life fully lived out in the teeth of its own limitations. You can, that is, be committed to wrestling with every kind of poverty and grief, and against every failure and disappointment, and find yourself pain-fully justified that way. It shows good faith of a frightening kind, courage, persistence. Gertrude Morel is more real than Isabel

Archer, and altogether more admirable. She neither gives up nor pretends; she enters the struggle and makes that her life. Nobody can say she hasn't 'lived'; she has, terribly, by the end. The effect is to make one go back to that expression 'a bad marriage' and ask if she and her husband hadn't overall, in sheer hot blood, black bile, tears, and the occasional shed blood, made it one kind of *real* marriage, if not a good one. People in her situation would be shocked to be told that, their own sense of grievance, waste and strife being so strong. But we remember from another story one of the great things in Lawrence. Another miner's wife, now a widow, contemplates the body of her husband, his life ended in a pit accident. They have been locked in the same struggle as the Morels. The sudden death shocks her into a higher sense of the reality of the life. It is no accident that Tolstoy's questions are asked: and the blindness and waste, being fully faced, are given dignity:

> . . . she knew what a stranger he was to her. In her womb was ice of fear, because of this separate stranger with whom she had been living as one flesh. Was this all that it meant–utter, intact separateness, obscured by heat of living? In dread she turned her face away. The fact was too deadly . . . He was no more responsible than she . . . For as she looked at the dead man, her mind, cold and detached, said clearly: 'Who am I? What have I been doing? I have been fighting a husband who did not exist. *He* existed all the time. What wrong have I done? What was that I have been living with? There lies the reality, this man.' And her soul died in her for fear: she knew she had never seen him, he had never seen her, they had met in the dark and had fought in the dark, not knowing whom they met nor whom they fought. And now she saw, and turned silent in seeing. For she had been wrong. She had said he was something he was not; she had felt familiar with him. Whereas he was apart all the while, living as she never lived, feeling as she never felt.

> *(Odour of Chrysanthemums)*

That can be the meaning of a life: misunderstood struggle, failure, defeat. Marriage as fight to the death; it happens all the time. It can be tragic, as Lawrence shows, but it need not be contemptible: it has the dignity Emily Brontë saw in love as fight to the death. If Isabel is returning to that fight, in that good faith, she has our sympathy; if she is to make the judgement that Osmond in his smallness is not worth fighting with, and must be left, we could understand her taking on herself the burden of that responsibility. If she is just going to sit out thirty years because she can't publish her mistake to the world, she is an egoist like Osmond.

Sexuality in Literature:
Lady Chatterley's Lover

Lady Chatterley's Lover takes the explicit description of sexual acts into English literature, and will always be important for that reason. Since the celebrated trial in which it was publicly vindicated as a serious book, writers have been free to describe these acts, using such words as come naturally to them, and we have had a lot of would-be liberated description, which you may either think of as the equivalent of sporting journalism (boxing and tennis reporters are given to colourful 'literary' passages in an effort to convey the technicalities and physical excitement of the sport) or as more anxious than healthy in its obsessed determination to 'describe'. Mere description is not serious; *Lady Chatterley's Lover* is not concerned merely to describe.

Prudishness was harmful to literature, when it stopped a writer saying what he needed to say. We may doubt though, whether Henry James felt he needed to say anything about the sexual relationship between Isabel Archer and Gilbert Osmond. We understand from the book that they had a child; it died in infancy; there have been no more pregnancies. We gather that they sleep apart. They are cold and distant with each other, we see; there is a conflict of wills; there is a suppressed opposition on both sides. The relationship is blocked; it could scarcely have a sexual expression. The two things go together; we are given the external, social expression; and the other thing can be dropped out of sight. One can say with some confidence that James couldn't handle it, so his discretion is a kind of wisdom. But a blocked relationship is likely to become a malignancy, and silence about its sexual aspect is one of the ways in which the book is starved of reality.

Wuthering Heights, on the other hand, shows feelings flowing freely and spontaneously, and expressed outspokenly, and so in a

way (I must seem unfair to James) Emily Brontë doesn't *need*
particularly to dwell on the sexuality. It is presumed as activity in
the same silent way as in James it is ignored as inactivity. The
directness of speech and the physical violence allow us to infer an
equally direct sexual feeling. Actual consummation between
Heathcliff and Catherine is not suggested: in fact a painful
frustration of active longing–especially in him–is the central
strand of their relationship and an element in his viciousness. But
Catherine herself is as naturally a sexual being as she is naturally a
charmer. There are ways of showing this without heavy-handed-
ness. Catherine is talking to Nelly, on the night of Heathcliff's
sudden reappearance, which has transformed her life, and caused
Edgar to feel the jealousy of the suddenly threatened relationship:

> 'The event of this evening has reconciled me to God, and
> humanity! . . . Oh, I've endured very, very bitter misery, Nelly!
> If that creature [Edgar] knew how bitter, he'd be ashamed to cloud
> its removal with idle petulance–it was kindness for him which
> induced me to bear it alone: had I expressed the agony I fre-
> quently felt, he would have been taught to long for its alleviation
> as ardently as I–However it's over, and I'll take no revenge on his
> folly–I can afford to suffer anything, hereafter! Should the
> meanest thing alive slap me on the cheek, I'd not only turn the
> other, but I'd ask pardon for provoking it–and as a proof, I'll go
> make my peace with Edgar instantly–Good night–I'm an angel!'
>
> In this self-complacent conviction she departed; and the success
> of her fulfilled resolution was obvious on the morrow–Mr Linton
> had not only abjured his peevishness (though his spirits seemed
> still subdued by Catherine's exuberance of vivacity), but he
> ventured no objection to her taking Isabella with her to Wuthering
> Heights, in the afternoon; and she rewarded him with such a
> summer of sweetness and affection in return as made the house a
> paradise for several days . . .

That is full of understated insight. Catherine is transfigured by
Heathcliff's return, and in her childlike way cannot see why Edgar
is dismayed. His opposition to her delight makes him 'that
creature'–a childish petulance in her. But because she is transformed, delighted, she can bestow herself on Edgar none the less,
and 'making her peace' with him must mean the way in which
married people naturally and wordlessly make peace. That in turn

appeases Edgar. That a new love sometimes galvanizes an old one, so that some of the liberated feeling transfers, to the benefit of the lesser or older love, is a common observation. It is a strangely equivocal benefit, and in due course an Edgar may realize what is happening and be simultaneously tortured and delighted, somewhat like Othello in his imaginings. In that situation a Heathcliff may observe with anguish that what he thinks due to him goes to Edgar; Edgar may realize that he is a surrogate for Heathcliff. The second Catherine is conceived in that state: hence the horror and hatred which she inspires in Heathcliff. She is a reminder of what Edgar had that he never had but ought to have had, as well as being the living image of the lost beloved—a torture to him on both counts.

Tolstoy had the same grasp of implicit realities, which are as much emotional as physical. We remember with a chill that dream of Anna's:

> She had one and the same dream almost every night. She dreamed that both of them were her husbands and both made passionate love to her. Alexey Karenin wept when kissing her hands and kept saying 'How wonderful it is now!' And Alexey Vronsky was there too; and he too was her husband. And wondering why this seemed so impossible to her before, she kept explaining to them, laughing, that it was much simpler that way, and that now both of them were happy and contented. But this dream weighed on her like a nightmare, and she woke up in terror.

'She kept explaining to them laughing, that it was much simpler that way.' The dream-Anna thinks like the waking Catherine Linton, who also sees that simplicity. But Anna awake is an adult; she knows the reality of the incompatible demands of the two men, who are not servants of her will, and won't fall into an attractive pattern of docility just to keep her happy. As for 'How wonderful it is now!', we remember that the Karenins sleep together; the last chapter but one took place in their bedroom. We also remember the earlier indication that 'it' was not 'wonderful':

> Punctually at twelve o'clock, when Anna was still sitting at her writing desk finishing a letter to Dolly, she heard the even steps of her husband in his slippers. Karenin, who had had a bath, and brushed his hair, came in with a book under his arm and went up to her.

'It's time, it's time,' he said with a significant smile and went straight into the bedroom.

'And what right had he to look at him like that?' thought Anna, recalling the look Vronsky had given Karenin.

Having undressed, she went into the bedroom, but not only was the animation that had been simply gushing out of her eyes and her smile no longer there: on the contrary, the fire in her now seemed quenched or hidden somewhere deep inside her.

What has happened between this earlier moment and the dream is that Anna and Vronsky have become lovers. Indeed, the very chapter which ends with Anna's dream starts with this:

That which for nearly a whole year had been the sole desire of his life, taking the place of all his former desires; that which for Anna had been an impossible, dreadful, and for that reason all the more fascinating dream of happiness–that desire had been fulfilled. Pale, with trembling lower jaw, he stood over her and implored her to be calm, without knowing himself how or why.

'Anna! Anna!' he said in a trembling voice. 'Anna, for God's sake!'

But the louder he spoke, the lower she dropped her once proud, gay, but now shameful head, and she bent lower and lower and sank from the sofa on which she was sitting to the floor at his feet; she would have fallen on the carpet if he had not held her.

'Oh God, forgive me!' she said, sobbing and pressing his head to her bosom.

Although that is, for a nineteenth-century novel, pretty outspoken in its willingness actually to envisage a scene of physical passion, and illicit passion too, the emotion sounds very conventional, and we are inclined to think it false for that reason. It is as if Tolstoy wanted to emphasize the guilt and not the joy; as if he were being sternly moralistic with himself, refusing to enter into something he knew to be joyous because he also knew it to be wrong. So he forces the tone:

And the murderer throws himself on the body with a feeling of bitter resentment and as though with passion, and drags it off and cuts it to pieces; so he too covered her face and shoulders with kisses.

In the paragraph about the dream Tolstoy does not have to cover

himself against criticism; he is interested in notating a psychic
strangeness, and can show what he knows to be true, in all its
complexity. Anna, we infer, feels with Vronsky, in their lovemaking,
what she had wanted to feel, but had never felt with Karenin. This
is not some vulgar modern notion about orgasms; it is a free
outward movement of love, an unselfconscious heartfelt abandonment. Feeling that, she is also regretting that she couldn't feel it
for Karenin. She would have wanted to, because of her earnest
regard for him, her wish to be in a right relationship with him.
Hence the dream, where two wishes are equivocally fulfilled.

When Karenin finally realizes what has happened, and tries to
keep up a façade so that the world will not know (it is the world
he fears), 'he could not see why his relations with his wife should
not remain almost the same as before'.

'But,' Anna said timidly, looking at him with dismay, 'our
relations cannot be the same as always' . . . 'I cannot be your wife
when I . . .' she began.

He gave a cold, spiteful laugh.

'I'm afraid the kind of life you have chosen has affected your
ideas . . . I was very far from the interpretation you give my words.'

Anna gave a sigh of relief and dropped her head.

'I must say, though,' he went on, getting heated, 'that I can't
understand how, being so independent as you apparently are and
informing your husband outright of your infidelity, you find
nothing as reprehensible in it as you seem to find in performing a
wife's duties to her husband.'

It *had* been a duty–there is the difference. He had in the little
scene of going to bed been the demanding husband, expecting his
'marital rights', as he might the next morning expect his hot water
and breakfast. He also shows the inadequacy of merely conventional notions–how they simply don't meet the needs even of a
'conventional' relationship.

But Dickens shows us what a tyranny they can be. There is
much in *David Copperfield* at which we goggle; it may seem so
strange now that we may not believe it is seriously meant; but it
would be a mistake to call it hypocritical simply because it is so
conventional. I am thinking for instance of the thrilled revulsion
from the Fallen Woman–that is to say, the admired and loved
Little Em'ly, who is a creature of some delicacy of feeling, and

who develops through her ordeal some strength of character. She is charmed by, and loves, James Steerforth, and gives herself to him. That can't be presented; it has to be translated into a social meaning: she is instantly transformed in the moral scheme from dream doll-child into an object of horror. But it isn't just horror; it is excitement. She has done 'it'; it is the adolescent thrill. The men feel instantly that she is either fair game or a matter for sad head-shaking; and the women feel (being instructed by the men to feel it) that if they enter the same room they are in danger of having their purity smirched. As a decent person, David is painfully divided, but he pays more than their due to the conventional taboos. His own regressive urge is powerfully reinforced by social values, by notions about sexless 'purity': why else does he marry a child, who is psychically unable to reach puberty? He and Dora have a baby, but it miscarries; Dora isn't made for sex and child-bearing, and it kills her. Em'ly, on the other hand, having felt love and acted her love out in the body, is virtually doomed to prostitution unless Daniel Peggotty can catch her before she drops into the abyss. In fact there is some rallying round of the kind which being a family enjoins; in the end Em'ly can be packed off to Australia, rehabilitated in her uncle's selfless love and with everybody else heavily conscious that they are tolerating her re-admission; but the notion that she might there love again, love a better man, marry him and make a good life is explicitly rejected. This is the 'damaged goods' legalism, rigidly enforced to the death.

It remains that James Steerforth's power over Em'ly and her response to his charm is the only straightforward sexual love in the book, and is set against the other strange forms which love takes. I don't suppose Dickens consciously meant to do so, but he shows a world in which distorted passions, strange regressions, and peculiar relationships are accepted socially because they don't offend the rigid sexual convention: be married, and anything goes. If you are not married, it may be normal but it's not acceptable. The bitter quasi-religious zeal with which the sexual conventions are upheld remains a deep meaning for this society; and the damage which is accepted in consequence is a mark of faith, not hypocrisy.

At the surface level it is a world of male dominance, its nastiest symbol being Uriah Heep's slavering hunger for Agnes Wickfield. The double-standard is elaborately deployed. We remember though, that one of the transcendently real moments is that where

Rosa Dartle discovers that Em'ly was not just a toy; that Steerforth had (so far as he could) loved her; that Em'ly had loved him. Mad with jealousy, it is Rosa who wants Em'ly whipped, degraded, prostituted. The conventions institutionalize and support real human feelings. They are partly bad ones. They offer the instruments of punishment to possessiveness, jealousy, anger, in men and women of Rosa's force of will. To a Karenin they offer only apparent certainties, which collapse painfully, leaving him unsupported when he is face to face with 'Life', as Tolstoy says.

The great power of convention is that it tells people what to think, and allows them to channel all their feeling one way. Identify yourself with conventional feelings, and you are able to range the impulses of the self (for once) with the judgements of society. It's like a passion, with built-in self-approval. You are able to flash out, wholeheartedly, like Rosa Dartle, at offenders. When the complexities of actual experience irresistibly impose themselves, as on Karenin, 'Life', in the sense of what actually happens in the real world, demonstrates how merely conventional the conventions are. One is left with nothing to fall back on; one has to make one's own sense of the occasion, to face the truth of other people's unconventional feelings. The actuality of desire, and joy in desire: joy you may not have, and desire which excludes you—this is disturbing to the self, settled in its own way of reading the universe. These shocks and reactions hurt in nothing so much as in sexuality, where the fundamental relationship between selves, whether dominant or submissive, has dangerous forces massed at the thinnest tissues which are the frontiers of being; where people actually 'connect' with each other, feel they may be united, feel they can be made whole or annihilated. Hence the importance for the novel or the drama of dealing adequately with sexuality—not so much in terms of the act itself, which is essentially a limited set of physical movements, but in terms of the act's meaning.

To get to the meaning, however, you may have to come close to the act in its direct expressiveness—not at any rate be frightened of envisaging it. Here Flaubert had imaginative courage. *Madame Bovary* too was prosecuted for obscenity in its time. What may have frightened its first readers was this sort of thing:

> More and more they came to talk about things which had nothing
> to do with their love; the letters that Emma sent him dealt with

flowers, poetry, the moon, the stars–the simple expedients of a waning passion, trying to whip itself up again with external stimulants. Every time she looked forward, on her next meeting, to a profound happiness, and then confessed she had felt nothing out of the ordinary. But the disappointment was quickly effaced by fresh hope, and Emma came back to him more passionate, more greedy. She threw her clothes off brutally, tearing at the thin laces of her corset, which slipped down her flanks with the swift sound of a snake sliding. She tiptoed to the door on naked feet to see if it was shut, and then with one movement let all her clothes fall;–and pale, silent, grim, she slipped into his embrace, with a long shudder.

That is what a strip-tease performance claims, but necessarily fails, to be: a demonstration of the woman's sexual power right to the end; the use of the body to cast a spell, to arouse, to dominate and then to appease, but always to control. It is a performance, and the element of whipped-up self-excitement shows that if it is first a performance for the other person, it is finally a performance aimed at oneself, to keep the relationship going. This is part of Emma's treadmill, that the lover has to be kept under the sexual spell. It shows how the sexual relationship mirrors the relationship as a whole.

If we look back to Racine and Shakespeare, we may reflect that until our own day sexual acts could not be simulated on the stage. Our contemporary dramatists and film-makers are now able to attempt to catch up with the novelists. Leaving aside the question whether simulated (or–when it comes–real) sex on the stage is capable of serving a dramatic effect–whether it could really convey its meaning to the audience, and if not whether it isn't necessarily a distracting and inevitably degrading side-show, one can ask the related question–is it absolutely necessary? Without any literal enactions, *Othello* is drenched in sexuality: the drama can do without the actions because Shakespeare could convey the whole meaning in the poetry. Much of the speech *is* sexual activity. Certainly the speech is extraordinarily direct and free, searingly so. More importantly, it can carry the inner meanings of Iago's and Othello's obsessions: the nature of the relationships being fully deployed in the words, they don't need to be directly expressed in acts–which cannot on the stage be so expressive for those not taking part. Acts are not so directly under the control of the play-wright. It is feelings, words, which give them meaning. Shake-speare's poetry fulfils the role of the novelist's narrative medium or the opera-composer's music.

Othello shows a world in which love and sexual possession are identified. The possessiveness implied in the sole right of access to the woman's body is shown to be potentially a degrading obsession, but simply to say that and look no further is to refuse to see that it is a real and powerful feeling: a force of the self which is so widely shared that societies endorse it as a value. Othello's love and his sexuality are not divided into compartments: and in that he is a 'normal', one might almost say an admirable man. As he says, at that moment when our feeling naturally flows towards him, it is the fountain from which his current springs (a metaphor which is itself sexual) and the fear of rejection, of loss of access to that source, disintegrates him. There are plenty of people who would say that if his suspicions had been justified, his reactions–even his violence–would have been understandable, even right. Sexual rejection is damaging; to be deceived is hurtful; to have one's love or faith or commitment repudiated is a trauma like bereavement. No book (surprisingly) has dealt entirely justly with the deceived husband, who is always presented as somehow inadequate, so that we can sympathize with the wife. On the other hand, insecure male possessiveness remains a corroding weakness, a defect of the psyche, even though at various times and places it has been socially endorsed. In any case, Shakespeare blows up the whole position by taking it at its most extreme: Othello's suspicions are totally false. His reaction to the external temptation Iago offers is total surrender to his own internal chaos. Sexuality in that kind of state becomes an obsession; and it is Shakespeare's peculiar moral genius here to develop the situation entirely in terms of horrified imaginings, expressed verbally in poetry which shows the whole mind's convulsion. Like Karenin, but more disastrously because of his greater strength of being, Othello has lived in the armour of a social self, shielded by convention. When the conventions are knocked aside and the armour is pierced, he is not only vulnerable, he is totally without internal resource. He has no force of personal feeling for the woman he loves adequate to counterbalance all the feeling that flows against her. He has no ideas of her worth, of her feeling for him, to set against suspicion; he hasn't even sufficient

M

idea of his own worth; he is convinced of loss, deceit, betrayal. The degree to which she is only a body, only a target for his own sexuality; the degree to which therefore his sexuality *must* be anxious, rapacious, aggressive–we see that when he murders her as the only way of keeping her to himself. What is enacted in the play is a profound instruction in the relationship between sexuality and insecurity, and the way in which the weakness of a certain kind of energetic nature necessarily expresses itself as violence. It is terrifying in its inevitability, and incidentally in the richness of its documentation of the related perversities: voyeurism, scatophily, necrophilia. Shakespeare had nothing to learn from present-day psychology, everything to teach: in particular how closely and naturally these extremes of behaviour come to the surface in the words we use.

The atmosphere of *Phèdre* is as heavily laden with sexuality as *Othello*, and its most appallingly symptomatic moment is the one where Phèdre suffers a kind of involuntary orgasm as a result of the cathartic power with which her passion for Hippolyte expresses itself to him. She has been unable not to tell him of her love, not to press herself upon him against her own conscious will; she sees his revulsion and seeks punishment at his hand, and suffers the last ignominy of being pleasured in imagination at the very thought of being killed by a man who is horrified at her love for him. It is a humiliation only Racine could have imagined, and testifies both to his knowledge and his horror of that knowledge. As in *Othello*, sexual passion deprives people of power over themselves; they can only give themselves to it. But Phèdre is not a primitive like Othello, she is the horrified spectator of her own disintegration. And the orgasm is a deeply appropriate metaphor: it comes unasked from far within, it takes total possession, it shakes the whole being, it is a pleasure, it is like death. It is shown as an evil which destroys wholeness of being. One is bound to think that for Racine sexuality is inseparable from a religious sense of sin, and that this separates him from Shapespeare. It is a natural consequence that Racine saw love as evil, as Shakespeare did not. The religious horror of sex as possession by the wrong gods lies behind the puritanical wish not to think about it or look at it. Dickens's Rosa Dartle is a descendant of Phèdre; hence her jealousy and complicated hatred of Em'ly, for she would have been a sinner too, far more abandoned and far more conscious of the hatefulness of her joy.

That strangeness about the late nineteenth century (a complexity, not a simple hypocrisy) means that people of my generation and earlier have a complicated feeling for *Lady Chatterley's Lover* in consequence. It was important that someone should have done what Lawrence did. For us, until the book was freely published, it circulated like the scriptures of an alternative religion. The words were used; the actions were named. The book also seemed to stand for a new, 'free', more honest and more healthy world. When it became publicly available we saw that it wasn't as great a book as we had thought, and because it is morally and emotionally inadequate in ways which can be shown, we may now over-react against it. But there are fine things in it–it is not in any case all of a piece. Some of the best things are to do with the sexual encounters.

The coarse view of the book–the view of conventional puritans, who can be surprisingly coarse (no, on second thoughts, it's not surprising)–is that the book, glorifying adultery, consists of a series of 'bouts'. The difference is that some take place indoors, others outdoors, in the rain, and so on. But all sexuality is sexuality: same organs, same actions.

But not the same feelings, and *that* is the important thing. Nothing, for instance, could be more surprising, nor more profound, real and touching than Connie Chatterley's first yielding to Oliver Mellors. I go on thinking it is one of the greatest things Lawrence wrote, one of the great things in the language. They are aware of each other, but only at the beginning of awareness. They have hardly spoken, and only rather distantly. The relationship is not easy, not friendly: each is aware of being separate, different. He has some sense of her misery, but can't afford in his own misery to spare much conscious sympathy. But there in the wood, watching the pheasant chicks, little centres of life, coming out of their shells, holding one in her hand, there wells up inside her a wave of grief for her own thwarted life (not that she is conscious of it in those terms) and her tears fall. In his own separate sadness he can't fail to see this; in the old Biblical phrase his bowels yearn towards her. He makes love to her in the hut, and it is plainly not– not yet–an expression of love, of desire. It is an expression of wordless physical sympathy, the simplest, deepest human solidarity. He offers her the instinctive support for which he doesn't yet have words, he offers her the kindness of the body, its warmth;

he puts her back in touch with the world by lending her himself as a channel. Some kind of religious term is needed to do justice to this aspect: he ministers to her. It can't be said at this stage that they commune with each other; but certainly something is mediated to each, they are put in touch with something beyond them. And on his part it is essentially giving, not taking. Mellors expresses it to himself later in the book: 'I stand for the touch of bodily awareness between human beings, and the touch of tenderness'. At the beginning, it is almost entirely impersonal; certainly there is no scope for Othello's demandingness, since neither has a claim on the other. Yet they meet at this level.

As the relationship develops, the sexuality changes its meanings, to express what is passing between the two as they fluctuate towards or away from each other. This is partly a matter of Connie's making demands, and Mellors's resisting them. He has been more deeply damaged by his life than she has been, and he is reluctant to engage again in a conflict with the world or with another self. Hence his curious self-withholding, his irony, his reversion in and out of dialect, to keep himself apart. She is more spontaneously willing to commit herself, she wants a deep relationship: this is both a demand of the self and a readiness to expose the self to danger. Their sexuality therefore expresses his personal reserve and her more freely-flowing but anxious outgoing. Inevitably there are blocks and unconscious dissatisfactions. Their second love-making for instance, is a failure: she fears she has gone too far, and wants to dissociate herself, while he is perhaps opportunistic.

This sort of difficulty even reflects back on the words used. He uses the old 'dirty' words freely, and we feel an odd vibration in them. It is part of his reserve that he uses these words against her: they are a challenge to her (can she accept them; can she accept *him*?); they are also a weapon. If she can't accept him, then the dirtiness of the words will be a limiting definition on what they have had together. It's 'warmhearted fucking' he says: which means you can either write it off if it passes, saying at least it was warmhearted; or you can if it is successful and becomes something more let the warmheartedness have the credit for the achievement.

Connie more instinctively pursues her need. What she wants is only expressed by, and is not limited to, the lovemaking. She wants him to commit himself to her as she is willing to commit herself to him. It comes out, inevitably as something like a demand, which can be frightening to a man who has suffered already from demandingness, who is also more experienced and damaged than she and quite honourably wishes not to damage her.

Yet his suffering has already been such that he needs curing. As he says himself at one moment 'It heals me all up that I go into thee' (a profound remark: the positive of Othello's negative). He is wounded as she is, and in need; the bodily kindness he first offered her is what he needs himself. And more; but to the end of the book he never comes round as frankly as she to admitting his own need. The sexuality on his part is therefore offered as self-sufficient and self-justifying, a meaning in itself. Instinctively she knows better.

But the fact that he uses it as an end in itself, offers to make do with it, not to look beyond, means that it is both the first and strongest link between them and a potential danger. It is not just that once he shows a maniac obsessiveness about simultaneous orgasm, and a curious horror of women who take their satisfaction slowly or separately. There is also that 'night of sensual passion' where Lawrence drops his directness and becomes curiously indirect, even flowery. It becomes clear that Mellors does all sorts of things to Connie, rather comically hinted at, or unconsciously revealed, in this piece of exclamatory prose:

> And what a reckless devil the man was! really like a devil! One had to be strong to bear it. But it took some getting at, the core of the physical jungle, the last and deepest recess of organic shame. The phallus alone could explore it. And how he had pressed in on her!
>
> And how, in fear, she had hated it. But how she had really wanted it! She knew now. At the bottom of her soul, fundamentally, she had needed this phallic hunting out, she had secretly wanted it, and she had believed she would never act it. Now suddenly there it was, and a man was sharing her last and final nakedness, she was shameless.

That's all rather flatly stated as a past event, and a given meaning. What one might deduce from it is that element of aggressiveness in Mellors, that wish to impose himself, to put the woman 'in her place' which lurks behind his resentment of his coarsely strong-minded first wife. Connie is more submissive, and is here made to submit, and to rationalize her submission.

One can't make too much of it, since we aren't given more than the flat statement. But it links with other things about Mellors which make one take him as very human, and therefore neither fully self-aware nor as fully in command of himself as he thinks. The dirty words, the dialect, the 'night of passion', the mentalism of 'here tha shits and here tha pisses', are signs of his wish to keep a distance, to keep a male superiority, even to hit out and wound. These are ways in which other male characters of Lawrence's show their struggle to maintain a footing with their women, whose domination they fear. Fearing that, they are frightened of commitment to them.

But commitment is what Connie wants. Mellors fears it as life breaking him open ('If I've got to be broken open again, I have', he says grimly fairly early on). Like others of Lawrence's men, he offers the other ideal: 'Living is moving, and moving on'. But she wants a permanent relationship, to live with him, to bear his child. In other words, though the book is from one point of view the record of an adulterous affair, it is from her point of view a search for a true life-commitment. Connie has no child to complicate the issue for her; her relationship with her husband has become meaningless to the point of horror. She is able to attempt what Anna Karenina attempted, with a better chance of success – except that one might wonder to what degree the Mellors we have had presented to us is finally going to be willing both to accept a permanent commitment and to accommodate himself to a Connie who is not in the last resort the sort of submissive creature one part of him wants. That lies outside the novel; we merely speculate; but we say to ourselves that there is no reason to see him as anything but 'difficult to live with' because he is dangerously insecure. But it is clearly their future to try that, whether they succeed or not. Success for Connie Chatterley would be to be able to look back on her second married life as Mrs Bolton does on her only, and sadly brief one:

> 'And I kept expecting him back. Especially at nights. I kept waking up thinking: why, he's not in bed with me!–it was as if my *feelings* wouldn't believe he'd gone. I just felt he'd *have* to come back and lie against me, so I could feel him with me. That was all I wanted, to feel him there with me, warm. And it took me a thousand shocks before I knew he wouldn't come back, it took me years.'

'The touch of him,' said Connie.

'That's it, my Lady, the touch of him! I've never got over it to this day, and never shall. And if there's a heaven above, he'll be there, and will lie up against me, so I can sleep' . . .

'But can a touch last so long?' Connie asked suddenly, 'That you could feel him so long?'

'Oh my Lady, what else is there to last? Children grows away from you. But the man, well! . . . Ah well! we might have drifted apart, who knows. But the feeling's something different. It's 'appen better never to care. But there, when I look at women who's never really been warmed through by a man, well, they seem to me poor dool-owls after all. . . .'

'The touch of him' and 'being warmed through by a man' are sexual metaphors of a kind, but it is the sexuality of sustained married love, more kindness than passion, as much peaceful as active, making the warmth of the double bed that children climb into in the morning, as if to nest with their parents, so learning something about the security of the body's warmth. That is what Connie Chatterley has been deprived of and wants, and in recognizing it she has an instinctive wisdom that her lover lacks.

12

Lawrence and 'that which is perfectly ourselves'

You have only to compare *Anna Karenina* with *Lady Chatterley's Lover* to see how much finer Tolstoy's book is. There are whole dimensions left out of Lawrence's. Compare, for instance, Tolstoy's depth of understanding of Karenin, and Lawrence's treatment of Clifford Chatterley. In both books it is part of the situation that the husband is a failure, both as husband and man, so that the action springs from the wife's deep sense of unfulfilment. But if he were simply intolerable, there would be no interest in the situation: a mistake is recognized and corrected. In life, nothing would be as simple as that, because feelings would be involved: grief or anger on one side, complications of shame and guilt on the other. Tolstoy does full justice to the situation by showing that Karenin has depths as well as limitations; and there is the terrible complication caused by Karenin's being galvanized into a more open and therefore more vulnerable being by the very fact of losing Anna. He has needs too; he becomes a person with a power of feeling which increases his claim on her.

Clifford Chatterley is a type Lawrence spent his life brooding over. He is seen at his deepest as Gerald Crich in *Women in Love*. He recurs as Rico Carrington in *St Mawr* – a cruelly comic picture of the same sort of person. With Gerald Crich Lawrence made a painful effort to enter into the whole set of feelings, and his Lawrence-figure Rupert Birkin feels a deep love for Gerald. With Rico Carrington the type has dwindled to a satiric target, and Lawrence is right outside, sardonic and fierce. With Clifford Chatterley Lawrence performs the Flaubert operation – despising his own creation and being wantonly cruel to it – even rigging the plot so as to do him moral injuries. Think, for instance, of the way in which Mrs Bolton, the miner's widow whose memories of her own marriage are a strong positive note in the book, is made at the end to undergo a degrading kind of incestuous surrogate-mother's marriage with Clifford. The loss of Connie has threatened his identity; his tight self-control may become hysteria; Mrs Bolton helps him to weep. That could be an imaginative kindness; but Lawrence turns it into a manipulative ploy, in which the woman is glad to be given this great crippled child, whom she can baby in moral as well as physical ways. It is a profound imagination on Lawrence's part, but it is partly willed and partly the product of his own deep fears and suspicions. Those too run through his books. The dominant woman is the Mother in some dangerous way, and he always fears the re-establishment of that dominance. Here it bobs up at the service of his wish to degrade Clifford. It is a mark of determination, though not necessarily a conscious one.

Or compare Vronsky with Mellors. If Vronsky is limited, rather worldly, rather simple in his manliness, too narrowly the officer and gentleman, we also see his strengths: his energy, decisiveness and intensity, and because of them a capacity to become deeper and broaden his range. He is committed, and grows with his love. It starts as an 'affair', to be taken as such things are taken in his circle: something dashing and ephemeral, what the Italians call *fare bella figura*: something to be observed half-admiringly as part of the social show, a performance. It becomes a passion, the centre of his life, and he learns to accept it as an obligation. Tolstoy shows his code of honour visibly deepening from something which is entirely a matter of narrow social attitude (like paying one's gambling debts before one's tailor's bills) into something which a career must be sacrificed to. It is his tragedy that he accepts as a duty, merely self-imposed, what he would have wanted to accept as a duty which his whole world endorses. It is also his tragedy that Anna won't let him accept his commitment to her as a duty, and let herself rest in that sense of his honour.

Mellors has depth, in that we feel he is a more complicated character than Vronsky, but he has less moral weight because of his capacity to shrug off or avoid allegiances. He too is manly, also a soldier, but not at all a gentleman–and none the better for that. It is clear that he is exhausted and hurt by his life and his marriage; so his hesitancy in accepting the new commitment to Connie, and starting the cycle of attachment all over again is understandable. But his revulsion from his earlier attachments makes the success of the new one an open question. His account of his emotional life, we see with a shock, is the last part of *Sons and Lovers* told in rapid and distorting flashback, in an ugly language which betrays obsessions, fears–even manias: certainly not the language of maturity, which is acceptance of self and acceptance of others' selves.

Then there is the matter of children. We tend to forget that Mellors has a little girl; but there she is, in a brief scene, carefully established as a calculating little minx, spoilt and unlikable; and then kept out of sight lest we should think her father heartless. But then, how do children *really* get 'spoilt'? If we did not know from ordinary life, there is Anna's son, Seryozha, at the end of his experience in *Anna Karenina*, deeply hurt by what has happened, wanting not to be hurt further, learning therefore to deny his feelings. In other words, he is going to turn out like his father, and the harm will go on being transmitted.

To do Lawrence more justice in this discussion, one must widen the focus and look at the really great novels and stories. But two of the limitations of *Lady Chatterley's Lover* need to be faced as limitations in his work as a whole. First there is this blankness about children and family life. It must spring from some deep fear or horror. In his second book, *The Trespasser*, we see the first of those portrayals of married life with children as a horrifying trap: his hero is married to a bitter jealous wife, and burdened with children. They represent an absolute bar to anything else: he is cornered, and kills himself. In the much later *Aaron's Rod*, Aaron Sisson is in the same situation. His blocked relationship with his vindictive wife is shown with the same clarity–though there is a germ of compassionate understanding for her aggrieved narrowness and dogged clinging. Aaron leaves his family because he has a deep sense that, as Mellors says, living is moving, and moving on. He thinks with shame of the hurt he has done his wife; he comes to feel that he is committed to her and can't ultimately be linked with anyone else. But as for his two little girls, who are again presented as spoilt and possessive, little harpies waiting to get their hooks into some man, he never thinks of them again. Lawrence didn't know what it was to be a father, and couldn't imagine it. As for being a mother, he knew too much about that from having been his mother's son. Aaron has an extraordinary conversation with Rawdon Lilly, the Lawrence-figure in *Aaron's*

Rod, in which like naughty boys they spill their resentment of the woman with children. It is pure jealousy, itself childish. Think of Dolly Oblonsky's feeling for her children: it is normal and satisfying, and serves importantly as emotional ballast. Lawrence saw that seldom: he lived through something like his own childhood again in *Sons and Lovers*; and there are some movingly imagined scenes in *The Rainbow*–the most touching being Tom Brangwen's stepfatherly relationship with the little Anna, his wife's daughter by a previous marriage. For the most part, though, children are something his heroines are about to have in the end (as in *The Lost Girl*, *Lady Chatterley's Lover*) or a tiresome complication, or just not there.

The other, related thing clearly established in *Anna Karenina* is the need for the couple, the family, to be rooted in the world, to be linked with other people, and to be doing something which makes the married relationship part of the world. I don't accept the foolish argument that Levin as 'mere' landowner is a parasite or ornament. Running his estate is a deep preoccupation; he is a real leader of his community and feels his responsibility as he should. His ability to be concerned with other people is the best thing about him. Vronsky wants that relationship too, but is cut off from his peers by his irregular relationship with Anna, and finds himself unable, despite his hospital-building and local government activities, to win his way back to a real role in society; so that he and Anna are cut off from a social life they both need. The love of Connie Chatterley and Mellors is equally a cut-off thing: hidden, out of the world. What they will establish when publicly together is an open question at the end, but Mellors is rootless and disaffected, hating the world of industrial life in twentieth-century England. How can you fit yourself back into a society you have written off?

This too runs through Lawrence's work. It announces itself towards the end of *The Rainbow*. Ursula Brangwen in that book has a natural wish to be usefully occupied, to fit in; she sees it in almost religious terms as being part of 'purposive mankind', taking her share in 'the great human endeavour'. That natural wish makes her become a teacher, where her idealism is tested and strained. She learns that teaching in one of the old elementary schools is not a matter of lovingly leading little children across the meadows of knowledge. It's a tough school, with tough cynical teachers working the machine, and tough children refusing to be easily passed through. She even comes to the point of using violence on a particularly repulsive child; so having to face realities in herself as well as the people she works with. That is all marvellously shown; Ursula comes through, tempered. But at the end of the book she is overwhelmed by traumas; her failed relationship with Anton Skrebensky is the deepest of these at the personal level, but it also reflects something not personal, or projected outwards on to the world as a whole. It resolves itself into a horror of the settled life of England, and horror of its inhabitants, seen as crawling insect-like beings. Those who accept their life, who settle for ordinariness, who fit in, seem to her to be nobodies like Anton Skrebensky, not really there, certainly not people she can identify herself with. She collapses into a kind of breakdown. The end of the book sees her coming out of it, and offers a hopeful symbol of the future, the rainbow of the title, which is quite unjustified by what has gone immediately before, much as one would like to accept it.

All this is not fully grasped by the reader, because it isn't fully presented by Lawrence as something to be understood. It comes from his own horror at the time; it is merely felt. *The Rainbow* and *Women in Love* were originally to be a single novel but were divided at this point, and *Women in Love* was reworked. There are odd consequences. For one thing, Ursula and her sister Gudrun start *Women in Love* as people with a set of attitudes taken over from *The Rainbow*. But both are undamaged personalities; the person who carries into *Women in Love* Ursula's horrors and difficulties is Rupert Birkin, the Lawrence-figure. Ursula herself has turned into one of Lawrence's Frieda-figures. But the immediate point is that when Ursula and Birkin decide they are committed to each other for life, that they have found the one person with whom they wish to make a life, what do they do? They both resign their jobs. So much for 'the great human endeavour'. Their opting-out springs from settled attitudes, and is presented as so natural that we may not think it is really very unnatural. They are to set off on a life of wandering detachment from everything but each other–with on Birkin's part the faint hope that they might somewhere find one or two congenial people and make a little community, and the further complication that he is deeply attached to Gerald Crich, who offers male companionship, but severed from its normal context, which

is work. It is in shared endeavours–and, with good fortune, in
professions or jobs which offer an adequate sense of social purpose,
that men (and for that matter women) find companionship, respect
and affection for each other as colleagues, these things being tested
by the kind of tempering that Ursula underwent in the previous
book. All that is dropped, yet Birkin characteristically and
honestly feels the need for it.

The impulse to leave, to shake the dust off, is repeated again and
again in Lawrence, and is a limitation. What makes Lawrence *want*
to leave he shows with great power: he is one of the writers who
show us most clearly what is wrong with modern life. But he
hasn't anything to offer but despair. As he says in *St Mawr*:

> What's to be done? Generally speaking, nothing. The dead will
> have to bury their dead, while the earth stinks of corpses. The
> individual can but depart from the mass and try to cleanse himself.
> Try to hold fast to the living thing, which destroys as it goes but
> remains sweet. And in his soul fight, fight, fight to preserve that
> which is life in him from the ghastly kisses and poison-bites of the
> myriad evil ones. Retreat to the desert, and fight.

Perhaps that's not meant too literally. Certainly there is no one in
the desert to fight but oneself; and the best self-conflict (which is
often necessary) takes place in people engaged with others;
principally those they marry, rear and work with. The desert,
taken literally, is a false destination. If we all went there, Lawrence
would have to come home, just to avoid us. Taken metaphorically,
it could only represent a state from which in the end one would
have to return to live with others.

In other words, Lawrence's insights are limited in two respects.
We cannot accept as comprehensive or normative a view of the
relationship between the sexes that takes no account of bringing
up children and earning a living in a society of other people doing
the same. We cannot accept a social criticism which finally shrugs
its shoulders and pads off into the desert, leaving us to get on
with it. Get on with it is certainly what we have to do.

For the sense of the natural order, the complete human cycle in a
settled community, we have to go back to *The Rainbow*, or beyond
it to the earlier *Sons and Lovers*. *The Rainbow* presents the only
happy family I can think of in the whole of Lawrence: the family
of old Tom Brangwen and his Polish wife Lydia, who achieve a

relationship which fulfils them and gives stability to Anna, the child of Lydia's previous marriage. It is set well in the past, and may be meant to be an idealized contrast with the present, as if that fulfilment were not now possible. In the next generation, Anna and Will Brangwen have a much more ordinary (i.e. troubled and not very satisfying) marriage; in the last generation their daughters, Ursula and Gudrun, have in *Women in Love* to establish something new, and by implication different. As in *Anna Karenina* two couples offer contrasting fortunes in their love-relationships. The women, Gudrun and Ursula, both enter the process with fixed attitudes: a revulsion from the ordinariness represented by their parents, their home, the world of work.

The achievement of Tom and Lydia is an imagined story, that is to say it corresponds directly to nothing in Lawrence's own experience. What Lawrence imagines is a dream of fulfilment as passionately intense as Dickens's dreams of childhood horror and rescue. It comes to an end at the moment of beautifully achieved humour at which Tom Brangwen gives Anna away at her wedding, has his vision of the meaning of his life, and makes his touching speech about the nature of marriage, punctuated by the comic asides of the rest of the family. That too is one of the great things in Lawrence—one of the great things in English. Lawrence seems to suggest it is a lost certainty.

There is a representative force of another kind in the account of Will's and Anna's marriage. It represents what Gudrun and Ursula—and presumably Lawrence—are trying to get away from in the second book. That episode too is a triumph: the long chapter 'Anna Victrix' in *The Rainbow* steps decisively beyond Tolstoy. The few pages in *Anna Karenina* on the early married life of Kitty and Levin are fine and touching, but what Lawrence does is altogether more massive, and is marked by his finding a special language for the wordless states of opposing selves, when the unconscious ecstasy of first union is past and the two fall into the unexpected conflict between egos. He enters into both people: Will's demanding dependence and its extraordinary occasioning (Anna wants to have some people in, and he is shocked at having to share her attention—that is how adults and babies are alike); the intensifying cycle of their unexpressed opposition; her triumph over him in her self-sufficient motherhood (always a horror for Lawrence); their struggle over his belief; their lapse into a mutual acceptance which is not at the deep level respectful of each other's separateness. And so Will takes his demands to his children; he takes solace in the young Ursula, so that the conflicts of one generation threaten to deform the next by making demands on it. Lawrence dealt with these things again–or with their results. But he never again entered into them in that total way as something he felt, and we feel through him. Rather he commented on the *effect*, in his sardonic style, from his external viewpoint. He dissociated himself from that sort of thing, from the common run. But perhaps that is in effect to dissociate oneself from some of the operations of the self–that is, from everybody.

At any rate Gudrun and Ursula know they don't want what their parents have, and don't hold the conventional ideals of marriage: the egoism for two; the life of the semi-detached–in affection as in home; the false ideal of living for the other; the demand that marriage should make one 'happy'–whatever that might mean; putting up with it for the sake of the children. That is all called in question: also the conventional passion with its clichés about the merging of identities, which really mean one ego locked on to the other; also 'settling down' into a life of mutual accommodation where the other person is 'known'. For knowing tends to mean controlling; being shocked by change; wanting the other person to be static, finished. For Lawrence even more than the romantics, that was literally death. Only dead things stop growing and changing; so with relationships.

There is a mixture of elements here. I have suggested that the account in *Sons and Lovers* of the marriage of the Morels, which might seem to support this wincing away from 'ordinary' marriage is much more powerful, ultimately more terrible: that what Gertrude Morel managed by living through a lifetime of very ordinary marriage with her kind of intensity lifts the whole thing to another level. What she did to her son Paul Morel is related to what Lawrence's mother did to him. If she damaged him she also made him. By that standard, the self-protective disgust at the idea of being ordinarily married which Ursula and Gudrun show at the beginning of *Women in Love* is adolescent over-fastidiousness (yet also shown to be such). And Birkin himself, who shares those attitudes, is reacting away from things that have damaged him, and damaged Lawrence, but which aren't completely summed up by their power to damage this person or that.

Lawrence's blankness about children springs from his horror of the woman whose fulfilment as a mother seemed to him to slight the father, to be a triumph over him (as with Will and Anna), or inclined her to treat the husband as a son (what we see inflicted on Mrs Bolton and Clifford Chatterley, where she becomes a mother to him as baby) or the son as a lover (as with Mrs Morel and Paul). This personal difficulty gives Lawrence's work a dimension of difficulty, struggle and resistance: and also some distortions. Lawrence didn't always manage to control his own bias, which was also the source of many of his insights. He shows the extent to which the writer is himself a self, whom we must listen to as we listen to other selves in life. We have to know, sometimes, how and *why* he is 'getting at' us.

The damaged personality who was Ursula in *The Rainbow* has turned into Birkin in *Women in Love*. He is recognizably a Lawrence-figure, but because he is 'in' the novel, and played off against other figures, he isn't to be taken as simply Lawrence ventriloquizing. He is dangerously near to Lawrence; but he is, we see, looking for a way out; he is searching for answers to his condition, being characteristically willing to move on from it. He is also open to the criticism implied in being played off dramatically against other people. The point of the novel is that exploratory effort: unresolved, perhaps baffled, at the end.

When Birkin in the strange night-scene in the chapter called 'Moony' throws stone after stone into the pond, obsessively trying to break up the moon's reflection and prevent it from reforming, he is symbolizing his fear of maternal dominance. (The figure perhaps also suggests how that attempt is necessarily defeated. The reflection will always re-form. The individual will cannot frontally assault nature.) His preoccupation would affect his relationship with women in love as the urge not to be owned, to keep a distance, to remain free. That is both a rational notion and (in him) the result of a fear.

The ideas, the stated concepts, which Birkin presents to Ursula spring in ways he does not acknowledge from his own damaged nature, its self-defences. Her resistance to his 'ideas' springs from her own more spontaneous freeflowing wish for an ordinary commitment which is not frightened of belonging, and can admit the urge to possess and be possessed. But that, of course, is just what he shies away from. Hence their struggle, which is creative.

What can they manage that is better? Can they find a mid-point?

The ideal Birkin presents to Ursula we recognize as fine, and for that matter necessary. The last pages of *Anna Karenina* show why. He wants the polarity between two centres of consciousness which are related like planets; attracted to each other by a gravitational pull, but also kept apart in their own orbits. The other person remains unpossessable, in some senses unknowable, a door out from the solitary self, a perspective into the universe. In that balance of commitment and distance 'that which is perfectly ourselves can take place in us'. This is a natural growth, neither forced nor deflected by the will, which is relaxed also in respect of the other person. Birkin asks Ursula to relax her will to be loved in the old way, which is a reciprocated demand, and to submit to this new relationship instead. (Actually, you can only do this as a conscious effort by exerting the will on the self. It is a kind of puritan conscientiousness about being undemanding. It would call for extremes of self-knowledge to circumvent the natural devices of the demanding self.) Ursula balks at the notion of 'submission', seeing it as a subtle ploy of the male will. It might be more to the point to see Birkin's position as a tactic of self-defence. She at any rate is a genuinely spontaneous person (with all the danger that implies) with a strong instinct for outgoingness in self-commitment, and a willingness to let things take a natural course. Hence their conflicts.

Another triumph of Lawrence's art is their quarrel and reconciliation in the chapter 'Excurse'. The symbolism isn't obvious—may not even be intended–but the rings that Birkin gives Ursula are fine finished things, like his opinions. She likes them, but finds all but one too constricting for her fingers. She and Birkin have a straight-up-and-down row in which their conflict explodes and is made real as a battle of wills; she vents all her jealousy and irritation, throws his rings in his face, and goes off. She then wanders back to him with a little peace-offering:

> 'See what a flower I found you,' she said wistfully, holding a piece of purple-red bell-heather under his face. He saw the clump of coloured bells, and the tree-like tiny branch: also her hands, with their over-fine, sensitive skin. 'Pretty!' he said, looking up at her with a smile, taking the flower. Everything had become simple again, quite simple. . . .

N

It is another of those profound gestures of meeting. Her flower for his jewels; perhaps meaning her natural spontaneous self, the instinctive wholeheartedness in which the person moves all together, set against his opinions, his agonies. For he is a divided person; his 'views' represent his deep wish to be spared the turmoils of relationship. He wants to get to a position by a conceptual flight and a verbal agreement, instead of getting there by living through the necessary process, which would include conflict and pain. He wants to be spared further pains of a kind he knows too much about already (like Mellors); so he wants to be unlike other people. She is braver; it is the bravery of the undamaged, the self-confident and the hopeful, but it is also wise. As she says, 'Yes, one does want that. But it must *happen*. You can't do anything for it with your will. You always seem to think you can force the flowers to come out. . . .'

The second Ursula, the girl in *Women in Love* as distinct from the girl in *The Rainbow*, is the characteristic heroine of later Lawrence, derived from his love of Frieda, his own wife. She is a recurrence, like the Lawrence-figure, and the Gerald Crich-figure. We see her also as Alvina Houghton in *The Lost Girl*, the countess Hannele in *The Captain's Doll*, and Connie Chatterley herself. She is sensitive, warm, brave, free-floating, curiously unattached yet willing to attach herself, self assertive without being self-regarding –in a word, spontaneous. The attractiveness of the type is obvious. The most attractive of them all is Connie Chatterley, whose warmth of feeling combined with her readiness to move on in life show great courage. But no sooner has one said that than one feels the limitation. Her sensitiveness can be curiously limited. Her absence of feeling for Clifford, her simple unconsciousness that he has a claim on her, her perception at the end that his violent feelings are merely repulsive to her and a ground for writing him off, and not a partial consequence of what she has *done* to him, these things are a hardness in her. We see it in other books. At the end of *The Lost Girl*, Alvina Houghton has gone to Italy with her chosen mate Cicio; she is pregnant by him, is bravely facing a new life in a strange country, utterly unlike her old Edwardian England. It is awe-inspiring Italian mountain country, bleak and tough. She is taking all that on, and we are impressed by her courage. Then she gets a letter from England, from her past. It is from the Dr Mitchell she had once made the mistake of getting engaged to. It was going to be a conventional marriage, 'settling down' into comfortable middle-class English life. She had realized the mistake, had simply jilted Mitchell and gone off. His letter is bitter and ugly, an outburst of self:

> Here was a pretty little epistle! In spite of herself she went pale and trembled. She glanced at Cicio. Fortunately he was turning round talking to another man. She rose and went to the ruddy brazier as if to warm her hands. She threw on the screwed-up letter . . . The world beyond could not help, but it still had the power to injure one here. She felt she had received a bitter blow. A black hatred for the Mitchells of this world filled her.

I think too of the first Ursula, annihilating Anton Skrebensky who is agonizingly in love with her: 'It seems to me . . . as if you weren't anybody – as if there weren't anybody there, where you are. Are you anybody, really? You seem like nothing to me.' And at the end of *Lady Chatterley's Lover*, Connie gets the Mitchell-reaction from Clifford. He produces his Gerald Crich–Rico Carrington physical symptoms: his blue eyes bulge and the whites turn yellow. He is a hideous face placed in front of the threatening demands of the universal self. She writes him off: 'It was useless. She went upstairs and told [her sister] Hilda the upshot. "Better get away tomorrow," said Hilda, "and let him come to his senses." ' That's that. It's just too easy, to be like that to people you have hurt or wronged. But these are people for whom Lawrence felt scorn and hatred, because they are expressions of the universal self. He wanted to get beyond that, we say; but did he? If the Mitchells fill you with 'black hatred' are you doing anything but respond to them in their own terms? If you think people are 'not there' or 'like nothing', are you not performing a characteristic operation of the self? Lawrence establishes with great care that Gerald Crich in *Women in Love* treats his industrial employees as merely instrumental, things to use, not people to consider. That is partly what's wrong with him. So the question is, is there a qualitative difference between Lawrence's heroes and heroines and his villains, and what is it? 'Anybody who is anything,' said Birkin, in the passage I quoted on p. 63, 'can just be himself and do as he likes.' This has to do with acting 'spontaneously on one's impulses'.

We can find a related intention in *Sons and Lovers*. 'To be rid of our individuality, which is our will, which is our effort – to live

effortless, a kind of curious sleep–that is very beautiful I think'–
Paul says that to Miriam Leivers. With the later love Clara Dawes
(who has an element of Frieda in her) something of that kind seems
to happen when they make love:

> All the while the peewits were screaming in the field. When he
> came to, he wondered what was near his eyes, curving and strong
> with life in the dark, and what voice it was speaking. Then he
> realized it was the grass, and the peewit was calling. The warmth
> was Clara's breathing heaving. He lifted his head and looked into
> her eyes. They were dark, and shining and strange, life wild at the
> source staring into his life, stranger to him, yet meeting him . . .
>
> To know of their own nothingness, to know the tremendous
> living flood which carried them always, gave them rest within
> themselves. If so great a magnificent power could overwhelm
> them, identify them altogether with itself, so that they knew they
> were only grains in the tremendous heave that lifted every grass
> blade its little height, and every tree, and every living thing, then
> why fret about themselves? They could let themselves be carried
> by life. . . .

'Life' is an ambiguous word. If you ask what it means here, you
see its dangers. The idea of an external wave which you allow to
carry you along is mere metaphor. 'Life' for Clara and Paul can
only be, literally, *their* life; and their life is themselves, with all
that that implies. You may think you are standing aside in your
conscious self to let your spontaneous self through, but suppose, as
Racine demonstrated, that what comes through is a monster? Or
suppose, in Lawrence's terms, that you are Clifford Chatterley,
Dr Mitchell, Anton Skrebensky, even Gerald Crich (who proved
Birkin's point by trying to murder Gudrun at the end of *Women
in Love*)?

This seems a difficulty at the heart of Lawrence's work. Because
he knew most people were limited, mere selves, he was forced to
divide mankind into two categories: a kind of aristocracy and a
proletariat. The difficulty is then to believe in his aristocracy, not
to find them constantly reverting to the norm: showing that they
are human. It is also troubling to find the proletariat being used as
something to prey on: being treated instrumentally. If that is
wrong socially and industrially, how can it be right humanly and
emotionally?

It is these facets which open Lawrence to the charge of being proto-fascist; and there was a part of him that was very willing imaginatively to entertain the idea of liquidating unnecessary or tiresome people. I have quoted (p. 189) the passage from *St Mawr* about 'the ghastly kisses and poison-bites of the myriad evil ones'— i.e. most people. Late in the story the little Welsh groom Lewis, riding through the English country with Mrs Witt, Lou Carrington's mother, breaks into fantasy and talks of his half-belief in a superior fairy race, the moon-people:

> They see people live and they see people perish, and they say, people are only like twigs on a tree, you break them off the tree, and kindle fire with them. You made a fire of them, and they are gone. . . . And they say: what do people matter? If you want to matter, you must become a moon boy.

That's fantasy, and only one note in an imaginative utterance of wide range; one doesn't want to be too literal about it. But the fantasy is entertained. If you compare the passage from *Sons and Lovers* you see that what is lost is the sense of solidarity: there we are all drops in the wave; now it is forgotten that we too are twigs on the tree, are people. I think of Birkin (admittedly in a bad mood, and people say such things in a bad mood) saying flatly 'Not many people are anything at all. . . . They jingle and giggle. It would be much better if they were just wiped out. Essentially they don't exist, they aren't there.' I think of Mellors (to come back to *Lady Chatterley's Lover*) saying to Connie that it would really be quite a good idea to shoot his wife and her husband: the first being just a bitch raveningly on heat all the time, the second a broken-backed creature that should be put out of its misery. Mellors is a game-keeper, and they are vermin: therefore. . . . Again, people say such things; especially people torn by an emotional involvement. Giving verbal rein to an impulse may save one from worse; and in any case one's impulses should be recognized. All the same, it's troubling. In the late short novel *The Virgin and the Gipsy* the vicar, an in-adequate man, sees his spontaneous and therefore superior (in Lawrence's terms) wife seek fulfilment with another man. The vicar himself, being damaged, turns nasty. He is written off as one of the 'base-born'. His daughter Yvette, also spontaneous and open like her mother, is one of the 'free-born'. The base-born are of course slaves; and their morality is slave morality. The free-born

N*

are noble, and free of that morality. We are in Nietzsche's world, then?

Nothing is unthinkable, and every possibility must be faced. Perhaps Ursula Brangwen's dismissal of Anton Skrebensky is the modern equivalent of 'Depart from me, ye accursed, into everlasting Hell'. Our culture is used to dividing people into two moral categories, sheep and goats, the elect and the damned. Fundamental to Lawrence's work is his notion of 'disquality'. People are not the same, are not therefore 'equal'; they are, or ought to be, individuals, and they ought to have the courage to be themselves, to discover what they need to become. Put like that, it seems acceptable truth—which suggests that it's the working out, the discovery that actions have consequences, especially for other people, that makes the difficulty, and forces one to assert, or to deny, that there are two kinds of people, and one kind doesn't matter.

13

Tolstoy and Lawrence: Some Conclusions

When Levin walks, slightly drunk, into the billiard-room of his old club in Moscow, he feels that 'his arms were swinging with quite unusual ease and regularity'. A little alcohol gives him this sense of being for once gracefully in his body and able to direct it skilfully because unself-consciously. By the time he leaves the club, he has had more to drink; the moment of poise has passed, and he is now 'swinging his arms rather peculiarly'.

We remember how we first meet him in Stiva Oblonsky's office at the beginning of the book. He is very sober, much possessed by the thought that he must soon propose to Kitty and so have his life's happiness decided. Naturally ill at ease among towns-people who (he suspects) think him rather odd and countrified and angular and impulsive, he feels particularly awkward among these civil servants, all on their home ground, united and given status by their uniforms. Levin is wearing a new suit, and feels strange in it, and his sheepskin cap is not perhaps the best accompaniment. Moreover the doorkeeper, not knowing him, has turned him away once. It is only when he is welcomed by the suave Stiva and introduced, that the officials begin to accept him and take him as a person to be civil to; but even that is spoilt because one of them chooses to see in him only the half-brother of the celebrated Koznyshev. So Levin never recovers his poise. His sense of being at a disadvantage focuses itself–literally–on the long finger-nails of one official. He glares at them with horror and hatred. Unconsciously he turns this expression of the other man's superiority into the effete affectation of an idle townee, whom he can therefore despise in return. But at the bottom he knows he is upstaged, as we say.

That is all trivial in itself, but that sort of thing is the constantly renewed guarantee of Tolstoy's contact with the fine grain of actuality; his knowledge that everything we say, do, and think comes to us or out of us through the refracting element of the self. Levin's self-centredness is one of the important facts about him, and is thoroughly explored. For instance, his horror of death is the natural reaction (like the universal adolescent one) of an intense being-oneself: if you are aware of your existence to that degree, its annihilation is a horror. But you should have got over it by Levin's age; in him it's an immaturity. It leads Levin at first to feel that since he is going to die, nothing is worth while. He is educated here by Kitty: in the preesnce of the dying Nikolai Levin, where Levin shows horror and fear, she shows a naturally self-forgetful energy. Dying people have to be helped to die; have to be comforted and supported in the last experience of all; she does this from a deep instinct for the outward-moving gesture to others in their need: an instinct related to mother-love, an obvious, natural and wholly good spontaneity, unhindered by self.

The book shows Levin being educated in ways which can't easily be put in words. His egoism is not lost, but is converted – at least for a time – into a good relationship with the world. This is partly because the world supports *him*, and in nothing so much as giving him Kitty. In his moments of joy when she accepts him, he is easily convinced that the world shares his happiness. It is like mysticism (p. 107) but only superficially; fundamentally the world is at his service and his gladness is the intoxication of the self to which the world is tributary.

The self which imagines that the world shares its happiness is only a fortunate variant of the self which imagines the world is laughing at it. That is Karenin's case. His posture towards the world is basically that of the insecure self which fears what the world may do to it, needs protection and defences, and is always afraid that other people are one-up. If he has moments of self-assertion, they are hideous. We remember the moment when at his desk, alone in his study, he looks up and sees Anna's portrait. Characteristically, he feels it is jeering at him, asserting his inferiority. He can only fight back to a feeling of self-respect by asserting his official self. He dashes off a powerful memorandum about the inhabitants of the Zaraisky Province, demanding a commission to investigate the situation from the (a) political, (b) administrative, (c) economic, (d) ethnographic, (e) material, and (f) religious points of view. The fierce energy that goes into that stabbing enumeration builds him up again; 'getting up and taking a turn round the room he again glanced at the portrait, frowned, and smiled contemptuously'.

Levin and Karenin are related in that way. The difference, certainly, is also part of their nature. Levin's diffident self-consciousness is one of his attractions, but it doesn't make him sensitive to others. If he is able to transcend it, it is by a kind of courage, energy, persistence of questioning; what is called 'heart' in the book. Fundamentally he is braver than Karenin, more willing to fight. And so, of course, is Anna. Her courage, her 'heart' is what links her to Levin, and to Kitty–who disapprove of her.

One of the profound things about *Anna Karenina* is that it makes these clear qualitative distinctions about people, while showing how they are also all human. I used the word 'best' of some people on p. 121; I don't take it back. Anna and Levin and Kitty and Dolly belong to an aristocracy of energy and seriousness–which includes Vronsky too, for all that modern readers don't like rich and noble guards officers with dilettante 'artistic' hobbies. These people are intensely committed to going where their life leads them, or in Dolly's case the opposite thing: holding on to what they have created.

Here is a clear link with Lawrence (also with Nietzsche and Stendhal, if one is taking a European view). In Lawrence too one sees the people singled out who are making the effort to be themselves, or realize themselves; who are willing to move forward where life takes them. In Lawrence too, one sees in his Frieda-figures the same admiration for the wholehearted spontaneity of the integral person moving together, what one wants to call natural, brave–even 'innocent' in the same way as Catherine Linton is innocent. The free outward gesture of the person acting entirely on impulse: that is Kitty assisting Nikolai Levin. And of course hers is a good impulse; we don't have any difficulty in approving it, and if we know or are related to a Kitty, we don't have any difficulty in loving them. In this way such adults are related to children in a good sense.

But it isn't always as easy as that. There are situations in which the same impulses can't be taken by others in that uncomplicated way. Anna's movement towards Vronsky is as deep, is fundamentally as good; but she is not free. And not all impulses *are* as good. Levin and Anna both have bad feelings; they are shown to be normally driven by the impulses of the self.

It was not that Lawrence didn't know about this. In a way he took it, like Tolstoy, as normal or basic, but he was interested in getting beyond it. If we are all selves, let us all strike out from there and see where life takes us. He wrote off the Karenins, in the end, as hopeless, and concentrated on the brave, showing them as free. They are innocent in that they simply follow their nature. If they can take the consequences, why can't others?

There are good reasons, and Tolstoy shows them. He would not divide the world in the same way into different orders of beings. That is, he would not, like Nietzsche and the later Lawrence divide the world into the sick and the healthy and let the healthy write off or prey on the sick. The constitution of the 'healthy' is firmly related to universal self-hood. In Levin's case we are aware of the precariousness of his happiness and success; in Anna's case we feel from the inside what it is both to be an 'aristocrat' in that sense, and to find that it leads naturally to defeat and death. 'Force of heart' is the mark of an élite, but it doesn't lead automatically to happiness and isn't taken as a right to success. Nor does it negate or supersede social morality: it redefines it. Tolstoy's moral universe is not an automatic assertion of the old rules, known, written down, and enforced as mere social judgement or legal sentence. Nor does it merely blow the old rules up. Morality comes from within: those like Anna who are deep enough to have a moral sense make their own judgements on themselves in the way they forward or thwart or end their own lives. Struggling for meanings, they sometimes find themselves condemned by their own discoveries.

If Lawrence is really putting himself behind Birkin in the claim that 'anyone who is anything can just be himself and do as he likes', Tolstoy might answer 'You put it too simply. People may do as they like; but *that* will define what they are, which is not just what they think themselves to be. They will be looking for and making their meanings, which will reflect back on them. They will not foresee the consequences, and must abide them. They are not solitary beings; their links with others will radically deflect their own development.'

It is a stumbling-block for modern readers that Tolstoy set at the head of his novel the text 'Vengeance is mine, I will repay, saith the Lord'. But no thunderbolts are needed for an Anna Karenina, who is made to suffer by being a sensitive being with a conscience and more than a single need: by being a social and moral being, fully human. Lawrence was shocked at Tolstoy's–as he saw it– willed manipulation of the story. Anna should have left Karenin as a demand of 'life', and she and Vronsky should have lived happily in the 'pride of their sincere passion'. The need for her child, any horror at what she had done to the child, any compunction for what she had done to Karenin–what of them?

But Lawrence's ethic looks like a narrow self-responsibility. Other people are responsible for themselves: I am not my brother's keeper. We are responsible to the 'life' in ourselves, and life is moving, and moving on, as Mellors said. There is an element of courage in this, and also an element of cowardice. The courage is the ability to face change in oneself and others, to come to the end of a stage in one's life and move into the next. Most people flinch from these necessary stages. But they may also have good reasons for hanging on: we may think of Heathcliff grimly clinging to his dream–or his illusion–for twenty years, because that is the meaning of his life and if he denies it his life is meaningless. For him a love for life is his demand on the universe. He's quite clear about that. Or we think of Dolly: she is *right* not to throw away what she has made and she alone can hold together.

Lawrence's first book, *The White Peacock*, deals with the *Wuthering Heights* situation. The young man George Saxton misses the love of his life, who marries another man. The choice was wrong; both their lives are thwarted and unfulfilled. Lawrence must have come to feel that that clamping of the self for a lifetime round a single need was a refusal to grow on and change, and that is a powerful insight to set against Emily Brontë's. Yet the opposite extreme–Mellors's case–is a tramp's philosophy. You sink into 'life is moving, and moving on' as a self-protecting shiftlessness. If you are always willing to welcome the next stage, it could be so that you don't get too attached to this stage, so that you don't care too much, so that you don't get hurt. The wish to be entirely free-floating is the wish not to suffer and not to be responsible. It is the wish not to have any dangerously valuable emotional invest-ments, to make any deep claims, or to expose yourself to certain dangers–especially the loss of love. In Tolstoy's world that is to range yourself with Stiva Oblonsky, Koznyshev, Varenka; or to make the vain effort of Karenin, who wanted not to be hurt and thought he could protect himself, but was hurt all the more when life cracked his shell.

Lawrence's heroes and heroines have more courage than that; their responsibility to themselves is a responsibility to something that at their best they may be taken to represent–to 'life' perhaps. Perhaps it is best to envisage his notion of self-responsibility in its grandest, most general and also grimmest aspect: as the natural growth of a single creature, alone, considered as native of a dangerous universe: like a plant, an animal, concerned only to be itself, to fulfil its own nature. This looks less like a selfishness, more like obedience to a natural law.

This too goes back a long way in his writing. His first game-keeper, Annable, in *The White Peacock*, said that we ought at least to be good animals. Of the animal Lawrence says in one place:

> The wild animal is at every moment intensely self-disciplined, poised in the tension of self-defence, self-preservation and self-assertion. The moments of relaxation are rare and most carefully chosen. Every sleep is watchful, guarded, unrelaxing, the wild courage pitched one degree higher than the wild fear. Courage, the wild thing's courage to maintain itself alone and living in the midst of a diverse universe.

And of the growth of plants he says it is 'that which is life itself, creatively destroying as it goes: destroying the stiff old thing to let the new bud come through'. Assenting to that offers no comfort other than that it is natural (especially if you happen to be the stiff old thing). But an important implication of the figure distinguishes it from traditional stoicism, where the tight little ego on the anvil of fate wills itself to be harder than the hammer. That is a form of glum self-approval. In the plant, the changes come from within, are your growth, and cast the old self off like a husk.

If you feel at one with that kind of universe, you have to accept all its manifestations; and a third crucial quotation is this, from 'The Crown', an essay in *Reflections on the Death of a Porcupine*:

> The tiger, the hawk, the weasel, are beautiful things to me; and as they strike the dove and the hare, that is the will of God, it is a consummation, a bringing together of two extremes, a making perfect one from the duality.

Actually, it is a creature of one species killing a creature of another species—which is an important distinction, here lost sight of. Predator and prey are only made 'one' in a digestive sense. One can assent to that as a fact without being sentimental about it—as I think Lawrence is, here, with the inverted sentimentality of mystical toughness.

And in the end, one has to ask: to what extent do these insights and parallels apply to people? Do we fit into the universe as plants, as animals, or as human beings who are social creatures and crucially distinct from plants and animals in our humanity? If it was good that Lawrence reminded us that we belong, it is now time to remind ourselves how we are unique. We have had much about our animal nature from the cruder kind of ethologist: it's doubtful if they even do justice to the animals *as* animals, but in any case the parallel will only be clinched when the first scientific-journalist bird writes *The Feathered Ethologist*. More to the point here, one wants to ask Lawrence whether he sees Connie Chatterley and Mellors as the human equivalents of the tiger, the hawk, and the weasel; and Clifford Chatterley as dove or hare? That is, are the naturally superior human animals entitled in forwarding their own nature to prey on the inadequate, the weak, the damaged, the stunted? Or just to shrug them off? I think again of Linton Heathcliff making his claim to be dealt with justly, even if love for him is not possible.

Or take another of Lawrence's favourite metaphors: the seed or nut which leaves its husk on the parent plant, falls through an alien element, the air, comes to ground, lodges, sprouts, dies to itself and becomes another plant. That seems more profound, more adequate. For Lawrence it symbolizes the willingness to lapse out, to be taken beyond oneself; and it does it better than Mellors's rather contemptible notion of moving, and moving on. It is a parable-figure in the New Testament, we remember, signifying new commitment, self-forgetfulness, receptivity to the life-giving truth. Tolstoy could have pointed out that this image could be interpreted his way too: the seed has to lodge if it is to sprout; that is, it has to come to rest in order to fulfil the law of its being; in coming to rest it passes its life into the next generation. Fulfilment of one's nature is not entirely self-referring: one does not simply pass from stage to stage endlessly. At a certain point one yields one's place to others—not just in death, though that is the natural final succession.

Does it come back to words like 'demand'? The person who goes through life demanding only his own fulfilment is a predator, an immature egoist. Certainly the person with fixed and constant demands is not spontaneous, since there is neither spontaneity—except of Othello's kind—nor growth. Spontaneity, F. R. Leavis once wrote, is 'life that discovers by living its own nature and need'. That kind of tentativeness, of braveness and openness, could be represented by Anna Karenina, who discovered that her nature was not simple, and her needs conflicted with each other. Lawrence's Birkin has a potential for the same tragedy, for he too senses conflicting needs in himself: he wants a permanent relationship with one woman (he is quite clear about that): he wants a relationship which fulfils certain prior conditions he has elaborated in his own mind; he wants that relationship with Ursula, who has impulses in conflict with his; and he is prepared in advance to say 'if one repents of the marriage, it is at an end'. He has no ideas at all about children; he wishes no settled place in a community. All that is set out; brave, tentative but mainly hopeful openness is set against the hard conflict of selves between Gerald Crich and Gudrun, which moves rapidly to its end in Gerald's defeat and death (like Othello, like Phèdre) and *Women in Love* ends on a baffled questioning note. It is closer to Tolstoy than Lawrence knew.

Birkin is divided and conscious of difficulties in a way in which many of Lawrence's main characters aren't. Lawrence grew up and began to write in an England—a Europe—in which the individual identity was threatened with submergence by the social ideal—whether of class, functional social status, or the stereotypes of institutional religion. What you ought to think and what you ought to feel were laid down from without, mostly by the people Dickens represented in *David Copperfield* in the Murdstones. You could spend a life trying to be 'good' in the approved way, and find only that you felt nothing at all, or didn't know what you felt or had denied your real feelings and spoilt your life; you knew what you ought to want, but didn't really want it, didn't know that, and didn't know what you *did* want. In those circumstances Stendhal's heroes, Nietzsche's imaginings, must have seemed a new heroic ideal, a liberation: people who know exactly what they want, and have the force of nature to acknowledge their own will, to accept themselves and fulfil themselves: Racine's

Phèdre turned inside out, or Catherine Linton made 'respect-able'.

Simply taken, it's a narrow ideal, a mere reaction against the convention. Tolstoy got well beyond it in *Anna Karenina* in a way Lawrence didn't often manage. One can only think it was because Tolstoy was aware of a wider range of needs and fulfil-ments than Lawrence, and came quickly to see that you could want incompatible things; more especially that you could want to be responsive to others' needs as well as your own. Lawrence deals too often with the solitary self; Tolstoy deals with the self that needs as a condition of life and happiness to be related closely to others and set firmly in a whole world.

I have done Lawrence an injustice by taking him more as a whole—with his tentativeness in some places, his overcertainty in others, his wrongness in others—and setting that against the single book in which Tolstoy achieved balance, clarity and inclusiveness. If you take the whole of Tolstoy into account, you get distortions counterbalancing Lawrence's will to distortion in the opposite direction. At this point it might be more just to point to what Tolstoy and Lawrence have in common. They are both funda-mentally seeking some place in which to root a religious view of human life. It is a religion of this world; it looks for its sanctions in 'life' itself. Reverence for that principle, awe at its manifesta-tions, its mysterious laws, links the two. Both early and late in Lawrence's work you can find great moments in which the idea of responsibility to the single lonely self is transcended. For instance, there is the moment in *The Rainbow* where Tom Brangwen out in the open at night at lambing-time is aware that he does not belong to himself. At the end of *St Mawr* Lou Carrington, waiting in the desert for life to run clear again, is in touch with the same source. What is impressed on them here is a humility, the sense that they must be at the service of something not themselves.

That is one way in which Lawrence gets beyond Nietzsche: that and the steady willingness always to put his spokesmen in dramatic situations where other characters not only answer them back but have an independent strongly-held life stance which makes them real opponents. If we look back over all the books I have been dealing with, Nietzsche is in any case answered. What sort of people in real life act as supermen? Iago, for instance, is beyond good and evil; or Murdstone has related instincts in his sense of a right to control others; or James Steerforth, who can use them. Surprisingly, Gilbert Osmond is a well-considered species-type. The world exists down there below him, looking up at him with awed respect for his 'fineness' while he looks down on it with contempt. He is himself, a self he has cultivated; he has his demands, which are for a kind of power. The world gives him his demands: Isabel Archer symbolizes them as things to possess: youth, beauty, wealth, 'style'. But Osmond's demand on the world is shown as what it is: an aggressive variant of being Karenin. If you feel so strongly about the world, it is because you are secretly its slave. Karenin too wanted to feel 'above' the world—so as to be safe from it. Osmond wants to be 'above' the world because the regard of the world means everything to him. Its great ox-eye turned on him fills him with satisfaction. His apparent contempt is merely an anticipatory self-protective device in case the world doesn't admire him as much as it ought to, shows him up as small. That is a familiar operation of the self.

Perhaps the most impressive and human of these people is Heathcliff. But we are shown fully what he is, and how he became it. We have no inclination to accept his energetic self-imposition, his cruelty, his explosive will, as anything but the working out of a nature which is damaged in basic respects, surprisingly vulnerable under the surface, and profoundly attached to an imagined good which is outside itself.

Indeed, the Nietzschean hero is fundamentally undermined by the notion of the self. If we go back to Racine, we see the notion of the conscious will sapped at source. These people may think they are imposing themselves or realizing themselves; really they are just more powerfully driven than others; and, with or without self-consciousness, they are potentially dangerous to society—except that they can be counted on to thwart themselves.

Lawrence and Tolstoy both set against that hopelessness the possibility of good spontaneity, and the possibility of growth. They both have the realism to deny the 'pure selflessness' of the Victorian ideal. But we are not in Racine's world of merely predatory egos locked on to each other—we see that happen, but we also see the counter-forces: the ability to offer love (and Heathcliff too can manage that), the willingness to undergo change; or the willingness to opt for fidelity. Tolstoy manages to keep constantly in view the underlying impulsions of the self; he is not therefore open to the charge—as some of Lawrence is—that he is ignoring the ways in which the will serves the mere self. Lawrence in any case was not ignorant or impercipient about all that: indeed there is a sense in which he takes it as given and goes on from there. We are all selves: but there is disquality between selves: which kind of self do we set above others? That which is willing to move on, to grow, to stay a living process. That gives us an aristocracy, and Tolstoy knows the element of truth in this: these are the people with 'heart'. But Tolstoy then takes the further step: though you must follow where your 'heart', where 'life' leads, you will find you cannot be closed to others.

It is not true therefore that everything is sanctioned in the name of 'life'. Merely to grasp your fulfilment is to be back among the mere selves. More growth is needed than is taken just to grow away from one stage. The very self is not appeased by merely having its demand fulfilled; indeed it is only appeased by being helped to grow against its own resistance, so that it reaches better peace with the world.

It comes down to this perhaps: we are not free. People who think they are free turn out only to be free to be themselves. That is a kind of slavery quite as bad as slavery to the old ideal of the social self. The part of us nearest to being free is the conscience, the intelligence, the will. Self-knowledge can be clouded or distorted by the self, but not entirely annulled. The mind that knows its good is outside itself, can conflict with the self that wants (so to speak) to eat up that good, to take it within in a self-referring process. To know that one's good is separate from oneself; that is one step. To want its good as much as one's own is another. The moral life begins there. Growth is necessary, but it also needs a direction. The self that does not merely deny itself, but can grow on to the point where it knows its needs, but also knows it cannot incorporate them, can neither deny them nor become totally dependent on their satisfaction, can recognize different needs and avoid being torn apart by them, is an adult.

Or do I just mean 'fortunate in its disposition, and fortunate in its circumstances'? The symbolic gesture with which I should like to close this book is not the father running to embrace the prodigal, or Lear and Cordelia kneeling to each other: emblems of spontaneous outgoing or hardwon mutual forgiveness. It is Anna Karenina standing alone, her hands at her temples, holding her hair and pulling it, and finding that the pain brings her back from reverie to consciousness. The consciousness is of being pulled apart. That is a condition in which people have often found themselves; and some people always will. I wish to say flatly that the modern cliché-idea that self-conflict is harmful and unnecessary is false. It is not true that in any situation of difficulty it is only a matter of discovering where 'life' or the 'blood' or 'true happiness' lies, and opting easily for that. Lawrence, or a cliché-response to Lawrence, lies behind this attitude, and the same body of clichés lies behind the rejection of a true self-consciousness, a positively directed will, and a sensitive conscience.

Tolstoy's emblem reminds those who need reminding that it is possible, and frequently occurs, that people are torn between two goods, that in such circumstances they cannot simply *know* where 'life' leads, because it leads both ways; that they cannot identify themselves with a single impulse; that what their conscience tells them is as true as it is unacceptable, that obeying their conscience is as necessary to their 'fulfilment' as obeying the other need; that they cannot therefore be wholly 'fulfilled', still less 'happy'.

The other thing they discover is the falsehood of the distinction (Lawrence's distinction) between 'the blood' or 'the body' and 'the mind'. When Lawrence used the old distinction it was in a valuable way: the moral life had been centred in the conscious will taken as the agent of the externally defined or imposed social identity, and allowed to tyrannize the life of natural impulse (Murdstone again). But the old distinctions were themselves false, and in reasserting the rights of the downtrodden element in that untrue polarity, Lawrence prolonged a false dichotomy. The key passage is this familiar one:

> The body's life is the life of sensations and emotions. The body feels real hunger, real thirst, real joy in the sun or the snow, real pleasure in the smell of roses or the look of a lilac bush: real anger, real sorrow, real love, real tenderness, real warmth, real passion, real hate, real grief. All the emotions belong to the body, and are only recognised by the mind. We may hear the most sorrowful piece of news, and only feel a mental excitement. Then, hours

after, perhaps in sleep, the awareness may reach the bodily centres, and true grief wrings the heart.

(from *Apropos of 'Lady Chatterley's Lover'*)

But that isn't 'the body'; it is the whole person, another aspect of the self. It is false that we are two split-off elements, mind and body, one having real feelings and one having false feelings. We are a single consciousness; the idea that we feel some things in the body and others in the mind is related to the equally false dichotomy between 'thought' and 'feeling'.

Yet it is true that we do, and must, feel conflict. But Anna Karenina knows that it is not her body against her mind, or her blood against her reason, or even her private impulse against her social conscience. A conflict as simple as that might be more easily lived with or resolved. It is her self against her self; one need against another. The conflict calls into question her whole sense of living identity and purpose, so that she has to ask 'who am I, what do I love, what do I know?' One cannot urge her to 'opt for Life' as if one course would 'only' damage someone else, since any course will damage someone else (Karenin, Vronsky, her child, herself, are all at risk), and any course will damage some part of her.

In the presence of such conflicts we have no wisdom in the sense of answers; we can only recognize the anguished extremity. I can imagine no society, no set of institutions, no system (or lack of system) of relationships between the sexes, in which such conflicts do not occur.

Bibliography

TRANSLATIONS

The English version of *Phèdre* quoted in chapters 4 and 5 is that by R. C. Knight, in the Edinburgh Bilingual Library, published by The Edinburgh University Press in 1971. The translation, into English blank verse, seems to me the best available. Robert Lowell's *Phaedra* (Faber, and Farrar, Straus and Cudahy) is more free and colloquial, sometimes strikingly acute, but usually paraphrastic. The two translations together give the reader without French some idea of the original.

The translations from *Madame Bovary* are my own.

Anna Karenina is quoted in the Signet Classic version of David Magarshack, published by the New American Library (New English Library in Britain), 1961. If the reader compares the Penguin translation by Rosemary Edmonds, he will usually find the convergences and divergences instructive.

CRITICISM

For *Othello* I have used as basic interpretation F. R. Leavis's essay 'Diabolic Intellect and the Noble Hero' in *The Common Pursuit* (London, 1952). See also the essay on 'Tragedy and the "Medium" ' in the same book.

On *David Copperfield*, see the chapter by Q. D. Leavis in *Dickens the Novelist* by F. R. and Q. D. Leavis (London, 1970).

On *Anna Karenina*, see the article by F. R. Leavis in *Anna Karenina and other Essays* (London, 1967). I have also found R. F. Christian's *Tolstoy: a Critical Introduction* (Cambridge, 1969) helpful.

On *Wuthering Heights*, see the monumental article by Mrs Leavis 'A fresh approach to *Wuthering Heights*' in *Lectures in America* (London, 1969). The parallel with Roché's *Jules et Jim* is particularly fruitful.

On Lawrence's work generally, see F. R. Leavis's *D. H. Lawrence: Novelist* (London, 1957). This is excerpted usefully in the Penguin Critical Anthology *D. H. Lawrence*, ed. H. Coombes (1973), which also contains J. C. F. Littlewood's essay 'Son and Lover' to which I am indebted.

GENERAL

Denis de Rougemont: *Passion and Society* (London; second edition 1956, paperback 1962). Now an old book but still valuable as a statement of a radical Catholic position. Passion is treated almost as a delusion which would not be universally entertained but for the seductive power of literature and the arts.

Lionel Trilling: *Sincerity and Authenticity* (Cambridge, Mass. and London, 1972). Brief and stimulating on related topics. Note the final chapter on 'The Authentic Unconscious', especially on Freud's movement away from his early and false compartmentalization of consciousness and the reifications it produced. Professor Trilling none the less refers in the book on several occasions to the alleged id as 'the locus of our instinctual drives', 'wholly obedient to the inexorable pleasure-principle'. If Freud came to recognize this as nonsense, so may we.

Index

of running themes and allusions; the main content of each chapter is not analysed